Practical Approaches in Treating Adolescent Chemical Dependency: A Guide to Clinical Assessment and Intervention

Practical Approaches in Treating Adolescent Chemical Dependency: A Guide to Clinical Assessment and Intervention

Paul B. Henry
Editor

The Haworth Press
New York • London

Practical Approaches in Treating Adolescent Chemical Dependency: A Guide to Clinical Assessment and Intervention has also been published as *Journal of Chemical Dependency Treatment*, Volume 2, Number 1 1988/89.

The Haworth Press, Inc., 10 Alice Street, Binghamton, NY 13904-1580
EUROSPAN/Haworth, 3 Henrietta Street, London WC2E 8LU England

Library of Congress Cataloging-in-Publication Data

Practical approaches in treating adolescent chemical dependency : a guide to clinical assessment and intervention / Paul B. Henry, editor.
    p. cm.
    "Has also been published as Journal of Chemical Deoendency Treatment, Volume 2, Number 1 1988/89."
    Includes bibliographies.
    ISBN 0-86656-709-7. — ISBN 0-86656-813-1 (pbk.)
    1. Teenagers—Substance use. 2. Substance use—Treatment. 3. Adolescent psychotherapy. I. Henry, Paul B. (Paul Bernard), 1943-
    [DNLM: 1. Substance Dependence—in adolescence. 2. Substance Dependence—therapy. WM 270 P8945]
RJ506.D78P7   1989
616.86—dc 19
DNLM/DLC
for Library of Congress

89-1660
CIP

Practical Approaches in Treating Adolescent Chemical Dependency: A Guide to Clinical Assessment and Intervention

CONTENTS

ABOUT THE EDITOR

Paul B. Henry, MDiv, brings extensive treatment and administrative experience to his role as Director of Marketing and Development at New Beginnings at Cove Forge in Williamsburg, Pennsylvania. He co-founded Today, Inc., an adolescent treatment center in Bucks County, Pennsylvania, and served as Executive Vice-President until 1983. Since that time he has consulted with the New Beginnings program at Cove Forge and was responsible for the development of the Cove Forge Adolescent Program.

Mr. Henry is the editor of the *Journal of Adolescent Chemical Dependency*. He has been a consultant to the Alcoholism Control Administration for the State of Maryland for the development of adolescent treatment services and to the Bergen County (New Jersey) Department of Health, as well as a consultant/trainer for the Office of Drugs & Alcohol Programs, the Pennsylvania Department of Health, and the New Jersey Department of Health. He teaches courses on alcoholism counseling and continues to consult with numerous professional organizations,school, and industries related to human resources development and alcohol treatment. In addition, Mr. Henry is on the faculty of the Rutgers (University) Summer School of Alcohol Studies and is an adjunct faculty member at Chestnut Hill College and Utah Summer School of Alcoholism.

Foreword

The addictions treatment field is a little more than two decades old. In that time, as we have developed a disease approach to understanding the addictive process, much of the money, time, talent and research went into an exploration of the adult alcoholic. But at last adolescent chemical dependency is being recognized as a sub-speciality within the addiction treatment field. It was not long ago that we heard statements such as "adolescents can't be addicted," or "adolescents should be treated with adults because aren't all addicts (alcoholics) the same?" Statements like these were commonplace until we began to think about the dynamics of normal adolescence and the severe disruption that any regular and prolonged usage of mood-altering chemicals can have upon these processes.

As we began to consider the dynamics of adolescence, we recognized that this is a unique age. Those of us who have gone through a relatively normal adolescence can remember the difficulties of growing up. We remember experiencing many painful changes. We felt the pressure of wanting to belong and the pain of feeling left out or of being different. We wanted to excel and please our parents and other meaningful adults, and yet at the same time we felt the need to be on our own . . . to do things differently. We did not like being compared to someone else. We wanted to be recognized as individuals. We wanted to be free of our parents and at the same time we often felt confused and alone without their guidance.

Adolescence is a difficult time for most. But these struggles are important and necessary to the developing adolescent, if he or she is to mature as a responsible young adult. Yet some kids do not get this chance. They become emotionally bonded to chemicals. In the midst of these struggles, they try a mood changing chemical and they experience a euphoric feeling almost immediately. This allows them to escape from their struggles; it allows them to lay aside the painful searching for identity, relationships and values that is so

1

necessary for adolescence. They give in to a chemical high as the solution to their seemingly impossible struggles, and in so doing they give up essential elements in the growth process of adolescence.

The adult who begins using alcohol or other drugs after the adolescent tasks are completed has already established an identity and has begun to form interpersonal relationships that are based upon interdependence. That is why we can look at the process of recovery and call it rehabilitation. We are rebuilding or rehabing. But the adolescent who begins using chemicals in early adolescence or, as we now too often see, in the preadolescent years has little or no identity or stable relationships upon which to build in therapy. Therefore, with the chemically dependent adolescent, we are not looking at a rehabilitation process, but rather habilitation. This demands that we seek different treatment strategies than those we have used with the adult.

Practical Approaches in Treating Adolescent Chemical Dependency: A Guide to Clinical Assessment and Intervention has been written to provide the person working with chemically involved youth with a text that is a hands on approach. We have set out to draw upon the practice of seasoned professionals and to demonstrate to the reader the current state of the art in adolescent treatment.

The book begins with a look at the "Basics of Adolescent Development for the Chemical Dependency Professional." Alan Cavaiola and Carolann Kane-Cavaiola provide a very comprehensive overview of the dynamics of adolescence and the destructive impact that chemicals have upon kids. In very clear fashion they describe the ways in which chemical dependency interferes with developmental tasks and they outline the treatment considerations that the counselor needs to consider to effectively help these youth.

In the second article Alan Cavaiola joins with Matthew Schiff to consider the adolescent at risk for chemical dependency. All of us who have worked with chemically involved youth know that there is a variety of at risk behaviors which adolescents present. This chapter overviews not only the obvious at risk behaviors, but also those which we may tend to overlook. The inclusion of clinical vignettes illustrates the issues that the clinician must face in dealing with these kids.

David O'Connell continues the emphasis upon the at risk adolescent by examining some effective programs and interventions that have been utilized across the country. The reader is directed to a number of programs that provide effective programming in prevention, intervention and treatment.

Increasingly it is important that we seek the most appropriate treatment for each adolescent and that we confirm the initial conclusion that a particular youth is chemically dependent. The counselor who works with youth needs an understanding of the issues involved in assessment and a specific procedure which he/she can use to increase his/her own effectiveness in making accurate assessments. Jane Nakken provides that procedure for assessment. Her article is a guideline for anyone responsible for doing assessments with youth.

Matt Green provides the reader with a specific model of intervention that knits together the community and the school. The Newton Youth Drug/Alcohol program which Matt directs has been helping alcohol and drug involved kids since the late 60s. His program has been highly acclaimed in Massachusetts and throughout the northeast. In his article he provides the reader with a look at how his program works. The emphasis upon a total community approach is extremely necessary if we are to make a profound impact upon the culture of chemically involved youth.

Inpatient treatment for adolescents is different than the traditional adult program. The elements that are essential for adolescent programming are described by George Obermeier and myself. Particular insight is provided into the need for attention to physical recovery and nutritional concerns. These are elements that have been overlooked within adult programs, but are, we believe, essential to an adolescent program.

Many communities do not have access to alternative day programs for chemically dependent adolescents. Traditionally adolescents have not done well in outpatient programs because such programs have not been able to provide the intensity and structure that chemically involved youth need in order to develop "clean" time. Frank Edwards and Lou Huston describe a program in Gastonia,

North Carolina that was developed with the assistance of the Rotary Club as an effective alternative to inpatient treatment.

All of the available data tells us that at least 60 percent of our chemically dependent youth come from homes where alcoholism or other addictions are present. This means that we need to work with families. Yet too often we work with youth in isolation or give up on the family. Emily Schroeder provides us with a look at therapy with the chemically dependent family. As the reader examines this article, he will note that Emily has provided a clear and concise method for getting started with families.

Peter Cohen has taken the groundbreaking work of Stephanie Brown and Terrence Gorski in relapse prevention and applied it to adolescents. In doing so Dr. Cohen recognizes the uniqueness of adolescents. To read his stages of recovery adapted to the developmental needs of adolescence is a must for anyone working with recovering kids.

Eileen Smith Sweet has contributed an article on issues in the treatment of chemically dependent minority adolescents. While there is much that is similar in adolescents everywhere, minorities in the United States, as in other societies, face special needs. Utilizing her experience as a psychologist in working with minority youth, Dr. Sweet shares her insight and sensitivity to this population with us.

Philip Gifford presents what I believe will be the most controversial aspect of this book. His article takes a very intensive look at the historical development of both A.A. and N.A. Based upon his analysis he presents an argument for utilizing N.A. as the choice support group for recovering adolescents. His bold claim that, "I believe that A.A. is almost never the more appropriate Twelve Step recovery program for adolescents now that N.A. is more generally available . . ." is certain to spark debate and arouse some intense feelings. Yet I have always believed that a challenge to our thinking is always in order, and Philip Gifford's article is presented in that vein.

Practical Approaches in Treating Adolescent Chemical Dependency: A Guide to Clinical Assessment and Intervention is a first step in defining the parameters of inquiry in order that we might better equip ourselves to work more compassionately with this

group that desperately needs competent and committed professionals to reach out and comprehend their turmoil and pain. I will be
satisfied if this book has led to a greater understanding of chemically dependent youth and if those of us who are committed to helping have increased our knowledge as a result of this book.

Paul B. Henry, MDiv, AAMFT

Preface

The 1980s are experiencing a renewed interest in adolescents especially concerning alcohol and drug use. Since adolescence is characterized by rapid growth and development, an understanding of the needs and interests of this period of life is essential if we are to develop programs for youth. The reality of adolescent alcohol and drug use also needs to be identified if the techniques and strategies are to be helpful. Unfortunately many of society's messages to adolescents frequently contain only what adults think teenagers need to hear rather than the messages and alternatives that are important to the young person growing up in today's world.

The U.S.A. is an ambivalent and often misinformed society about alcohol, its use and problems. Though our young people grow up in a drinking society, alcohol use is rarely discussed. It is as if we expect them to suddenly learn and know all that there is about alcohol and its effects, why it's consumed, how to minimize risks, and how to deal with alcoholism at some magical time. Adults have often been uncomfortable in talking about alcohol because they've been unsure of the facts about alcohol and their feelings about its use, disconcerted by their own personal drinking habits and patterns, and unclear of what to say to the young. Parents often overlook the fact that they have offered their child a drink during a celebration or family event and are content in characterizing adolescent drinking as what occurs when they're with other adolescents. The broader and more accurate definition of drinking as consuming alcohol, regardless of where and with whom this occurs, needs to be considered.

Understanding adolescent drinking is necessary to design programs and work with this population. The reality is that a portion of our youthful population (approximately one-third) have either never consumed alcohol or may have tried alcohol on occasion but are not regular users. These young people need to be able to socialize and interact in a drinking society. Program development and strategies should address the needs of this group of adolescents. Many young people are introduced to alcohol at home and continue the practice by drinking when they're with their friends. Approximately two-thirds of the adolescents (high school seniors) indicate regular use of alcohol. Much of the drinking occurs at parties with other adolescents, raising issues of concern. An important item for attention is that approximately one-fourth of the adolescent drinking population indicate that they drink to the point of intoxication about six times a year. This clearly places the individual in a situation of risk for himself and others. Minimizing intoxication should be a primary goal for society. However, it must be noted that the majority of these young people are not alcohol problem people, they are adolescents who are at risk to experience a problem related to alcohol.

Many of the concepts related to drinking apply to drug taking in society. Drugs are part of our society and we are ambivalent and/or misinformed about drugs and their use. Adults often only consider illegal street drugs as drugs and ignore over-the-counter substances and prescribed medication. As with alcohol, we must broaden our understanding of drug taking to gain insight into our youthful population. Most children are introduced to over-the-counter and prescription drugs at home. The use of these drugs is usually to feel better and to eliminate pain. In general, this use is most often non-problematic and does not generate societal concern. However, an attitude toward and patterns of drug use are established. This concept needs to be considered when setting up information campaigns and designing drug education programs.

Though some young people indicate that they have tried an illegal drug, a smaller percentage have established a pattern of regular use. This clearly indicates that there is a percentage of our young people who are experimenting with drugs and not maintaining use. This at-risk behavior needs to be discussed in programs directed at the young, along with implications of getting high. A major area of concern is the multiple substance use that often occurs at a gathering of young people. Alcohol and other drugs may be used concurrently and create a high-risk, problematic situation for the young adult.

Alcoholism and drug dependency also need to be identified in the youthful population. The young person who is dependent on alcohol and/or other drugs is often hidden; he/she may be misdiagnosed as having another problem. This young adult may mask symptoms for a time and/or pretend that his/her use of alcohol and drugs is just like everyone else's. It is imperative that society focus on the meaning of significant changes in the life of an adolescent and, as early as possible, attempt to identify the reason for the changes in attitude, personality, style of dress and appearance, participation in activities, friends, health, grades, etc. The alcohol/drug dependent young person is experiencing problems with regular activities and may also be withdrawing from some. This young person may be attempting to blame the changes in his/her life on others at home or at school, and often acts in inappropriate ways. It is essential that programs of assistance and help be developed for these young people to enable them to receive the treatment required for recovery.

Alcohol/drug problem adolescents are the group on whom this text is focused. *Practical Approaches in Treating Adolescent Chemical Dependency: A Guide to Clinical Assessment and Intervention* provides information and strategies for individuals attempting to identify, treat, and work with this population. Paul Henry, MDiv, noted for his work in treating young people, has assembled needed and practical approaches for dealing with the chemically dependent young. The articles flow in logical order beginning with the adolescent years, at-risk behaviors, assessment of alcohol/drug problems, techniques for school and communities, strategies for families, and essential elements to consider for adolescent treatment. The text will aid parents, educators, and professional youth workers in gaining an understanding of the chemically dependent adolescent; it also offers techniques and strategies for those directly concerned with adolescent treatment.

Gail Gleason Milgram, EdD
Professor/Director of Education and Training
Center of Alcohol Studies
Rutgers University

Basics of Adolescent Development for the Chemical Dependency Professional

Alan A. Cavaiola, PhD, CAC
Carolann Kane-Cavaiola, MA, MSA

Perhaps no other work within the chemical dependency treatment field brings with it both the frustrations and rewards as counseling adolescents. Most professionals may be ambiguous in regard to doing some particular type of counseling or working with a particular age group, however, most are clear in their perception of whether or not they can work with teens. A speaker, for example, at a recent national conference on adolescent chemical dependency, concluded his thorough, insightful presentation by stating, "Thank God, I don't have to work with them."

Given the proliferation of adolescent chemical dependency to epidemic proportions in the U.S. and given the multitude of mood altering chemicals available to them, it becomes of utmost importance for the chemical dependency professional working with teenagers to have well-honed assessment skills. This includes having a strong, practical knowledge of adolescent development. How else is one able to differentiate between behaviors that may seem either "crazy," "chemically-induced" or primarily the result of a condition known as "adolescence."

Too often what we have witnessed when there is a lack of working knowledge regarding adolescent development is that the counselor will use their own adolescence as a data base. This can be dangerous for several reasons. First, a counselor with a skewed data

Alan A. Cavaiola is Clinical Director, Monmouth Chemical Dependency Treatment Center, 152 Chelsea Avenue, Long Branch, NJ 07740. Carolann Kane-Cavaiola is Executive Director, J.F.K. Center for Drug and Alcohol Prevention and Treatment, 73 Green Street, Woodbridge, NJ 07095.

11

base or one in which there is a lack of information may have difficulty in relating to variations in his/her client's upbringing. A counselor who grew up in a single parent family or as an only child will have experienced adolescence differently than his/her client who grew up with an intact family or with many siblings. Second, dangers arise when counselors may not have worked through key developmental issues or tasks. For example, the counselor who has not worked through issues of dealing with authority effectively, may be prone to overidentifying with his/her client to the point of "going to battle" with his/her parental authority figures or excluding valuable family systems information.

In the following pages, we will attempt to define and explain those developmental characteristics, issues and tasks that are part of adolescence.

DEFINING ADOLESCENCE

Adolescence is often defined chronologically to span the teenage years, however, while the onset of adolescence is usually specific, its ending is rather ambiguous. Adolescence can be defined as the psychological response to the biological event of puberty within a particular social/environmental/cultural context. The biological event of pubertal onset therefore marks the beginning of adolescence, however, the termination of adolescence is less well defined. One way to view this is that the more enriched the species, the longer will be the period of childhood. In today's society; college, graduate school or other professional training and apprenticeships all keep the individual in a suspended state of adolescence, however, with the goal of attaining a higher level of enrichment for the individual.

Adolescence is perhaps best known as being the state of "storm and stress," terms which were first coined by American psychologist, G. Stanley Hall. Early psychoanalytic writers viewed adolescence as a transiently disturbed, maladjusted state. Yet, Anna Freud (1958) presented the view that this disturbance is "normal" and that the absence of disturbance was more of concern. More recently, however, this viewpoint has come under dispute. Conger (1983) for example, questions labeling *"normative* transient adolescent upheavals as a disturbed state . . ." (pg. 5). He puts forth the observation that "transient variations in mood, thought and action occur in the normal course of adolescence . . ." (pg. 5). Conger cautions, however, that we not be tempted to view nonnormative, nontransient disturbances as normal, especially when they may indicate actual pathology.

The "storm and stress" theory was also questioned by Offer and Offer (1975) in a landmark study. They concluded that not all adolescents go through extreme upheaval and turmoil. They were able to group most of the adolescents they studied into one of three categories: (1) The continuous growth group (23%) was comprised of well-adjusted adolescents, who were able to meet the demands of this stage, (2) The surgent growth group (35%) was also comprised of reasonably well-adjusted youngsters, who may have had difficulty in coping with unexpected trauma and, (3) The tumultuous growth group (42%) was more characteristic of the adolescent turmoil hypothesized by the "storm and stress" theorists.

Environment plays a key role in adolescent development. Growing up in the rural Midwest will produce much different experiences than growing up in New York City, or metropolitan suburbs. Family milieu will also play a significant role. For example, Baumrind (1968) found distinct differences in adolescents who grew up with authoritarian parents (autocratic, obedience-oriented) versus authoritative parents (democratic but not overly permissive). Those adolescents growing up laissez-faire or with egalitarian parents (controls and boundaries lacking), were thought to be a highest risk for chemical abuse (Jessor and Jessor, 1974). More recent, the impact of growing up in homes where parents are chemically dependent have recently become to be understood more (Woititz, 1984).

THE TASKS OF ADOLESCENCE
AND OTHER COMMON DENOMINATORS

Most developmental stage theories include a series of developmental tasks or challenges which the person must master in order to attain continuous growth. Most are familiar with Freud's Oral Stage in which the infant must, during the first two years or so of life, be able to obtain a sense of satiation and security in order to be able to then relinquish the breast and move on to the next state. If frustrated, the child is said to become fixated at this stage, which will hamper future growth.

Adolescence involves accomplishing a series of important tasks which become critical for growth to occur in adulthood. First, adolescents must adjust to the physical changes of puberty. Changes in hormonal level, height, weight, onset of menstruation, concerns about masturbation all become part of the concerns which plague adolescents. There are also many concerns about what is appropriate sexual behavior. It is noteworthy that although most chemically dependent adolescents indicate they are sexually active, many have apprehensions regarding sex and are misinformed about basic human sexuality. Adolescents must also learn to master sexual and aggressive impulses as part of this task.

The next task involves separation from parents and being able to gain a sense of independence and competency. Issues of separation are perhaps the most important and the most difficult. In order for a healthy separation to occur, both parents and adolescent must be emotionally prepared to accomplish this task together. It has been hypothesized by family systems theorists that adolescent rebellion is a byproduct of difficulties in separation. Rebellion may therefore, signal enmeshment in which the child is not free to separate. In general, dysfunctional families will encounter problems in achieving separation. When the dysfunctional state revolves around alcoholism, the separation process is usually encumbered, as family roles become more rigid. The hero son or daughter for example, remains loyal to that role in order to maintain balance or homeostasis within the family.

Adolescence also marks the beginnings of developing effective social and working relationships with same and opposite sex peers. Wanting to be a part of a club or clique of same sex peers is a very strong drive as the child moves into adolescence. Being identified as "accepted" by virtue of club colors or wearing similar fashions is the most common manifestation of this desire. This identification with same sex peers allows the adolescent an opportunity to discover the opposite sex on a back drop of the peer groups well defined acceptable characteristics. Much is discovered, however, when the "ideal" and the "idealized" are experienced close up. In reverse of this even more can be learned as in the popular movie, *Breakfast Club,* adolescents from different peer groups were only able to discover what they had in common when forced through "administrative detention" to get to know each other.

The next task involves selection and preparation for a vocation. Here decisions regarding career, education, training, apprenticeships, become of utmost importance in shaping the entrance into the work world and adulthood. Parents and counselors sometimes feel that they are nagging or preaching regarding the importance of career decisions, however, they cannot be stressed too highly. In this realm, it is not unusual for adolescents to have either grandiose career plans or more typically, no plans whatsoever.

Values begin to develop and crystalize as one moves into older adolescence. Although there may be a rejection or rebellion against parental values, once the "dust settles" most adolescents take into adulthood the values they were taught growing up. Even religious and political affiliations tend to be similar. As the cliche goes, "the apple does not fall far from the tree."

Finally and probably the most important task is in developing a sense of identity. For Erik Erikson (1968), one of the first developmental stage theorists, the quintessential task of adolescence is the establishment of a sense of identity as a unique person. If this is not attained, role confusion and identity confusion results. The adolescent must find a personal answer to the question, "Who Am I?" This is accomplished through the adolescent's experimentation with different lifestyles, resolutions of bisexual conflicts, and breaking from childhood dependency.

In looking for other common denominators, there are several issues which help to characterize adolescence, which will be mentioned briefly. (1) *The Need for Power.* Teenagers are acutely aware of their nebulous position in our society. They lack status. They are neither children nor are they adults even though some may be more adultlike than childlike. The title of David Elkind's (1984) book perhaps best sums this issue up, *All Grown Up and No Place to Go.* It also seems that as our society has become more affluent and automated, the less need there is for adolescents to help support households. The school year calendar of having summer vacations was originally developed as part of our agriculture heritage in which children and teenagers were needed to help harvest the crops. In some European countries, formal schooling ends at age 16, followed by choice of vocational school, mandatory military service (for males) or for a few college. (2) *Nonconformity*. This fits in with the need for autonomy. To break from the established culture this is usually most evident in fashion, hairstyle, hair length, music and language when compared with the choices of their parents. (3) *Need for Freedom*. All adolescents share a desire of longing to be free and to have freedom of choice. This fits in again with separation issues. However, this need also coexists with a (4) *Need for Structure*. It has been a common observation in residential adolescent chemical dependency treatment programs, that as much as they complain initially, adolescents seem to feel comfort and secure with the high degree of structure. Another way to view this is in terms of the strict codes of behavior found in delinquent gangs. (5) Finally, the *Need for Peer Acceptance*, as mentioned earlier, is a drive so strong that it will overpower the adolescent's sense of morality, ethics and connection with the family, even that of a nurturing, loving family system.

Thus far, we have been discussing adolescents as a relatively homogeneous group. However, professionals working with adolescents know there is a vast difference between a 13-year old and an 18-year old, an 8th grader and a high school senior, or the "worldly drop-out." Here, we will be referring to distinctions in early, middle and late adolescence.

Early adolescence covers approximately ages 13 to 15. These are ages of emotional lability, frantic and phrenetic activity which seems relentless. The group rules and usually the most pathological member of the group is looked up to as a leader. It is therefore, not unusual for teenagers to be quite cruel at these ages. Anyone, who is "different" because of physical, mental disability, ethnicity or culture, or physical appearance, becomes the subject of ridicule. Many can remember with a degree of embarrassment taking part in the heartless ridicule.

Middle adolescence (ages 15-17) is characterized by more settling in, i.e., more introspective and self-conscious behavior. Here adolescents are still peer-oriented but the most pathological teenager is usually no longer intimidating the group. Cruelty becomes less frequent as group members are now able to tell one another to "knock it off." Steady relationships and dating take on utmost importance. Constant bickering, arguing with parents and siblings, most of the time will be critical and negative.

Late adolescence (ages 17-19) is characterized by more settling down. This is where the "tasks" become more focused upon. At this point, decisions regarding careers, relationships, issues of separations are in the forefront. Those adolescents who do not progress become Peter Pans, so to speak. They never really grow up. In late adolescence, one begins to realize that life does not hold limitless possibilities.

ADOLESCENT THINKING: WHY ADOLESCENTS ARE NOT MINI-ADULTS

Those chemical dependency professionals who have worked with both adolescents and adults are aware that many of the treatment techniques and strategies that are effective with adults are not with adolescents. Often this is because of the inherent differences in adult and adolescent thinking. Much of the writing of David Elkind (1984), has been devoted to exploring the cognitive differences in adolescents. Based upon Piaget's theory, it is noted that adolescents are beginning to move from concrete operational thought, i.e., here and now, concrete syllogistic logic to formal operational thinking which involves the capacity to engage in propositional thinking, go beyond the here and now, understand abstract concepts and subjects. Elkind points out that the adolescent's new ability to reason abstractly and to imagine the ideal and perfection is why they become hypercritical of parents, authority, and cultural institutions such as church, school, etc. Being able to imagine the perfect parents or perfect family and now realizing that yours is not perfect makes for a critical, argumentative adolescent. The media has been all too happy to put forth an idealized image of family life, e.g., Ozzie and Harriet, The Brady Bunch, Family, Happy Days, even Eddie Munster seemed pretty happy and content in an atmosphere of family harmony. The adolescent's idealism also accounts for his/ her uncanny ability to pick up on the slightest hypocrisy in adults while often being unable to live up to his/her own expectations. To an adolescent expressing an ideal is equal to living up to it.

Also characteristic of teenagers is self-consciousness. This newfound dilemma is based upon the adolescent's ability to "think about thinking," to think about what goes on in his/her mind and to imagine what's going on in the minds of others. Because of their self-centered concerns, adolescents assume that everyone else is similarly concerned with them. This is what Elkind refers to as the "imaginary audience," which is characterized by always feeling on stage, that everyone is always watching you. If you have ever witnessed a young adolescent pretending to play an imaginary guitar or drums, it was most likely being performed before an imaginary audience.

Another characteristic of adolescent thinking which is especially important as a defense in chemical dependency is the "personal fable." The fable goes something like this, "Bad things happen to other people but not to me," or "Other people will grow old and die, but not me." The fable is within all of us to some extent, but has its origins in adolescent thinking. Revising the fable to accommodate reality is what makes risk-taking and risky drug-taking so appealing. It also makes alcohol and drug education with early and middle adolescents superfluous.

THE IMPACT OF CHEMICAL DEPENDENCY ON ADOLESCENT DEVELOPMENT: TREATMENT CONSIDERATIONS

Maturational development is generally regarded to be impeded or halted when adolescents become chemically dependent. Therefore, one may be counseling a chronological 20-year old, who is emotionally 14 years old. This section explores some of the reasons why development becomes affected so dramatically.

Baumrind and Moselle (1985) provide an excellent overview on the impact of chemical abuse on the developing adolescent. They point to the concept "developmental lag" as explaining how this impediment occurs. Here, it is hypothesized that alcohol and drugs interfere with growth by obscuring differences between work and play contexts; promoting a false sense of reality; reinforcing a sense of being "special" or having limitless possibilities; enabling avoidance of realistic confrontations with the demands of society; obscuring social reality, rules and mores; maintaining homeostasis within the family while pretending to be moving towards independence and separation.

The chemically dependent adolescent essentially lives in a world mostly made up of fantasy and personal fables. The inability or avoidance in confronting the demands of the environment was best exemplified by a 15-year old chemically dependent male, who retreated to the fantasy world of the game, "Dungeons and Dragons" whenever confronted with conflict. In this fantasy world, he was no longer powerless, and would always win out against adversity. Adolescents whose drugs of choice are primarily in the hallucinogen category often reveal several of these "developmental lag" characteristics, precisely because of this constant retreat from reality.

Also important is the notion of chemical dependency maintaining homeostasis. Although it appears that the chemically dependent adolescent is independent, this often is a facade. It is easy to mistake rule-breaking and total peer-orientation with independence. Therefore, these adolescents will masquerade as independent and confident in their ability to handle themselves in any situation. Often this pseudo-maturity is shaken as soon as practical plans for independent living are discussed. Co-dependent families often reinforce dependent behavior by enabling the adolescent to avoid dealing with the natural consequences of his/her actions. These family rules are rigid and entrenched. Reilly (1984) provides a good analogy of the family therapist's role of preparing the family to "boast" their adolescent into a "launch sequence" provided the proper conditions are conducive for a "countdown." In order to prepare the family for liftoff, they must be able to negotiate issues of separation and fear of loss.

Baumrind and Moselle (1985) also indicate that "Amotivational Syndrome" and "Psychosocial Dysfunction" are consequences of prolonged drug use. AMS was usually associated with prolonged marijuana use. While these authors do not consider marijuana use as the cause of AMS, they propose that "prolonged marijuana use by young adolescents intensifies and consolidates AMS" (pg. 55). This usually results in underachievement, lack of vocational goals, school dropout, inconsistent job histories and lowered energy levels. Yet, marijuana (and most other mood-alterers) will produce a false sense of power and achievement, which gives the adolescent the illusion of accomplishment. In differentiating the "normal" adolescent's idealistic fantasies of limitless possibilities from the chemically dependent adolescent's illusions of achievement, one must look at how each will respond when their fantasy is confronted or under attack. The nonchemically dependent adolescent will usually begrudgingly make some concession, while the chemically dependent youngster will persist and defend the illusion endlessly. Eventually, the nonaddicted youngster will move out of illusions of being special, having unlimited possibilities and fantasies of achievement without effort. The chemically dependent adolescent will remain locked into these illusions.

Psychosocial dysfunction results from prolonged drug use because adolescents will use drugs to "achieve states" which otherwise would occur in everyday interaction in human relationships. Chemically dependent adolescents therefore, have difficulty in empathic communication, which is the result of not being able to take the role of the other. A prolonged state of egocentrism results. Relationships take on more of an exchange connotation, i.e., "What can you do for me?" or "I will turn you on if you turn me on." Social understanding is confused and distorted.

This egocentrism also manifests itself in the user's lack of taking responsibility for behavior. It becomes necessary to project blame outward in order to protect an already fragile sense of self-esteem. Many chemically dependent adolescents will compensate for low self-esteem and self-derogation (Kaplan, 1980), through flights of grandiosity. Alcohol and drug taking will produce momentary periods of self-enhancement according to Kaplan. In some instances, this low self-esteem factor can be a means of motivating adolescents to accept treatment and to work on those aspects of self which are despised. In the author's doctoral dissertation (Cavaiola, 1985), it was noted that chemically dependent adolescents entering residential treatment exhibit significantly low self-esteem, which eventually improves with treatment, however, clinical observations suggest that those adolescents who score as being satisfied with themselves upon entering treatment, do worse. This can be interpreted perhaps as the absence of motivation for change.

Finally, chemically dependent adolescents fail to achieve a sense of personal identity according to Baumrind and Moselle. As was indicated earlier in the writings of Erikson, personal identity develops as the result of exploring different roles and life paths. Unfortunately, chemically dependent adolescents are not good explorers or "genuine" risk takers. For example, one of our patients thought nothing of driving through the suburban streets of a New Jersey town at 80 mph under the influence of cocaine, but was afraid to ask a girl for a date or go for a job interview when he was abstinent. It is precisely this lack of "normalizing" experiences which keeps the chemically dependent adolescent locked into his/her addiction and from developing a sense of identity. "Street images" often take the place of a genuine personal identity.

Proceeding through the tasks of adolescence, mentioned earlier, involves many anxious, painful, lonely moments which all become part of the adolescent experience. However, the chemically dependent adolescent knows exactly which drug will alleviate anxiety, deaden pain, or obscure feelings of loneliness or alienation. Unfortunately, the price is emotional stagnation, impaired cognitive development and immaturity.

Many of our chemically dependent adolescents, who have suffered some trauma such as the death of a loved one, or who have endured physical or sexual abuse, are at even a greater disadvantage in that they have two issues to work through before they can begin to grow and develop again: (1) acceptance of their chemical dependency, (2) acceptance and resolution of the trauma. Grief work cannot and will not take place without sobriety. The denial that is manifested in chemical dependency provides total protection from their feelings.

Sobriety brings with it hope. We have seen recovering adolescents make tremendous strides in their growth as they moved from the confusion and apprehensions of early sobriety into having a sense of stability in their recovery. This was brought to light when one 18-year old had returned to counseling after being into recovery for longer than a year to discuss career decisions that were facing him. He was beginning to catch up, to deal with age-appropriate tasks. Fortunately, his family had continued to grow as well, in order to allow and encourage his progress and upcoming separation.

CONCLUDING REMARKS:
TREATMENT IMPLICATIONS

The chemical dependency professional working with adolescents must be keenly aware of the issues that are central to adolescent development. Often counselors become frustrated by the adolescent's struggle for power or his/her denial which seems to be entrenched in his/her very being. The keys to breaking through this denial are naturally different from those used with adults by virtue of the fact that adolescents think differently from adults. The counselor must not become personally involved in the power struggle. The program cannot impose an endless set of rules. Simplicity, clarity and consistency are paramount when translating a philosophy into an operating program. The treatment milieu must include daily time for high energy, accelerating activity. However, staff must have the expertise to do more than just lead calisthenics and shoot baskets. Generally, chemical dependent adolescents do not have positive body images and organized games and activities must be sensitive to that and not demand too much at first.

Recognizing the important battles and diffusing or avoiding the unimportant is a critical task for the adolescent chemical dependency staff. Counselors will sometimes get locked into "content" of a particular problem and may therefore miss the adolescent's real issue or concern. One particular case comes to mind of an adolescent who constantly focused on concerns regarding his facial expressions and mannerism. This eventually lead to his disclosing fears of being homosexual. Clinicians working with adolescents must have resolved their own authority issues since they will definitely arise in this environment. Staff need to possess the ability to have fun. Adolescents as we have noted are quick and cruel at pointing out hypocrisies and deficiencies in others. The clinician unable to admit his own personal contradictions, weak points and generally laugh at himself when appropriate, may not have the sense of humor necessary to do this work. By presenting ourselves as infallible, we may be reinforcing the adolescent's belief that adults should and must be perfect.

Expectations for the adolescent's behavior need to be judged relative to appropriate adolescents, not by what is considered to be appropriated by adult standards. For example, expecting the dress to be clean and neat, does not mean suit and tie, appropriate language may not mean a total elimination of "profanity" from their vocabulary.

Since normal adolescent development means "testing," it is important to have a series of checks and balances within the staff itself so as not to react too quickly with therapeutic discharge when you might possibly be on the verge of "passing" the test and getting close to a breakthrough with an adolescent patient. Just as it is the role of the adult to set limits, it is the role of the adolescent to test them. Developing a rapport with an adolescent client often appears very different from that of an adult. As much as confrontation works with adolescents, it is often not the only way to break into their trust, certainly it is not the quickest. Often firmly advocating for them (not to be confused with rescuing) gets you closer to a relationship that will soon allow you the opportunity to confront. Sometimes we may have to take off our counselor hats, in order to achieve rapport. In a recent interview with a particularly angry and resistant adolescent (who was fearful of being in a residential program), we found a common interest to talk about in skiing. This paved the way for a therapeutic relationship.

It is important to recognize both the similarities in adolescents as well as the differences. As was indicated earlier, middle and late adolescence each bring certain characteristics and unique challenges to the individual clinician. Mixed groups of boys and girls and same sex groups, need to be fluid options in treatment, since these stages each bring differing needs for that exchange and help personal growth. Adolescents in treatment are often amazed that they can relate to someone of the opposite sex and that they share similar feelings. Program structure must allow for the staff to act intuitively and shift the therapeutic interventions on a weekly or daily basis if need be.

In assessing and treating adolescent chemical dependency, it becomes of utmost importance to recognize where that youngster is in the developmental process. Where are they stuck? Where is their family stuck? What hurdles must the adolescent negotiate successfully in order to resume growth. It is precisely the role of the chemical dependency counselor both to help the adolescent on the road to recovery as well as to help point the direction and to help the adolescent avoid pitfalls, sidetracks and detours.

Great care in treatment planning needs to be given to balancing the individual counseling and family counseling time. The treatment group is not to be viewed an alternative for that individual work as it very well may be in an adult facility. Adolescents rarely get "positive" as quickly as adults seem to in a residential setting.

We as professionals, are the key and need to continuously provide and repeat often the consistent message, "Easy does it, but do it."

REFERENCES

Baumrind, D. (1986). Authoritarian vs. authoritative control. *Adolescence*, 3, 255-272.

Baumrind, D. and Moselle, K.A. (1985). A developmental perspective on adolescent drug abuse. In *Alcohol and Substance Abuse in Adolescence*. Ed. Stimmel, B., New York: The Haworth Press, Inc., 41-67.

Cavaiola, A. (1985). *Life Stress, Personality Correlates and the Effect of Treatment on Adolescent Chemical Dependency*, Unpublished doctoral dissertation. Hofstra University, Hempstead, New York.

Conger, J.J. (1983). *Current Issues in Adolescent Development*. APA Catalog of Selected Documents in Psychology, 6, American Psychological Association. Washington, D.C.

Elkind, David (1984). *All Grown Up and No Place to Go: Teenagers in Crisis*. Reading, Massachusetts: Addison-Wesley.

Erikson, E.H. (1968). *Identity: Youth and Crisis*. New York: Norton.

Freud, A. (1958). Adolescence. *Psychoanalytic Study of the Child*, 13, 255-278.

Jessor, S. L. and Jessor, R. (1974). Maternal idealogy and adolescent problem behavior. *Developmental Psychology*, 10, 246-254.

Kaplan, H.B. (1980). *Deviant Behavior in Defense of Self*. New York: Academic Press.

Offer, D. and Offer, J. (1975). *From Teenage to Young Manhood*. New York: Basic Books.

Reilly, Dennis M. (1984). Family Therapy with Adolescent Drug Abusers and Their Families: Defying Gravity and Achieving Escape Velocity. Journal of Drug Issues, Inc., 2, 381-391.

Woititz, J. (1984). Adult children of alcoholics. *Alcoholism Treatment Quarterly*, 1, 71-99.

Adolescents at Risk
for Chemical Dependency:
Identification and Prevention Issues

Matthew M. Schiff, MD
Alan A. Cavaiola, PhD, CAC

INTRODUCTION

National statistics point to the proliferation of alcohol and drug abuse among today's adolescents. The National Institute of Drug Abuse (NIDA) (1985), reports 1 in 20 high school seniors use marihuana or alcohol daily. It is estimated by the National Institute of Alcohol Abuse and Alcoholism (NIAAA), that 1.3 million teenagers between the ages of 13 and 17, abuse alcohol and other substances. There have been alarming increases in emergency room and crisis intervention visits which totalled approximately 60,000 per year (Beschner & Friedman, 1982). Increasing admissions to adolescent chemical dependency treatment centers and varying hospitals correspond to these statistics.

As chemical dependency becomes increasingly accepted as a primary diagnosis in adolescence, very little information and data is being collected about those teenagers who are most "at-risk" for chemical dependency. This article discusses "at-risk" populations and various methods of prevention directed toward them.

Essentially, there are two major groups which we need to be concerned about. The first is comprised of those young people who are affected by familial chemical dependency. This is the "Number

Matthew M. Schiff is Director of Child and Adolescent Psychiatry at Monmouth Medical Center, Long Branch, NJ. Alan A. Cavaiola is Clinical Director of Monmouth Chemical Dependency Treatment Center in Long Branch, NJ.

One'' factor for placing a youngster at risk for chemical dependency. This risk factor, however, is plagued by nature versus nurture debates. One side focuses on the chaotic, inconsistent, and poorly nurtured environment of a child in an alcoholic family. The other side focuses on adoption studies and possible genetic influences. According to the American Academy of Child and Adolescent Psychiatry, 1986, there are approximately seven million children of alcoholics in the country today. The second group is made up of those children who are "at-risk" or vulnerable because of a host of life or physical stressors. In the sections that follow, these two "at-risk" groups will be examined more closely.

AT-RISK POPULATIONS: FAMILIAL-HISTORICAL LOADING FOR CHEMICAL DEPENDENCY

Adolescent chemical dependency often presents clinicians with a confusing diagnostic picture. Accurate history taking in the form of a three generational family genogram is essential in sorting out etiological factors. Familial lines to chemical dependency have become an accepted tenet over the past decade. Basically, chemical dependency "breeds" chemical dependency. Cotten (1979), for example, reported that a person treated for chemical dependency is six times more likely to have had a chemically dependent father. Adoption studies, such as Bohman (1978), show a 20% correlation between alcoholic biologic fathers and their alcoholic offspring. It appears that the greater the genetic commonality, the greater the likelihood of chemical dependency, for example identical twins versus fraternal twins (Kaij, 1960). Also, an offspring with two alcoholic parents has a greater likelihood of becoming alcoholic than a son or daughter with one alcoholic parent. Statistics from inpatient adolescent chemical dependency centers (Harrison & Hoffman, 1987; Schiff, Cavaiola & Harrison, 1984) report high rates of parental and grandparental alcohol and drug dependence. Historians must be able to differentiate family problems or stressors which may have been alcohol or drug related, such as accidents, hospitalizations and legal/social difficulties.

The practical applications of the genogram should tease out other pertinent, yet less obvious factors, such as hyperactivity, conduct disorder, and affective disorder. Bohman (1978), Cantwell (1972), and Goodwin (1975), uncovered a 15 to 20% correlative link between male alcoholics and their hyperactive, conduct disorder offspring. Historical difficulties in this area include accidents, early legal trouble, school behavior problems, distractibility, and impulsivity histories.

Woodruff (1979) and Paton, Kessler and Kandel (1977) took the previous research of depression and manic depression in families and added the fact that up to 25% of chemically dependent treated patients had pre or post depressive periods. Early history can include depressive symptoms such as poor sleep induction, early morning awakening, interrupted nightmarish sleep, poor appetite, bulimia, suicidal thought or action, crying spells, anhedonia, phobias, anxiety attacks and substance use for depressive relief. Manic type symptoms such as pathological gambling, over-spending and indiscriminate, often multiple partner promiscuous sexual behavior histories can occur. Detoxification can lead to an exacerbation of some of these symptoms.

A case example involving affective disorder is illustrated:

Norma, a 17-year-old, began drinking and smoking marihuana at age 12. Subsequently, she used noninjectable stimulants at least 30 times. Unmanageability in school and at home occurred. Mood control problems, since third grade, included episodic depression, separation fears, anhedonia, crying spells, and periodic suicidal thought. Norma's father had a history of depression, withdrawal, and agitation. Norma's first trial on antidepressants occurred at age eight. The chemical dependence started at age 12 with pubertal onset and the birth of a newly born sibling. The substance use served to lessen emotional pain and anesthetize moods. The depression worsened, bringing on stimulant use, isolation from peers, and high amounts of guilt over increased promiscuity. After a period of detoxification, early morning awakening, sleep disturbance, guilt, depressed mood, and inability to manage peer group discussion had increased dramatically.

Hyperactivity, conduct disorder and affective disorder are often deeply hidden by denial, deception or adoption. Careful family history taking and clinical observation prevent misdiagnosis or possible reasons for chemical dependence relapse.

AT-RISK POPULATIONS: INTERNAL OR EXTERNAL INTERFERENCES

There is a second group of adolescents who are at high risk for chemical dependency, which occurs without the predominance of a chemical dependency family history, such as that discussed in the previous section. Interferences are defined here as unavoidable environmental influences, family and community stressors and creative, developmental, and neurological characteristics, which set the adolescent up for increased vulnerability to mood-altering chemical involvement.

The Alienated or Peer-Scapegoated Adolescent

This first subtype of at risk adolescent, is best characterized by the type of teenager who does not fit in with any existing peer subgroup. Although the names change, high school cliques are omnipresent. The "jocks," "preppies," "punks," or other cliques that would form around specific interests, such as students who are in the school band or drama club etc. These groups require some level of social skill for entrance. This is not the case, however, with the "burnouts" or the "space cadets," in which the only requirement for inclusion is alcohol or drug taking behavior. This is often where we find the adolescent who feels alienated or different from his/her peers. They may have been subject to ridiculing or teasing from other adolescents as is the case of the peer-scapegoated teenager. This particular group of "at risk" adolescents is easily identifiable long before the onset of any mood altering chemical use. They are essentially the "loners" or the "lost child" within their social and family milieu. Unfortunately, unless there is some other co-existing problem, such as school failure or learning disability, these students will usually go unnoticed.

It is of interest to note that the literature pertaining to mood-altering chemical abuse and alienation is varied. Kamali and Steer (1976) found that drug use was not significantly related to escapism or boredom in high school students that they studied. On the other hand, Lasky and Ziegenfuss (1979), did conclude that substance users showed significantly higher alienation scores than nonusers. These authors, however, do raise an interesting distinction between what they label as "social anomie" and "personal alienation." Although social anomie may be characteristic of adolescents in our society given their lack of status power, it appears that the adolescent at-risk for chemical dependency more often suffers from personal alienation.

Also involved in this "at-risk" category are those adolescents who have lost interest in school and traditional work values. Donovan, Jessor and Jessor (1983), concluded that those adolescents who continued to manifest alcohol problems into young adulthood were characterized by lower values placed on achievement, lower expectations of academic achievement, and higher acceptability of socially unacceptable behavior.

Attention Deficit Disorder—Learning Disabled Adolescent

This next group of "at-risk" adolescents is comprised of those teenagers who do not fit in with a particular peer group because of differences in cognitive, attentional, behavioral control, and peer relations skills. Characteristics of this group include impulsivity, disruptiveness, and action before thought. When these factors collide with pubertal onset, middle school entrance, and the increased availability of alcohol and drugs, the potential for chemical dependency is tremendous. Wood, Wender and Reimherr (1983) had assessed the prevalence of an attention deficit disorder, residual type, in a population of young adult male alcoholics, who were studied while they were in residential alcoholism treatment programs. They found a 33% prevalence rate of attention deficit disorder, in childhood (and in adulthood) within their population. It was concluded that attention deficit disorder may be associated with increased risks for development of alcoholism. In an earlier study, Tarter, McBride and Buonpane (1977) found in a subgroup of adult alcoholic patients a much higher frequency of minimal brain dysfunction; now renamed attention deficit disorder, than other subgroups studied. In a five year follow-up study of hyperactive children, it was noted that the hyperactives were found to drink alcohol more frequently than a matched group of children who have difficulty in school for reasons other than hyperactivity (Blouin, Bornstein & Trites, 1978). All the aforementioned studies point to the "at-risk" nature of children and adolescents with attention deficit disorder.

The risks can be generationally cyclized by the mother who drinks or uses drugs in pregnancy. This often causes some stage of fetal alcohol and/or drug syndrome in pregnancy. Sokol, Miller and Martier (1981), and Steinhausen, Nestler and Spohr (1982), report that 50% of any drug or alcohol related pregnancy will have facial, skeletal, or neurological abnormalities. These pregnancies occur frequently in the U.S.; one in 75, according to Little and Streissguth (1982).

A case sample which best illustrates this type of adolescent is presented:

> Lawrence R., is a 15-year-old, third of five children, from a middle class, immigrant family who began using alcohol and marihuana, following entrance into the middle school in 6th grade. The developmental history reveals an over 9 lb. birth weight. During early childhood, Lawrence's mother consistently complained to doctors and teachers of her child's inattentiveness and possible hyperactivity. At age 12, a 93 full scale I.Q. on the WISC-R revealed deficits in visual memory, visual motor integration, and verbal abstraction, despite superior range spatial relation scores. His reading and spelling achievement scores were two years below grade level. The test results plus early birth history, indicated neurological impairment factors and early attention deficit disorder themes. It was also significant that Lawrence was the only one of five children to demonstrate any problems with alcohol or drugs, similarly no one within Lawrence's extended family had ever had a problem with alcohol or drugs.
>
> From sixth grade alcohol and marihuana use, Lawrence went on to use cocaine, amphetamines, and LSD, at least 40 times each. As his chemical dependence progressed, he turned

from an inattentive, passive, disorganized, day-dreaming child into an aggressive, antiauthoritarian, law breaking child. He entered the chemical dependence residential program on probation for possession and theft.

Both the nonfamilial and familial attention deficit disorder and learning disabled child share feelings of being different from his/her peer groups. Often, the learning disabled child who has been classified by the Child Study Team within his/her school, perhaps as Perceptually Impaired or Neurologically Impaired, feels that he/she is flawed or "retarded." They are often failing academically and socially. Very few of these youngsters who have come into residential treatment have accurate information regarding their learning disability or academic strengths and weaknesses. Mood-altering chemical abuse becomes a way of assimilating into the main stream of their school and peer group. It is often unfortunate, that the very drugs of choice of these learning disabled youngsters, will only exacerbate their learning difficulties (Miller, 1985). A good example of this is the youngster who has problems with organization and memory, who will abuse marihuana, which will have an even more devastating effect on these abilities.

Gifted and Talented Adolescent

The gifted and talented youngster is at-risk for chemical dependency in low percentages. Stress for perfection, need for something different, lack of individuality and creativity in educational programming, and sensitivity to their own delicate perceptiveness increase the chances for chemical dependence. These children are often labeled incorrectly by other frightened or competitive peers as "poindexters," "nerds," "oddballs" or outlandish trendsetters. This can cause social ostracism and isolation. Drug and alcohol abuse then becomes attractive to these youngsters as a way of gaining entry into more desirable cliques or peer groups. The following is a case example which illustrates the plight of the gifted child:

Rachael is a 16-year-old, oldest of two children, who began using alcohol and marihuana at age 12. Rachael had been a straight "A," creative student throughout grammar school, however, upon entering middle school, her grades had begun to falter. One of her teachers had become aware that Rachael was the subject of ridicule by some of her peers because of her high grades and increasing weight control problem. As she moved from middle school into high school, Rachael had become more rebellious, both at school and at home. She would stay out past curfew and was beginning to fail several of her subjects. At the same time, her mood-altering abuse continued to increase and Rachael began to experiment with several other substances. Her great interest and productive talent began to decline. She gave up her previously treasured music lessons. Her entrance into treatment was precipitated by Rachael's being referred to a student assistant counselor within her school because of her attitude and poor school achievement.

Each of the aforementioned groups share in common, the bond of being made to feel different because of anomalies that have occurred in their intellectual or physical development. It appears also, because of social and personal alienation, that these adolescents are attracted to mood-altering chemical abuse perhaps as a means of gaining entry into an accepted peer group or clique. It is often the case that these youngsters may project attitudes of arrogance or hostility which only serve to mask underlying feelings of insecurity with fears that their defenses will be unmasked to other social teens.

Adolescents from Dysfunctional Families

With this particular group of "at-risk" adolescents, we are referring to families that are dysfunctional for reasons other than chemical dependency. These families' children may be exposed to extreme marital discord, a long, drawn out divorce or visitation and custody battle, in which children become pawns; or enmeshed with one and even two parents.

Stanton and Todd (1982) were one of the first authors to discuss the addict's role as "martyr" within dysfunctional, over-meshed families. From a family systems perspective, the addict stays "sick" in order to keep the focus on himself/herself, and, thereby, holds together a dysfunctional marriage or liaison. Within our treatment setting, we have often seen adolescents whose onset of drug and alcohol abuse coincided with threats of a marital separation and family breakup. In instances like these, it is not unusual for the parents to rally around their adolescent son or daughter as their lives become increasingly more unmanageable due to chemical abuse. It was of interest to note that the family roles which are so often referred to in the family alcoholism treatment literature (Black, 1981), were originated by Virginia Satir to describe the coping reactions of children within any kind of dysfunctional or stressful family. In a residential program, we have seen a cross-representation of adolescents who have adopted various family roles, i.e., hero, mascot, lost child, scapegoat, in families where other chemical dependencies were nonexistent. These children and adolescents are "at-risk" by virtue of the stressful conditions that exist within their family. Prior research points to the correlations between stressful life events, as perhaps being a precursor to adolescent chemical dependency. Duncan (1977) found higher levels of stress during the year preceding the onset of illicit drug use in a group of 31 drug dependent adolescents. Cavaiola (1985) found that chemically dependent adolescents had significantly greater life stress scores when compared to a control group of nonchemically dependent adolescents, however, there was a nonsignificant difference between the groups in regard to stressors that predated the onset of alcohol and drug use. (These stressors often included family factors such as divorces, remarriage, illnesses within the family, unemployment, or death of a family member.) This suggests that there were far more stressful events that happened around the time of use or as a consequence of mood-altering chemical use within the treatment group. Obviously, not all adolescents who experience a high level of life stressors become chemically dependent, however, they do constitute an "at-risk" group.

Other types of family dysfunction have also been linked to adolescent chemical dependency. Lack of parental supervision (Hawkins, Lishner & Catalano, 1986), inconsistent rules, negative communication patterns and absence of praise have also been found to correlate. Similarly, positive family interaction and family bonding may impact positively on prevention.

The following are two brief case examples which best illustrate the type of family dynamics which are often found in chemical dependency treatment programs:

> *Dawn* is a 15-year-old, high school sophomore, who was referred into treatment by the court after shoplifting with some friends. A pretrial evaluation revealed that Dawn had been drinking heavily and abusing marihuana, cocaine, and hallucinogens since age 12. She lives with her mother and maternal grandmother. Dawn's parents separated when she was a toddler and since that time she has only seen her father only once. Although it was suspected he was chemically dependent, this could not be substantiated by the mother.
>
> Dawn has always felt that she has "two mothers." At times, she will feel close to her mother; however, that only occurs when her mother and grandmother are fighting. At times, Dawn sees her mother as a sister, while at other times she will see her as a strict mother. As Dawn was entering puberty, she felt that both her mother and grandmother had become even more strict. They refused to let her go out or socialize with friends, especially boys. Dawn began to experiment with drugs in school. She would lie about babysitting jobs in order to be with her friends and get high. As Dawn's chemical abuse increased, so did her defiance and acting out until the courts became involved and referred her into treatment.

> *Jimmy* is a 16-year-old, high school junior who was referred to residential treatment by the courts because of drunk driving without a license. Jimmy began drinking and taking drugs when he was around eleven. He currently lives with his natural father and his paramour.
>
> Jimmy's parents had been having arguments and fights since he was around nine years old. He overheard an argument in which there were accusations of infidelity. Jimmy recalls being afraid that his parents would split up, however, by the time they did, when he was ten, Jimmy was somewhat relieved. He continued to see his father, although his mother retained custody. Jimmy recalls feeling caught in the middle

between his parents and it was not unusual for him to try to mediate arguments or try to get his parents back together. His getting into trouble at school became a means of getting his parents to talk, even though the focus was on him. Jimmy became enraged when his father began to date and again when he began living with a girlfriend. Jimmy felt displaced and unloved. He began to socialize with guys at school who were going through similar problems. In this group, Jimmy got into heavy drug and alcohol use.

Upon admission to the treatment center, Jimmy was pleased to hear both of his parents would be required to participate in family therapy.

Adolescents from Dysfunctional Environments

This population of "at-risk" adolescents is comprised of those youth who are considered disadvantaged because of poverty, high crime rate neighborhoods, lack of educational or occupational opportunity and lack of social mobility. Perhaps most represented within these groups are the minority and ethnic groups which are held back from assimilating into the prevailing culture. Often, these youth are not identified as being at-risk for chemical dependency because of their cultural differences. For example, in some Latino cultures, it is accepted and encouraged as a display of machismo or maleness, to get drunk on a Friday night. A young person growing up in that culture could be more likely to adopt that cultural value. Does this make the individual more at risk? This type of explanation was sometimes given to explain why there are higher rates of alcoholism in Irish cultures where it was acceptable to drink apart from the family, while in Jewish and Italian culture there were lower rates of alcoholism supposedly because drinking was part of family milieu. In any event, social, economic, educational and occupational disadvantages can and do make for high risk situations with regard to chemical dependency. These risks may be tied in to varying familial and nonfamilial risk factors that exist. The idea of an increasing risk factor matrix that can be scored through historical data and interview should be considered in the future.

The Traumatized Adolescent: Although this group can include an array of various cases, the preponderance of cases seen within our treatment programs, are comprised of those adolescents with complicated bereavement issues, or post-traumatic stress disorders which relate to having been the victim of physical and/or sexual abuse. In the first subgroup, we have noted from clinical observation that many adolescents that enter treatment have had major losses. This would include the death of a family member, close friends and significant others. There are often adolescents who are "stuck" in their grieving process, usually in the denial, depression, or anger stages. Mood-altering chemicals, usually of the sedative-hypnotic type, provide momentary and specious relief from emotional pain associated with complicated bereavement.

The following is a case illustration:

> Fred C. is a 17-year-old, high school senior, who was referred for chemical dependency evaluation and treatment by a student assistance counselor within his school. While Fred had begun experimenting with alcohol and occasional marihuana smoking at around age 15, it was noted that his experimentation at this time was nonproblematic. During Christmas time of his Junior year, trauma had struck Fred's family. His older sister was murdered by her violent, jealous boyfriend after a party to which they had gone. The boyfriend then turned the gun on himself and committed suicide. Fred could vividly recall the horror and disbelief that both he and his family had experienced upon learning of his sister's death. Fred could also remember being in shock through the wake and funeral, and vividly recalls his uncle leaning into the limosine after the funeral services, and stating to him, "You've got to be strong for your family." Fred's family had difficulty in talking about the death and each tended to isolate from one another. Fred recalls feeling both depressed and enraged, and yet, because the murderer had also killed himself, Fred had no one to want to direct his rage. For the next six months, he proceeded to drink and use drugs on a daily basis. Since he would often blackout, friends would tell him the next day of his reckless, daredevil behavior, in which Fred would defy death. It was not until Fred had begun to open up to the student's assistance

counselor about his dependence on mood-altering chemicals to cope with his emotional pain, that the school was then able to accept that he needed chemical dependency treatment.

Complications in the bereavement process note that many in-mourning families have a great deal of difficulty in talking about their grief, such as in the case illustration above. These adolescents often feel that they have lost more than one person. They have no one to turn to or talk with about their feelings. Unfortunately, they often harbor feelings of guilt, responsibility, self-blame, and anger which place them at even higher risk for chemical abuse.

The second group of traumatized adolescents who are at risk for chemical dependence is comprised of those youngsters who had been physically and/or sexually abused. This group overlaps the characteristics of severe trauma with significant familial risk. The majority of perpetrator to victim to observer cases occur in genera-tionally, abusive, chemically dependent families or extended fam-ilies. Cavaiola and Schiff (1987) studied inpatient abused chemi-cally dependent adolescents in eight week treatment programs and compared them to inpatient nonabused chemically dependent youth in eight week treatment and to high school attending students. Thirty percent of the first 500 adolescent admissions to inpatient chemical dependence treatment were abused. Sixty-eight percent came into treatment with clandestine elements still in place. Signifi-cant numbers of these children used harder drugs more frequently at two years on average earlier age (age 11). Potter-Efron and Potter-Efron (1985) found similar results in a midwestern chemical depen-dence treatment center with over 35% of teenagers reporting physi-cal or sexual abuse.

Kempe and Kempe (1984) found similar characteristics to Ca-vaiola and Schiff (1986) in regard to abused adolescents. Promiscu-ity with, at times, associated teenage pregnancy, runaway, school special classification and failure, delinquency, suicide attempts, homicidal ideation, and attempts at previous ineffective social ser-vice or mental health intervention, often accompanied chemical de-pendence in this group. Males were more prone to violence toward property, animals, and person. Females were more prone to promis-cuity, self-mutilation, and suicide gestures and attempts.

The following is an example of a sexual abuse case:

> Andrea D. was a 14-year-old, oldest of three, eighth grader who was admitted to an inpatient chemical dependence treatment unit following almost a year of alcohol and marihuana abuse. She had left a recent trail of lethargy, truancy, assaults on fellow students and family, school failure, school emotionally disturbed classification, and two pill overdose suicide attempts. She appeared to be following in family footsteps. Three grandparents are alcoholic and her father was a violently abusive, post divorce, alcoholic. He toted weapons including guns and used them as threats. He beat up the mother in front of Andrea. Only paternal sexual or violent abuse of Andrea was denied.
>
> Andrea's family history was followed and intermixed with the trauma of a physically forced sexual abuse. A teenage boy held her while a 19-year old penetrated her. Andrea was previously trusting and friendly to both boys and girls. She had been an excellent student and athlete. Post trauma, she changed peer groups and began using alcohol and marihuana for the first time. She developed a negative body image. She became mildly anorexic, angry, scared of retaliation from the boys' families, and pugilistic to others. She became sexually promiscuous without contraceptive or venereal disease prevention method use. Her behavior affected family, school, and community. She was brought into treatment through a legal entre from a detention center.
>
> Psychiatric and psychological evaluation showed denial, projection, suspiciousness and hostility. She demonstrated distorted body image, feelings of lack of protection, helplessness, and powerlessness. She only showed her difficulties in group in the 5th week of treatment as the secret surfaced.

The links of violent and sexual abuse are shown in this presented case. Generations of difficulties can produce a long term conspiracy of silence. The resulting morbidity and mortality that occurs from abuse will be presented in the next section.

RISK FACTORS IN VIOLENCE TRIAD
(SUICIDE, HOMICIDE AND ACCIDENT)
SYMPTOMATOLOGY

Kratcoski (1982), Duncan and Duncan (1971), Paperny and Deisher (1983), Silbert and Pines (1984), Sanchez-Dirks (1979) and Hindman (1979) have all documented the links of parental abusive chemical dependence to murder, family violence, sexual abuse, and prostitution. These problems often occur in and across generations.

In our prior research (Cavaiola & Schiff, 1986), chemically dependent previously abused youth were studied utilizing psychological test data and psychiatric evaluations. Low self-esteem, severity in psychopathology, and hostility trends were found. These trends along with difficulty in a group setting were links to the violence triad in these youngsters. Homicidal thoughts and actions occurred at least 35% more often in abused, chemically dependent adolescents. The figures are in the 10% range for accidents and actual suicide attempts. Approximately 10% had been involved in animal torture and cruelty.

An example of a violence triad case is presented:

Neal S. was treated in an inpatient eight week chemical dependence program. He was a 17-year-old, 12th grade, alternative school student. He had a four year history of daily alcohol and marihuana dependence along with increasing mescaline and lysergic acid (several hundred hits) abuse. He had frequent visual hallucinations on drugs, flashbacks while not on drugs, and aggressivity to person and property, at home, school and in the community. He often thought of killing his abusive, alcoholic father and would sharpen knives at home in anticipation of this event. He rammed a car into his own house. Despite outpatient psychological intervention, increasingly florid symptomatology occurred. He required three days of librium detoxification to stop the tremors and disordered vital signs of alcohol withdrawal (a pint a day consumption).

Neal had reason to react so violently. His father had given facial beatings to his mother which Neal had frequently observed. Neal was episodically similarly beaten. Neal was an abuse victim and observer. He lived with this hell for most of his life. His mother was psychiatrically hospitalized with severe depressions. Neal was left alone with his drunken, abusive father.

Neal's agitation calmed while in treatment. His flashbacks reduced. He began to understand chemical dependency through group, AA and NA meetings. He remained sober, even after inpatient treatment. He was able to defuse enough abusive history and anger to halt identification with his aggressive father, halt illegal fighting, and homicidal family thoughts. He neutralized enough aggression to finish high school, obtain a job and three years later join the armed services. His life ended tragically in a motorcycle accident in his fourth year after treatment with no autopsy information on alcohol or drug blood and urine testing. The authors will always wonder about this most unfortunate death.

The figures presented correlate to other pioneering studies in runaway shelters and other chemical dependence programs. Hindman (1979) warned that 25% of all murders occur intrafamilially. Drug overdose, self-mutilation, school fighting with objects or weapons, unexplained accidents, especially those involving cyclists, boaters, and pedestrians may involve chemical addiction which often goes unidentified.

Accidents can occur with episodic misfortune. Suspension of teenage judgement can tragically lead to morbidity and mortality. It worsens when semi-intoxicated teenagers are all "partying" together. Accidents, homicides, and suicides involve numerous non-chemically dependent innocent victims. People happen to be taking a walk or ride and are lost forever, felled by the most ferocious of all animal predators: the human being. Further victims of the violence triad at increasingly high risk, are those relatives and friends who have to travel the funeral or mourning path. A violent, unexpected death is always harder to mourn.

Slower, painful deaths can occur from AIDS infection. Teenage pregnancy with the added risk of a fetal alcohol or drug syndrome child can lead to the baby's abuse and death.

The violence triad affects many adolescents; however, often they are not readily identified. Police, court, social service, social work, psychology and psychiatric offices, school and emergency room are all places where the teenager can surface. All prevention efforts must understand the ubiquity of these difficulties.

PREVENTION ISSUES

With the ability to define "at-risk" populations, it then becomes possible to direct prevention and early intervention efforts towards these groups, in such a way as to make a positive impact. Those of us in the chemical dependency field are very much aware of the fact that no disease has ever been eradicated by treatment alone. The question remains, however, as to what would constitute effective prevention efforts. Another factor which needs to be considered is that the risk period for the onset of chemical abuse is getting younger and younger, both in the United States, as well as in other countries (Adler & Kandel, 1983). Unfortunately, prevention efforts have only recently begun to be empirically validated. It is noted that initial prevention efforts were perhaps effective in changing children's and adolescent's knowledge and attitudes regarding substance abuse, however, few of these programs had actually impacted on subsequent substance use (Malvin, Moskowitz, Schaefer & Schaps, 1984; Snow, Gilchrist & Schinke, 1985; Schinke & Gilchrist, 1985). As Schinke and Gilchrist (1985) had so aptly noted, "as with any young science, first substance abuse prevention attempts were crude and largely heuristic. Subsequently, each generation of prevention studies had displayed greater sophistication" (p. 596).

The concept of prevention has been used rather ambiguously. Having originated in the mental health area, prevention had been conceptualized as occurring on three levels; primary, secondary, and tertiary. In general, the goal of prevention is to intervene with individuals prior to the onset of the disease or disorder (Rosenberg & Repucci, 1985). The goals of primary prevention are essential to either: (1) enhance the person's overall psychological help and strengthen confidences, resources, and coping skills as a protection against the disorder, or (2) to reduce the rate of occurrence of the disorder (Bloom, 1979; Cowen, 1980). Secondary prevention efforts are usually directed more at those populations that are identified to be "at-risk." It is here that we feel, based upon our current level of understanding of those groups who are at high risk for chemical dependency, that more prevention efforts can be directed. Studies such as those done by Hoffman and Harrison (1987) and Zarek, Hawkins and Rogers (1987) also help to validate identifiable "at-risk" populations similar to those discussed in this paper. Unfortunately, however, while there is a plethora of studies directed at primary prevention (Schinke & Gilchrist, 1985), there appear to be few studies that focus on secondary prevention directed at "at-risk" groups and longitudinal outcome studies which study their efficacy.

There are also several areas where possible early intervention can take place with these "at-risk" populations. Schools probably provide the best arena for identifying and intervening with these "at-risk" youths. Teachers, school administrators, Child Study Team members, guidance counselors, and student assistance counselors all come in contact with the "at-risk" populations on an ongoing basis. Problems such as school failure, truancy, acting out behavior in the classroom, erratic performance, inattentiveness, depressive-type symptoms, as revealed in writing, poetry or art, social isolation and personal alienation, are all indicators of children who are "at-risk" for chemical dependency. However, schools often feel burdened by financial restraint or curriculum requirements which may interfere with the educational system's ability to become involved in prevention efforts. Here, it may be possible to combine prevention and early intervention programs with other prevention efforts such as mental health or child abuse prevention programming. Programs need to be directed towards enhancing psychological health and strengthening competencies, resources and coping skills.

Since young people are usually making decisions regarding whether or not they are going to use mood-altering chemicals by approximately 5th grade, it is recommended that primary prevention efforts be directed towards K through 6th grades. While secondary prevention efforts could be targeted to those K through 6th grade youngsters who are considered "at-risk." These students might benefit more from affective education, self-esteem building, and enhancement of coping skills programs. By the time students reach middle school years, it is much more appropriate to have early intervention programs which would be aimed at identifying those youngsters who have already begun to abuse mood-altering chemicals and who are exhibiting signs of chemical dependency. Early intervention teams coordinated by student assistance counselors, also need to be made available in all high schools. It is furthermore recommended, that the Child Study Teams, which are usually comprised of school psychologists, school social workers, learning disability specialists, physicians and medical consultants (child psychiatrists, etc.), include a student assistance counselor who specializes in chemical dependency counseling. They can identify and work with those students who are determined to be "at-risk."

Equally important in the role of secondary prevention and early intervention, are the legal, medical, mental health, and social services systems. In identifying children who are "at-risk," police, judges, probation officers, juvenile conference committees, and attorneys all need to be made aware of the "at-risk" populations discussed in this paper. Unfortunately, there are many instances where chemically dependent adolescents have become entangled in the criminal justice system; therefore, their chemical dependency has gone undiagnosed. In instances where the courts are willing to order youngsters for evaluation and treatment, a positive impact can be made prior to the onset of chemical dependency. Similarly, within the spectrum of medical care services, physicians, especially obstetricians, pediatricians, and family practice specialists need to be attuned to the characteristics of the "at-risk" populations and their prototype genograms. They need to be able to refer these youngsters for evaluation and counseling prior to the onset of chemical dependence (Schiff & Cavaiola, 1985).

Both mental health and social service professionals can serve as effective gatekeepers in the identification and early intervention with "at-risk" populations. Here, psychiatrists, psychologists, and social workers need to utilize three generational histories in order to identify chemical dependency patterns or patterns of other problems which may indirectly give clues to chemical dependency. Social service agencies involved in evaluating families where abuse and chemical dependence take place, must have well-trained personnel who are versed in the correlations and links between chemical dependency and physical/sexual abuse. Unfortunately, all of the aforementioned systems have traditionally been more attuned to treating disease and dysfunction. These authors highly recommend that we begin also to look at the children and siblings in homes where there is existing chemical dependency and high risk situations. Therapeutic decisions are chosen between working with a family, separating a family temporarily and separating a family permanently.

CONCLUSION

This article has attempted to create awareness about those various groups of children and adolescents who are most "at-risk" for chemical dependency. It is obvious that there are a great deal of overlapping risk factors which most likely synergistically place these youngsters at even higher risk. For example, an adolescent from a two parent alcoholic, nonmobile, culturally deprived, dysfunctional, abusive family environment, probably constitutes the highest risk factor potential.

Although, the authors have attempted to cite relevant research where available, it is obvious that a great deal of work remains to be done in further elucidating those who are at risk. Long term prospective studies are especially needed. Furthermore, prevention research with these "at-risk" populations is surely lacking.

It would be unfair to our readers, however, to conclude here without making mention of another group of "at-risk" individuals which deserves further consideration and study. This group is comprised of what Rutter (1987) and Garmezy (1985) refer to as the stress-resilient and invulnerables, i.e., individuals who are at high risk, but who do not become dysfunctional. In his most recent article, Rutter (1987), talks of certain "protective processes" which serve to reduce the impact of risk factors. He includes within the realm of protective mechanisms "those that promote self-esteem and self-efficacy through the availability of secure and supportive personal relationships or successful task accomplishment; and those that open up opportunities." In order to provide efficacious prevention programming, we need to know more about these "stress resilient" individuals. What inoculates them against disease or dysfunction in the face of high risk?

The multitude and overlap of "at-risk" individuals does indeed present a thick, at times overwhelming morass. The challenge of the eighties and in future decades needs to channel its efforts towards the prevention of adolescent chemical dependence and its numerous possible sequelae, i.e., homicide, suicide, and accidents. The cost of wasted talent, energy, and life is indeed staggering.

REFERENCES

American Academy of Child & Adolescent Psychiatry (1986), Children of Alcoholics. Facts for Families, II:6.

Adler, I. & Kandel, D. (1983), Risk periods for drug involvement in adolescence in France and Israel: Application of survival analysis to cross-sectional data. *Social Forces*, 62:375-397.

Beschner, G. M. & Friedman, A. S. (1982), "Young Drug Abuse — Problem Issues and Treatment." Mass., Lexington Books, D. C. Heath & Company.

Black, C. (1981), *It Will Never Happen to Me*. M. A. C. Publications, Denver, CO.

Bloom, B. L. (1979), Prevention of mental disorders: Recent advances in theory and practice. *Community Mental Health Journal*, 15:179-191.

Blovin, A. G., Bornstein, R. A. & Trites, R. L. (1978), Teenage alcohol use among hyperactive children: A five year follow-up study. *Journal of Pediatric Psychology*, 3:188-194.

Bohman, M. (1978), Some genetic aspects of alcoholism and criminality — a population of adoptees. *Archives of General Psychiatry*, 25:269-276.

Cantwell, D. P. (1972), Psychiatric illness in the families of hyperactive children. *Archives of General Psychiatry*, 27:414-417.

Cavaiola, A. (1985), Life stress, personality correlates and the effect of treatment on adolescent chemical dependency. Unpublished doctoral discussion, Hofstra University.

Cavaiola, A., Schiff, M., Diedrichsen, C. & Seay, J. (1986), Physical & sexual abuse among chemically dependent adolescents' personality correlates & behavior sequelae (in publication). Proceedings of 11th International Congress of Child & Adolescent Psychiatry and Allied Professions.

Cotton, N. (1979), The familial incidence of alcoholism. *Journal of Studies on Alcoholism*, 40:89-116.

Cower, E. L. (1980), The wooing of primary prevention. *American Journal of Community Psychology*, 8:258-284.

Donovan, J. E., Jessor, R. & Jessor, L. (1983), Problem drinking in adolescence and young adulthood. A follow-up study. *Journal of Studies on Alcohol*.

Duncan, D. F. (1977), Life stress as a precursor to adolescent drug dependence. *The International Journal of the Addictions*, 12:1047-1056.

Duncan, J. W. & Duncan, G. M. (1971), Murder in the family — a study of some homicidal adolescents. *American Journal of Psychiatry*, 127:1498-1502.

Garmezy, N. (1985), Stress resident children: The search for protective factors, in: *Recent Research in Developmental Psychopathology*. J. Stevenson, Ed Perganson Press, Oxford.

Goodwin, D. W., Schulsinger, F., Hermanse, L., Guze, S. B. & Winokur, G. (1975), Alcoholism and the hyperactive child. *Journal of Nervous and Mental Disorders*, 160:349-352.

Hawkins, J. D., Lisher, D. M. & Catalano, R. F. (1985), Childhood predictors and the prevention of adolescent substance abuse. National Institute on Drug Abuse, Research Monograph Series #56.

Hindman, M. D. (1979), Family violence. *Alcohol Health and Research World*, Fall, pp. 2-11.

Harrison, P. A. & Hoffman, N. G. (1987), Adolescent residential treatment intake and follow-up findings. CATOR 1987 Report, St. Paul, MN: CATOR.

Kaij, L. (1960), Alcoholism in twins: studies on the etiology and sequels of abuse of alcohol. University of Lund, Sweden, Dept. of Psychiatry.

Kamili, K. & Steer, R. A. (1976), Polydrug use by high school students: Involvement and correlates. *International Journal of Addictions*, II:337-343.

Kempe, R. S. & Kempe, C. H. (1984), *The Common Secret; Sexual Abuse of Children and Adolescents*. New York, W. H. Freeman & Co.

Kratcoski, P. C. (1982), Child abuse and violence against the family. *Child Welfare*, LXI:7:435-438.

Lasky, D. I. & Ziegenfuss, J. T. (1979), Anomie and drug use in high school students. *International Journal of Addictions*, 14:861-866.

Little, R. E. & Streissguth, A. P. (1982), Effects of alcohol on the fetus — impact and prevention. *Canadian Medical Association Journal*, 125:159-164.

Malvin, J. H., Moskowitz, J. M., Schaeffer, G. A. & Schaps, E. (1984), Teacher training in affective education for the primary prevention of adolescent drug abuse. *American Journal of Drug & Alcohol Abuse*, 10:223-235.

Miller, L. (1985), Neurological assessment of substance abusers: Review and recommendations. *Journal of Substance Abuse Treatment*, 2:5-17.

National Institute on Drug Abuse: U.S. Department of Health and Human Services, C83-07A, NIDA printing offices. Bethesda, MD.

Paperny, D. M. & Deisher, R. W. (1983), Maltreatment of adolescents: the relationship to a predisposition toward violent behavior and delinquency. *Adolescence*, 18:499-506.

Paton, S., Kessler, R. & Kandel, D. (1977), Depressive mood and illegal drug use: A longitudinal analysis. *Journal of Genetic Psychology*, 131:267-289.

Podolsky, D. M. (1985), Alcohol, other drugs and traffic safety. *Alcohol Research World*, 9:4:16-24.

Potter-Efron & Potter-Efron (1985), Family violence as a treatment issue with chemically dependent adolescents. *Alcoholism Treatment Quarterly*, 2:1-15.

Rosenberg, M. S. & Reppucci, N. D. (1985), Primary prevention of child abuse. *Journal of Consulting and Clinical Psychology*, 53:576-585.

Rutter, M. (1987), Psychosocial resilience and protective mechanisms. *American Journal of Orthopsychiatry*, 57:316-331.

Sanchez-Dirks, R. (1979), Reflections on family violence. *Alcohol Health and Research World*, 12-16, Fall.

Schiff, M., Cavaiola, A. & Harrison, L. (1984), Child psychiatry, prevention and chemical dependence. Prevention Symposium for The American Academy of Child and Adolescent Psychiatry Annual Meeting, Toronto, Canada.

Schinke, S. P. & Gilchrist, L. D. (1985), Preventing substance abuse with children and adolescents. *Journal of Consulting and Clinical Psychology*, 53:596-602.

Silbert, M. H. & Pines, A. (1983), Early sexual exploitation as an influence in prostitution. *Social Work*, 285-289.

Snow, W. H., Gilchrist, L. D. & Schinke, S. P. (1985), A critique of progress in adolescent smoking prevention. *Children and Youth Services Review*, 7:1-19.

Sokol, R. J., Miller, S. I. & Martier, S. M. (1981), Identifying the alcohol abusing obstetrical/gynecological patient—U.S. Department of Health and Human Services. *National Institute on Alcohol Abuse and Alcoholism*. Publication AH, pp. 118-1163.

Stanton, M. D. & Todd, T. C. (1982), *The Family Therapy of Drug Abuse and Addiction*. New York: Guilford Press.

Steinhausen, H. C., Nestler, V. & Spohr, H. L. (1982), Development and psychopathology of children with the fetal alcohol syndrome. *Developmental Behavioral Pediatrics*, 3:49-54.

Tarter, R. E., McBride, J., Buonopone, R. N. & Schneider, D. U. (1977), Differentiation of alcoholics. *Archives of General Psychiatry*, 34:761-768.

Wood, D., Wender, P. H. & Reimherr, R. W. (1983), The prevalence of attention deficit disorder: Residual type or minimal brain dysfunction in a population of male alcoholics. *American Journal of Psychiatry*, 140:1453-1460.

Woodruff, R. A., Guze, C., Clayton, P. J. & Carr, D. (1979), Alcoholism and affective disorders. In: *Clinical, Genetic and Biochemical Studies*, Jamaica, New York, Spectrum Publishers, ed: Goodwin, D. W. & Erickson, C. K. pp. 39-48.

Zarek, D., Hawkins, D. & Rogers, P. D. (1987), Risk factors for adolescent substance abuse—Implications for pediatric practice—Pediatric Clinics of North America.

Treating the High Risk Adolescent: A Survey of Effective Programs and Interventions

David F. O'Connell, PhD

Under the most auspicious conditions, the adolescent will arrive in young adulthood with a well developed sense of identity, a capacity for intimacy, and a strong sense of independence as a person. Along the way he/she will have moved beyond the family to form meaningful social relationships, formulated a personal set of values, and cast aside internal fantasies in favor of life's realities.

And if all goes well the adolescent will enjoy the status of young adulthood without dependence on alcohol or drugs. However, by the time a teenager graduates from high school there are nine chances out of ten that he/she will have used alcohol or some other psychoactive drug. Sadly enough one in ten teenagers graduating from high school will develop a pattern of abuse of psychoactive substances (Johnston, O'Malley, & Buchman, 1984).

But what makes these children vulnerable to the development of a serious drug and alcohol abuse problem, and how might helping professionals lessen the chances of these children developing chemical dependency?

This article seeks to address these important questions. Research has shown that certain groups of young people are at a greater risk to develop chemical dependency or abuse than are others. Research has also identified a number of cognitive, emotional social and behavioral factors associated with increased risk of teenage drug and alcohol abuse. This chapter will focus on high risk conditions for

---

David F. O'Connell is Consulting Psychologist at New Beginnings at Hidden Brook, Bel Air, MD, and is in private practice in Reading, PA.

49

drug and alcohol abuse as well as prevention and treatment strategies that have been found to be effective with young people at risk for chemical dependency.

GENERAL ANTECEDENTS AND RISK FACTORS FOR TEENAGE SUBSTANCE ABUSE

Research on predictors of adolescent drug use, risk factors that increase chances for drug abuse as well as characteristics associated with teenage drug and alcohol use has been carried out for over two decades (Hawkins, Linshner & Catalano, 1985). We now know those situations, characteristics and correlates which render certain adolescents vulnerable to drug abuse/dependence. The following is a discussion of these factors.

Physical Factors

Research shows that late maturing boys and early maturing girls in American society experience psychological distress that affects their self-esteem, sense of identity, and academic performance, and renders them vulnerable to chemical abuse (Hamburg, 1974). Late maturing boys, for example, show greater rebellious behavior, poorer self-concepts, greater rejection from peers, as well as greater general maladjustment than their early maturing counterparts. Early maturing boys on the other hand, tend to assume more leadership roles, are more socially popular, more involved in athletics, and are seen as more attractive by both adults and peers than are late maturing boys.

Early maturing girls encounter a different set of problems. Socially, they are defiant and are more alienated than their late maturing cohorts. They are seldom seen as socially popular and rarely attain leadership roles among their peers. They tend to lack social poise and have been described by researchers as submissive, nonassertive, and indifferent in social interaction. Late maturing girls, on the other hand, are more extroverted, poised, and self-assured than their early maturing counterparts (Jones & Mussen, 1958).

Late maturing boys and early maturing girls experience significant psychological pain during early adolescence. During this developmental phase they are egocentric and self-absorbed with their body image. For some of these children the psychological scars incurred in this developmental period will be carried on into late adolescence and adulthood.

Due to this psychological stress, this group of adolescents shows a greater vulnerability to alcohol and drug use. For example, alcohol and other sedative drugs may be used to reduce anxiety about body image or to buttress a lagging sense of self-esteem.

Cognitive/Emotional Factors

Adolescents with a low sense of well being, poor self-image, a high level of anxiety and/or depression, as well as a sense of alienation from others are all at risk for chemical dependency (Smith & Fogg, 1978; Ahlgren, 1980). Adolescents showing high levels of personality traits such as rebelliousness, impulsivity, and untrustworthiness, anger, immaturity, insecurity, egocentricity, and irresponsibility have been found to be at risk for alcohol and narcotic abuse (Braucht, Follingstead, Brakarch, & Berry, 1973).

Adolescents who report a high dislike for school have lower cognitive development, poor problem solving skills, and lower ego development show high risk for drug and alcohol abuse (Bachman, O'Malley, & Johnston, 1978; Kohlberg, LaCross, & Ricks, 1970). Academic failure as well as low academic aspiration has also been found to be associated with increased risk for chemical abuse (Hawkins et al., 1985; Jessor & Jessor, 1975).

An overview of the research on cognitive/emotional risk factors indicates that in general the greater personality maladjustment the adolescent shows, the greater the risk for chemical abuse problems.

Behavioral Factors

Delinquent or deviant behavior during adolescence predicts subsequent drug use (Johnson, 1979). Other behaviors that are associated with high risk for chemical dependency are: cigarette smoking, disciplinary problems at school, antisocial behavior, as well as absenteeism and running away from home (Smith & Fogg, 1978; Bachman, 1978; and Robins, 1978). A lack of social bonding with society has also been indicated as a risk factor (Hawkins et al., 1975).

Adolescents showing behavioral problems constitute a diverse group of young people. Many of these children have serious psychiatric disturbances. Some have very dysfunctional families. Still others may have serious learning disabilities. Substance abuse is often only one of a multitude of problems behaviorally disturbed adolescents experience.

Social/Familial Factors

Having friends who use drugs, having favorable attitudes towards drug use and early first use of drugs all are associated with drug abuse among adolescents. Hawkins et al. (1985), and Braucht et al. (1973), demonstrated that high use of alcohol among college students was found to be associated with high alcohol use among parents. A family history of alcoholism, criminality, family disorganization, parental drug use, and divorce are all associated with chemical use (Hawkins et al., 1985).

Any one of the above risk factors and any combination of them place the adolescent at risk for developing alcohol or drug abuse. Obviously the more strikes the adolescent has against him/her the higher the risk for all kinds of emotional, physical, and behavioral problems including chemical abuse. However, each adolescent is an individual equipped with a wide range of personality assets and personal strengths, as well as social, environmental, and spiritual supports that would co-determine the level of functioning, stability, and adaptability of the youngster. Without an *individual* evaluation of each adolescent, helping professionals in the chemical dependency and mental health fields cannot predict with any great accuracy whether or not a child will develop a chemical dependency problem.

It is clear that the development of chemical abuse and/or chemical dependency is a complex problem and the causative factors underlying it are ill understood at present. How does this factor affect the development of education and prevention programs to impact on chemical dependency in high risk adolescent populations? First of all, it is clear from the previous discussion that since so many different factors may predispose a young person to chemical dependency there are indeed vast numbers of adolescents, theoretically at least, at risk for chemical abuse. In order to have an impact on the problem broad based, multidimensional comprehensive education and prevention programs would be needed. These programs should also involve the cooperation of a number of youth serving agencies and organizations such as the family, juvenile probation departments, courts, schools, and community organizations. In the following section various existing prevention and treatment programs that have been found to be effective with high risk adolescents will be considered.

PREVENTION AND INTERVENTION PROGRAMS FOR HIGH RISK ADOLESCENTS

Recently there have been great efforts made at early identification of/and intervention with drug and alcohol abusing juvenile offenders. These programs have been conceptualized as alternatives to criminal prosecution. The *Court Referral Project* of New York City is an example of a mandated diversionary system for juvenile offenders. This program involves diagnosis, assessment, referral, as well as group therapy. This program has been described in detail by Nimmer (1970). A diversionary early intervention program, the *Alcohol and Traffic Safety Program* in the state of Ohio is another such program which focuses on early intervention with troubled youth. This program consists of twenty hours of education on drunken driving for delinquent youth institutionalized for major and minor felonies (Rohrer, 1984).

Iverson and Roberts (1980) report on an effective prevention program known as the *Juvenile Prevention Program*. This program utilizes family involvement and peer pressure to ameliorate personal and family problems, as well as to have an impact on problem behavior such as poor communication in families and manipulation by juveniles. It is a seven session, two hour weekly program. Research results on the effectiveness of the program indicate that participants show improved family communication, increased self-esteem, and increased drug knowledge, as well as decreased drug usage and decreased contacts with the legal system.

The above programs appear particularly appropriate and well suited for adolescents experiencing severe social and behavioral problems.

Community Based Programs

These types of programs are primarily aimed at youth with potential chemical abuse problems. They typically focus on alternative activities to substance abuse in the community. The staff works with youth and community personnel to assess community needs, identify resources, and promote projects that impart a sense of accomplishment in community service for youth. This enhances self-esteem, improves social relationships, and adds structure to their daily lives.

Cohen (1971) and Johnson (1980) have espoused the "alternative theory" for Community Based Programs. This theory holds that traditional drug prevention efforts attack only the symptoms of drug abuse and not the cause. They view drug use as a response to unfilled needs or experiential deficits. Cohen contends that unless society develops new opportunities and activities to meet the needs of adolescents, then drug use will continue unabated.

The *Yes Program* in San Francisco is an example of such a community based prevention program. The authors (Feldman, Mandel, and Fields) note that drug and alcohol problems form a part of a larger issue and problem in the community. This program stresses meeting young people in their respective communities through interesting activities. (For example athletics, dances, crafts.) The *Yes Program* includes client advocacy, referral, supportive counseling, group therapy, and the arrangement of special community programs such as block parties and exhibits.

Cohen (1985) has described other types of community based projects such as *CCDAC* in Idaho, *Channel I* in Massachusetts, and the *Alternative Pursuit Program* in Virginia. All of these programs view constructive, responsible activities as alternatives to juvenile drug abuse. The goals are to enhance self-mastery, self-esteem, social relationships, and involve youth meaningfully in their respective communities.

Community Programs are particularly appropriate for adolescents who show little commitment toward school, little interest in the family or community, show favorable attitudes towards drug use and have friends who abuse drugs.

School Based Treatment

Cohen (1985) notes that schools have distinct advantages over the other systems of socialization for youth such as families and peers and are good bases for prevention and intervention programs. In schools drug abuse is less likely to be denied and more likely to be dealt with through appropriate treatment. Good school based programs focus on treatment and education as a source of accomplishment for self-esteem enhancement. These programs can be linked easily with family based and community based programs.

According to Mai, Patrick and Greene (1980), school based programs should have the following three components:

1. Learning should take place in a structured environment where youth can receive support and encouragement for their efforts as well as individualized attention.
2. School subject should be relevant and meaningful for students (For example, life skills, career planning, vocational treatment, psychological development).
3. Opportunity should be provided to work cooperatively on projects with peers to decrease alienation and improve self image.

Examples of this type of program include the *Phoenix School* in Maryland and the *Door* in New York City. These programs are day treatment programs and seek to normalize the youth and his/her inner role in society by maintaining him/her in a school setting while providing psychotherapeutic and remedial academic help.

In the Phoenix School Program troubled youth are seen in separate facilities which allows for easier integration of the treatment and counseling components of the school. All teachers are trained in counseling techniques. Therapy is emphasized as important to the success of the program. Drug prevention efforts include counseling, guest lectures, and drug information seminars. Alternative activities are also included. Family members are encouraged to be involved in the program and work on the program goals. Social skills are taught and efforts are made to help adolescents build supportive peer networks in and out of school. Other programs such as the Door in New York City designed to serve dropouts and drug abusing youth, emphasize vocational training in addition to academic counseling programs. Workshops and special projects are geared to enhance a student's knowledge of personal, social, political, and vocational issues. Although there is a focus on chemical abuse, this issue is not directly addressed in these programs and the primary focus is on remedying structural defects in the student's life.

School Based Programs seem to be especially effective with and appropriate for behaviorally disturbed youth, youth suffering from academic problems, and youth with psychiatric or psychological dysfunction.

Day Treatment Centers

Pomerantz, Collins, Shapino and Carroll (1984) report on a unique treatment approach for high risk teenagers termed *Day School*. The aim of *Day School* is to enhance the teenagers feelings of personal control and self-efficiency and to develop an internal rather than an external locus of control. *Day School* is an alternative to residential treatment. Referrals come from children and youth services and juvenile probation departments. Both status offenders (for example truancy, running away, ungovernability) and criminal offenders (for example, theft, burglary, disorderly conduct) are eligible for the program.

This alternative school offers the possibility of introducing therapeutic alternatives and educational approaches throughout the school day. It is characterized by the following:

1. A combination of a full school program and a comprehensive treatment program.
2. It is a community based alternative to institutionalization.
3. It includes ongoing professional collaboration among many support systems.

The program has a small student body (about 26) which allows for lots of personal attention. The program has a strong behavioral focus. It utilizes a level system in which students progress up through predetermined levels of community responsibility based on their performance. Staff utilize immediate feedback, penalties, rewards, and concrete rules and structure to facilitate student progress. Confronting negative behavior in students forms a large part of the program. The staff members take on a parent surrogate role to help offset the student's poor family life. Focus is given to assisting students to see the connection between their behavior and negative consequences. There is also a high level of nurturing by staff (tender loving care). Strong religious values are emphasized. The *Day School* Program also includes a training program on parenting skills for the student's family.

Daily life in the day school involves continual confrontation of students. By utilizing a behavior incentive program of immediate awards and penalties the association of behavior and consequences is sharply connected in the youth's mind. The behavior programs are designed to develop a sense of self-efficiency and a sense of internal self-control. The program attempts to offset the great failure these youth have experienced in their daily lives. The program provides structure and limits. It also provides opportunities for social learning, decision making, and assumption of responsibilities for one's own life. The program emphasizes small successes rather than focusing on larger, loftier, but less practical goals.

Day treatment centers such as *Day School* appear to be particularly appropriate programs for behaviorally disordered youth with psychiatric problems that require the attention of mental health professionals. Youth with a developing chemical abuse problem and adolescents with severe academic problems are also candidates for these programs.

Peer Programs

Peers can have a significant impact on an adolescent's behavior values and attitudes. Peer Programs harness this influence to balance the impact of negative peer pressure. Research by Johnson (1980) suggests that Peer Programs promote higher motivation to succeed in school, greater achievement, higher self-esteem, and improved social relationships. Peer Programs are diverse in nature, content, and scope. As Resnik and Gibbs (1986) indicate, Peer Programs have similar goals. These are:

1. Addressing a lack of meaningful roles, activities, and opportunities for adolescents. Generating meaningful involvements, activities, and responsibilities for youth. Encouraging youth participation in life decisions, youth serving institutions and society in general.
2. Channeling peer pressure and the risk taking of youth to constructive ends.
3. Providing youth with social, interpersonal, and academic skills to help them cope with progress in life.

Some Peer Programs focus specifically on reducing drug abuse. Others are more general in nature and focus more on the correlates of drug abuse, such as low self-esteem, poor decision making skills, and lack of alternatives to drug use. These programs exist in school, communities, and street settings.

Spark in New York City is one of the most well established Peer Programs (Resnik & Gibbs, 1986). It makes use of a peer group discussion to confront and address problem behavior with high school students. It is essentially a counseling program. The program provides a support group for teenagers who lack a context to discuss problems or address self-esteem issues. The program appears to be particularly effective for disruptive unmotivated youth.

Another Peer Program, *Positive Peer Culture* is an intense program using a group counseling format designed to develop responsibility in adolescents through honesty, directiveness, and self-responsibility. Confrontation is used to develop honesty and self-awareness. The groups are designed to counteract and turn around a negative youth culture and use the power of the group in a productive way. The focus is on caring and responsibility. This program is particularly appropriate for low income, inner city youth. It is especially suited for "tough" youth.

Peer Teaching or Tutoring Programs are another type of Peer Program and focus on both teaching youth about chemical abuse and assisting academic underachievers.

Peer Counseling Programs as described by Samuels and Samuels

(1975) are programs that utilize peers in a helping capacity to assist other adolescents with self-understanding, values clarification, and communication skills.

Peer Programs appear to be particularly appropriate for adolescents involved in a negative peer culture. These include adolescents showing antisocial behavior, gang involvement, poor self-control, and personality disorders.

Drug Education Programs

Ideally, Drug and Alcohol Education Programs should be comprehensive developmentally focused and based on the knowledge of risk factors associated with chemical abuse. *Here's Looking At You Two Thousand* represents the state of the art in drug education programming and is particularly relevant for at risk children. Research on risk factors by Hawkins et al. (1985) has provided the theoretical basis for the development of this program. The program is designed to teach students information, special skills, and increase family adaptation and health. It includes refusal skills and other social skills that enable high risk youth to handle drug encounters. This program is developmentally focused and can be implemented in kindergarten through twelfth grade. Parental involvement is viewed as a crucial component of the program. The program is easy for teachers to understand and to implement. The curriculum makes liberal use of video games and other enjoyable activities to accomplish learning objectives. A unique feature of this program is the use of cross age teaching in which older adolescents teach younger students social skills, such as, refusal skills.

In this writer's estimation this program is the program of choice for at risk children and adolescents in the school setting. It appears to be the best of the broad based educational approaches to early prevention of chemical abuse.

The foregoing discussion is focused on prevention and treatment programs for adolescents who show many of the risk factors for chemical abuse that were considered previously in this article. In the following section various psychological disorders found in children and adolescents that increase the risk for chemical abuse are presented along with guidelines for intervention.

SPECIAL CONDITIONS ASSOCIATED
WITH CHEMICAL DEPENDENCY

Psychological Disorders

Adolescents who are diagnosed with a psychological disorder are at greater risk for developing chemical abuse/dependency than are other adolescents. Severe personality disorders, anxiety states, social disorders, and behavioral disorders all pose significant life adjustment problems for these adolescents. Many of these young people turn to drugs and/or alcohol to ameliorate painful affective states or to reduce inner-confusion.

Chemical dependency counselors need to be aware of the nature of these disorders when treating such adolescents for chemical abuse. Mental health professionals and school counselors need to be mindful of the risk for chemical dependency with these youngsters, the reasons for their abuse of drugs, and the effect that chemical abuse will have on the course of treatment with the adolescent.

In the following section a number of psychological dysfunctions common in adolescents are presented. A description of the central features of the disorder and treatment considerations are included.

Conduct Disorder

Adolescents with this disorder show repetitive, persistent patterns of misconduct in which the basic rights of others or major age appropriate social norms and rules are violated. Some examples of misconduct are: vandalism, firesetting, breaking and entering, rape and murder. Many of these young people come from socio-economically deprived backgrounds. Many have been physically and/or sexually abused as children and come from severely dysfunctional families.

Some of these adolescents have severe psychiatric problems such as depression or paranoia and the aggressive antisocial behavior is the adolescent's mode of dealing with deep internal problems. A number of these children are cognitively impaired and/or have learning disabilities. They experience school failure and alienation from the main stream of society. They find solace in antisocial behavior in the drug underworld, gangs, and other delinquent subcultures.

These teens often have a defect in their ability to feel for others and are seen as egocentric, manipulative, and showing little guilt or remorse for their antisocial behavior.

Treatment Considerations

For some conduct problems residential treatment may be indicated. The structure of these programs is important for containing antisocial behavior, limit setting, and providing healthy socialization. Day treatment centers and group homes are also appropriate programs. Regardless of the type of facility there should be psychiatric consultation available. Some of these adolescents can be extremely agitated and violent, especially under stress and/or when intoxicated and may need neuroleptic medication to stabilize them. The treatment program should also focus on chemical abuse through social skills training, behavioral therapy, and addiction education. Family therapy is indicated to modify chaotic, disruptive family relationship patterns. Parents of these adolescents often have a serious drug or alcohol problem. As children of alcoholics, these adolescents need special care to help them deal with family conflict, feelings of powerlessness and ambivalent feelings towards the alcoholic parent (Ackerman, 1983). Carpenter and Sandburg (1973) recommend the use of psychodrama and role playing with these patients to help offset guarded attitudes, minimal empathy, and the inability to use fantasy as well as poor communication skills. The use of music therapy and poetry reading in group therapy has been successful with these patients' and can focus on such themes as trust of parents, love, intimacy, and self-control. The concurrent group treatment of these patients' parents focusing on ventilation of anger and reparenting skills is also considered an important component of effective treatment. Concrete guidelines for prosocial behavior in group therapy and in the treatment community may be important. Structured relaxation and the use of guided imagery to develop feelings of confidence have been proven useful (Reardon & Tosi, 1977).

An important approach in group therapy is having the adolescent deal with anger, a confrontation, and other negative emotions without resorting to acting out. The goal is to help these adolescents raise their tolerance for negative emotions. These patients need to know the effects of psychoactive drugs on feelings and behaviors such as disinhibition, the blunting of feelings, and increased aggression. They need to deal with these feelings without the use of chemicals.

Identity Disorder

The central feature of this disorder is severe subjective distress resulting from an inability to maintain a coherent and acceptable sense of self. All adolescents experience some level of identity crisis but adolescents with this disorder suffer profound identity diffusion manifested by extreme confusion about life goals, career goals, friendship patterns, and loyalties. These young people struggle constantly with the question "Who Am I?" They feel empty, isolated, and show an inability to work and to develop intimacy. Some develop a negative identity by becoming involved in cults, gangs, and other groups. Most are preoccupied with religious and social issues. Many are suicidal. A number of these adolescents develop borderline personality disorder, a severe psychiatric disorder, when they become adults.

Treatment Considerations

These adolescents are very vulnerable to chemical abuse. Often they experiment with drugs and the drug subculture in a desperate attempt to forge some kind of identity. In addition to the anxiety reducing effects of depressant drugs, the self-esteem enhancing effects of methamphetamines and other stimulants, as well as the perception altering effects of hallucinogens have great appeal for these young people.

The treatment of choice is psychotherapy. This should focus on the development of interest and pleasures and should encourage growth and emotional development. The adolescent needs help in accepting all aspects of himself/herself including his/her imperfections. Ambivalent feelings need clarification and understanding.

Vocational and academic guidance and counseling is also very useful.

Overanxious Disorder

The central features of this disorder are diffuse anxiety, continual worrying, and sleep difficulties. Bodily complaints such as sore throat, respiratory disorders, rashes, and tics are common. These youngsters show obsessive thinking. They ruminate about self-confidence and performance, especially in academics and athletics. They often show deep concern about issues such as death, disasters, and accidents. They show pervasive apprehension and a poor tolerance for stress. In interaction with adults they continually seek approval and attention. They show an anxious, perfectionistic need to perform correctly and are preoccupied with conformity. This disorder runs high in families that show an over concern with achievement and conforming behavior.

Treatment Considerations

These adolescents are very prone to the use of alcohol/sedative medication to offset the often debilitating anxiety and distress they experience. In the counseling situation these adolescents often struggle with conflicts about loss of control and helplessness. In some cases a percentage of these adolescents may need appropriate anxiolytic medication to reduce high levels of subjective distress so that the child can take advantage of the therapy.

This type of adolescent needs supportive treatment. In addition exploratory therapy may help uncover the causes of the anxiety. These youngsters can also benefit from social skills training, especially assertiveness training focusing on refusal skills. Many of these patients show a kind of pseudo-maturity and feel superior to their age mates. They need assistance with socializing with adolescents their own age and should be encouraged to become involved in low stress social activities. Since many of these adolescents are pushed hard for academic or athletic success the focus in counseling should be on realistic successes, the patient's feeling about personal success, and self-acceptance of limitations.

Non-pharmacological antianxiety programs such as Transcendental Meditation (TM) and stress inoculation training are often helpful at reducing anxiety. Transcendental Meditation is especially helpful because it not only reduces anxiety, but increases self-esteem, improves academic performance, increases productivity, and promotes flexibility and adaptability in thinking. It may also reduce the distress caused by the physical manifestations of anxiety such as headache, sleep problems, and respiratory distress (Orme-Johnson & Farrow, 1976).

These youngsters typically make good patients and the prognosis for both the successful treatment of the anxiety disorder and associated chemical abuse is good.

Avoidant Disorder

The central feature of this disorder is pathological shyness and avoidance of social contact that interferes with social and emotional development. These adolescents typically avoid strangers. With caretakers and family members they can, however, show dependent demanding behavior. In family relationships the timidity and embarrassment seen in less intimate relationships is replaced by resentment, anger, and at times grandiosity. These adolescents often have severe losses in their backgrounds and may have had chronic medical problems as children. They are extremely inhibited as teenagers. In severe cases they show extreme isolation, depression, and can show self-mutilation and suicidal behavior. Internally, these patients feel anxious, tense, and helpless.

Treatment Considerations

The treatments of choice are family and individual therapy. In individual counseling the focus should be on assertiveness and increasing socialization. In family therapy the family needs to be helped to let go of the child and assist the child to become more involved with age mates. The focus should be on the child's individualism and growth. The adolescent needs assistance finding meaningful, successful relationships outside of the nuclear family. These youths should be encouraged to become involved in athletics and other extracurricular activities. A strong focus on self-esteem building is also necessary. Many of these adolescents were belittled by parents as they were growing up and have experienced a deep sense of failure in their lives.

Since social anxiety is extremely high, these adolescents may turn to the use of alcohol and other depressant drugs to ameliorate the anxiety. The disinhibiting effects of alcohol as well as marijuana and other psychedelics are a great lure for these youngsters to assist them with overcoming their shyness in social interaction. With appropriate therapy the need for these chemicals should sharply diminish or disappear.

Attention Deficit Disorder

The central feature of the Attention Deficit Disorder is the incapacity to remain attentive in situations, especially in the home and at school, where it is necessary to socially do so. Attention Deficit Disorder refers to a group of disorders in which hyperactivity, impulsiveness, and learning disabilities are prevalent. The problems of hyperactive children and adolescents are so pervasive that these patients constitute 50% of the referrals to the nation's community mental health centers.

The term Attention Deficit Disorder refers to a heterogeneous group of individuals many of whom show learning disabilities, emotional problems, neurological dysfunction, hyperactivity, or a combination of these. It is diagnosed most frequently in males and tends to run in families.

The essential features of this disorder include distractibility, inattention, and impulsivity manifested by such behaviors as hasty performance of school work, inability to sit still in the classroom, and in general an "acting before thinking" mode of functioning. These youngsters show difficulty organizing and completing work. They have problems concentrating on anything. Needless to say, this makes academic work and management in the classroom very troublesome.

Treatment Considerations

Many hyperactive children are maintained on some type of stimulant medications (for example, Ritalin) throughout their childhood years. This medication may be tapered off in adolescence. However, many adolescents do not "grow out" of Attention Deficit Disorder. Twenty percent of adolescents diagnosed with Attention Deficit Disorder as children need to be maintained on their medication throughout their teenage years and sometimes into adulthood. Many show what is termed as *residual* hyperactivity in young adulthood. These youngsters continue to experience the aforementioned problems but the symptoms are less severe in nature.

Because many have had medication all their lives these adolescents view psychoactive drugs differently than other teenagers. The leap from Ritalin use to the use of amphetamines, cocaine, and other stimulants may not be a great one. Because of this vulnerability, the adolescent needs drug education and drug prevention efforts.

Hyperactive teenagers may lead thrill seeking, reckless lives. They may be overly aggressive. In treatment, they need to have a very structured counseling environment. In severe cases day treatment or residential treatment is needed if aggressive acting out and the consequences of impulsive behavior are severe. In treatment these patients need to know rules and expectations explicitly. They need frequent praise and reinforcement for even minimal gains in counseling. Counseling should focus on authority issues which are prevalent with this disorder. Hyperactive children often have pervasive social and emotional difficulties secondary to their disorder. A thoughtful knowledgeable clinician is needed to assist these adolescents with their large variety of problems.

In chemical abuse treatment the focus should be on self-mastery and self-control, the dangers of drug substitution or cross-addiction (for example, Ritalin and methamphetamine use) and should include stress inoculation, Transcendental Meditation, or other activities that normalize the nervous system.

Other Disorders

Adolescents with learning disabilities, a history of sexual or physical trauma, eating disorders, and serious disorders such as schizophrenia and other psychotic disorders all are at a greater risk for chemical abuse than their healthier counterparts.

However, these disorders require highly skilled professional treatment and consideration of them is beyond the scope of this article. Professionals treating these disorders often overlook the possibility of chemical abuse and need to be more sensitive to it in providing sound treatment.

CONCLUSION

Adolescents at risk for chemical abuse and chemical dependency constitute a highly diversified group in terms of age, background, level of psychopathology, life adjustment, and coping skills. Mental health specialists, school counselors, addictions clinicians, and other professionals need to be aware of the special needs of these adolescents when implementing education, prevention, or treatment programs. Strong efforts at early identification of vulnerable adolescents and the design of appropriate prevention and intervention programs need to be made. Further research should focus on the effectiveness of existing programs and the development of more comprehensive programs for high risk youth.

REFERENCES

Ackerman, R. J. (1983). *Children of Alcoholics: A Guide Book for Educators, Therapists, and Parents*, 2nd Edition Learning Publications: Holmes Beach, FL.

Ahlgren, A., Norem-Hebeisen, A.A., Hockhauser, M., and Garvin, J. Antecedents of Smoking Among Pre-adolescents. Unpublished paper, the authors, 1980.

Bachman, J.G., O'Malley, P.M., and Johnston, J. (1978). *Adolescence to Adulthood: Change and Stability in the Lives of Young Men*. Ann Arbor, MI: Survey Research Center.

Braucht, G.N., Follingstad, D., Brakarch, D., and Berry, K.L. (1973). Drug education: A review of goals, approaches, and effectiveness, and a paradigm for evaluation. *Quarterly Journal of Studies on Alcohol, 34*, 1279-1292.

Braucht, G.N., Brakarch, D., Follingstad, D., and Berry, K.L. (1973b). Deviant drug use in adolescents: A review of psychological correlates. *Psychological Bulletin, 79* (2), 92-106.

Carpenter, P. and Sandburg, S. (1973). "The Things inside: Psychodrama with delinquent Adolescents" *Psychotherapy: Theory, Research and Practice*, 10, 3, 245-247.

Cohen, A. (1985). Drug treatment in school and alternative school settings. In

A.S. Friedman and G. M. Beschner (Eds.), *Treatment Services For Adolescent Substance Abusers*. NIDA, DHHS Publication No. (ADM) 85-1342.

Cohen, A.Y. (1971). The journey beyond trips: Alternatives to drugs. *Journal of Psychedelic Drugs, 3.*

Feldman, H., Mandel, J., and Fields, A. In the neighborhood: A strategy for delivering early intervention services to young drug users in their natural environments. In A.S. Friedman, A.S. and G.M. Beschner (Eds.), *Treatment Services for Adolescent Substance Abusers*. NIDA, DHGS Publication No. (ADM) 85-1342.

Hamburg, B.A. (1974). Early Adolescence: A Specific and Stressful Stage of the Life Cycle. In Coelho, G.V., Hamburg and Adams, J. (Eds.), *Coping and Adaptation*. New York: Basic Books.

Hawkins, J.D., Lishner, D.M., and Catalano, R.F. (1985). Childhood predictors and the prevention of adolescent substance abuse. In C.L. Jones and R.J. Battjes (Eds.), *Etiology of Drug Abuse: Implications for Prevention*. Washington, DC, National Institute on Drug Abuse, ADM 85-1385.

Iverson, D., and Roberts, T. (1980). The juvenile intervention program: Results of the process, impact, and outcome evaluations. *Journal of Drug Education, 10* (4), 289-300.

Jackson, L. (1975). Alternative pursuits: Implications for drug abuse prevention: In: Senay, E., Shorty, V., and Alksne, H. (Eds.), *Developments in the Field of Drug Abuse*: Proceedings of the 1974 National Association for the Prevention of Addiction to Narcotics, National Drug Abuse Conference. Cambridge, MA: Schenkman.

Jessor, R., and Jessor, S.L. (1977). *Problem Behavior and Psychosocial Development: A Longitudinal Study of Youth*. New York: Academic Press.

Jessor, R., and Jessor, S.L. (1975). Adolescent development and the onset of drinking. *Journal of Studies on Alcohol, 36*, 5-13.

Johnson, D. (1980). Group processes: Influences of student-student interaction on school outcomes. In: McMillan, J., ed. *The Social Psychology of School Learning*. New York: Academic Press.

Johnston, L.D., O'Malley, P.M., and Buchman, J.G. (1984). *Highlights from Drugs and American High School Students 1975-1983*, NIDA, DHHS Publication No. (ADM) 84-1317.

Jones, M.C. and Mussen, P.H. (1958). Self-conception, motivations, and interpersonal attitudes of early- and late-maturing girls. *Child Development*, 29 (4):491-501.

Kohlberg, L., LaCross, J., and Ricks, D. (1970). The predictability of adult mental health from childhood behavior. In: Wolman, B., ed. *Handbook of Child Psychopathology*. New York: McGraw-Hill.

Mai, L., Patrick, S., and Greene, M. (1980). The Learning Laboratory. Treatment Research Monograph, DHHS Pub. No. (ADM) 80-928. Rockville, MD: National Institute on Drug Abuse.

Nimmer, R. (1970). The public drunk: Formalizing the police roles as a social help agency. *The Georgetown Law Journal, 58*, (6), 1097.

Orme-Johnson, D.W., and Farrow, J.T. Eds. (1976). Scientific Research on the Transcendental Meditation Program. Collected Paper Vol. I. MERU Press: West Germany.

Pomerantz, S.C., Collins, T.R., Shapiro, D.B. and Carroll, J. An Evaluation of a Day Treatment Model For Adolescents At Risk For Substance Abuse. Unpublished Paper. Coatsville Veterans Administration Medical Center, Coatsville, PA.

Rathus, S.A., Fichner-Rathus, L., and Siegal, L.V. (1977). Behavioral and familiar correlates of episodic heroin abuse among suburban adolescents. *The International Journal of the Addictions, 12* (5), 625-632.

Reardon, J., and Tosi, D. (1977). The Effect of Rational Stage Directed imagery on self concept and Reduction of stress in adolescent delinquent females. *Journal of Clinical Psychology*, *33*(4), 1084-1092.

Resnik, H.S., and Gibbs (1986). Types of Peer Program Approaches in Adolescent Peer Pressure. Theory Correlates and Program Implications for Drug Abuse Prevention. DHHS Publication no. (ADM) 86-1152.

Robins, L.N. (1978). Sturdy childhood predictors of adult antisocial behavior: Replications from longitudinal studies. *Psychological medicine*, 8 (4):611-622.

Rohrer, G., Elliot, J., and Geer, N. (1984). An alcohol education traffic safety program for institutionalized juvenile offenders. *Journal of Alcohol and Drug Education, 29*, 40-43.

Samuels, M., and Samuels, D. (1975). *The Complete Handbook of Peer Counseling*. Miami, FL: Fiesta Publishing Corp.

Smith, G.M., and Fogg, C.P. (1978). Psychological predictors of early use late use, and nonuse of marijuana among teenage students. In: Kandel, D. ed., *Longitudinal Research on Drug Use: Empirical Findings and Methodological Issues*. Washington, DC: Halstead-Wiley.

Issues in Adolescent Chemical Dependency Assessment

Jane M. Nakken, MA, CCDP

The treatment of chemical dependency in adolescents has grown tremendously in recent years, despite an apparent leveling off of daily chemical use patterns in this age group (National Institute on Drug Abuse, 1986). A new concept as recently as the mid-1970s, such treatment is now a major trend of the health care delivery system throughout much of the country. The number of new treatment programs, both freestanding and hospital-based, is increasing rapidly.

Their popularity is fed by a number of factors. One is that treatment works, perhaps more dramatically than other intervention, for adolescents who appear to be hopelessly immune to other kinds of treatment. In response to this "miracle cure," excitement spreads through the community of parents and kid-helping professionals, and more youth are referred for chemical dependency treatment, sometimes at early stages of chemical involvement. Demand for treatment beds grows. Another reason for the growth of treatment is that many health care organizations view adolescent treatment programs as an answer to financial problems. Hospitals, running with many empty beds, see these programs as good money-makers. This is a fortunate combination of factors for those in need of treatment. It has, however, also resulted in very serious challenges.

"Adolescent Treatment on the Hotseat" (Worden, 1986) read a recent headline in the *U.S. Journal of Alcohol and Drug Dependence*. The article was inspired by media scrutiny of admission and treatment practices at adolescent treatment programs throughout the

Jane M. Nakken is Senior Consultant for Hazelden Consultation Services, Minneapolis, MN.

country. The campaign, which included special reports on CBS News (Insight, 1986) and The Phil Donahue Show (1985), raised serious questions about the ethics of adolescent treatment providers.

Story after story illustrated the point that adolescent treatment providers are warehousing kids at the request of their parents or the courts, sometimes in locked units, without recourse or protection for their civil right to liberty. While some of these questions related to the care provided adolescents in treatment (such as placement in locked treatment units without benefit of a court hearing, refusal to allow parents to communicate with a child in treatment, and use of personally degrading "treatment methods" such as the wearing of self-derogatory signs and shaving of heads), the critical charges most often raised concern inadequate assessment and inappropriate admission practices.

What are these accusations? They include the following, stated here as their most extreme proponents presented them in 1985 during legislative hearings in Minnesota (e.g., Newlund, 1985) and in testimony delivered to the United States House of Representatives Select Committee on Children, Youth and Families (Smith, 1985):

1. Diagnosis ruins lives. Kids shouldn't be labeled chemically dependent at all, since most of them grow out of drug abuse problems. The label is permanent, and it causes major problems, such as inability to enlist in the armed forces or to be licensed in some professions.
2. Assessments done by treatment providers are self-serving. Diagnoses are often unjustified. In some programs, a youth may be admitted simply based on the request of parents, with the major admission criteria being ability to pay the bill.
3. Treatment is being used as a way to incarcerate kids for the convenience of adults. These critics say it is no accident that locked adolescent treatment centers became popular during the same time that juvenile justice reforms made it harder to lock kids up in the correctional system.

The publicity created a convincing impression that the chemical dependency treatment system hurts adolescents. Are treatment programs meeting a need, as suggested at first glance by the growing numbers of kids admitted to treatment? Or are they creating one by misdiagnosis and overtreatment of kids in order to serve self-interests? These questions and other challenges have been raised in the national media and state legislatures, where only brief mentions were made that there are high-quality programs. The media effectively painted the adolescent treatment field with a broad brush which left it looking suspiciously like a private system of incarceration run by self-serving interests and paid for with insurance dollars (Jackson-Beeck, 1985; Schwartz, Jackson-Beeck & Anderson, 1984). And it stands to reason that as chemical dependency treatment for adolescents becomes increasingly available throughout the United States, such scrutiny will increase.

This scrutiny presents the chemical dependency field with a challenge. We must let go of our indignant reactions, take down our defenses, and ask how it is that people are saying such things. We must look at ourselves, at the institutions in which we work and those we recommend to others, and ask whether these charges are true. Then we must look a layer deeper, and ask how we can prevent poor practice and safeguard good clinical care for chemically dependent adolescents.

To do this, we must translate our experience of successful treatment and our clinical knowledge into criteria and standards, and promote their acceptance as reasonable approaches to the disease of chemical dependency in youth. We must provide and reinforce clear definitions of quality in assessment and treatment practice from within the adolescent treatment field. If we fail to do this, we give the job to lawmakers and third-party payment sources, most of whom know little about kids and chemical dependency.

CURRENT STATE OF THE ART
IN ADOLESCENT ASSESSMENT

"Adolescent State of the Art Humbling" read a 1986 headline in the *U.S. Journal of Alcohol and Drug Dependence*. The accompanying article highlighted some of the concerns of treatment experts. Some of the issues highlighted were:

- Overreaction by adults to experimental chemical use by adolescents resulting in overdiagnosis and inappropriate late admissions to treatment;
- Use of psychosocial treatment approaches geared toward solving the problems underlying chemical use while kids continue to use chemicals and get into trouble;
- Disagreement among professionals as to the appropriateness of diagnosing chemical dependency in youth according to the traditional disease model approach;
- Inappropriate use of locked units;
- Whether adolescents should be treated separately from adults; and
- The establishment of ethical standards for advertising of adolescent chemical dependency treatment services.

All these are issues closely related to those being debated in the media and in the halls of public policy-making. Many of these questions are clearly the same as those which we asked about approaches to chemical dependency in adults, yet we struggle to find appropriate applications of the wisdom we have gained through working with adult alcoholics for over fifty years.

In today's health care climate, we don't have fifty years to get our act together as a field. We must take a good look at the information we have, set some clear standards, and practice them. Then we must put them to the test by evaluating outcomes. If we are diagnosing chemical dependency accurately, assessing treatment needs with respect to our client's individual situation, and providing good treatment, we should expect good outcomes in the majority of cases.

The Diagnosis Question

So far, there is no adequate consensus in the field even on this issue. The public statement is that chemical dependency is an appropriate diagnosis for adolescents. But much of the talk that goes on among professionals at conferences and meetings quietly undercuts the certainty of this position:

—"Sure, we all have to play the diagnosis game to get paid."
—"Adolescent chemical dependency is different."
—"Abuse and dependency—there's no difference in kids."
—"We know a lot of these kids will grow out of it, but they need help now."
—"What are we going to do with the kids who aren't really dependent but there's no place else for them to go?"
—"A little treatment never hurt a kid."

All of these comments are dangerous. They mean that we talk out of both sides of our mouths, and that we aren't clear about what we are doing as we continue to practice drastic and expensive intervention into the lives of the kids we work with. In making such statements, we are leaving the door open for sloppy assessment, over-diagnosis, and consequently, inappropriate treatment.

I'm not saying diagnosis with adolescents is easy. It's not. It requires knowledge not only about chemical dependency but about adolescence—a stage of life which in itself has been called a "chronic disease" by some, complete with its own symptoms. But I am saying we need not start from ground zero. Chemical dependency is a disease, and adolescents can have it. We know a lot about chemical dependency.

While definitions of chemical dependency vary, there is general agreement on several points:

—it is a disease with progressive and chronic symptoms;
—it is characterized by compulsive use of mood-altering chemicals;
—it causes negative consequences in all life areas.

Chemical dependency is a disease in which the afflicted person is consumed by a relationship with chemicals which becomes more motivating than any other relationship, goal, belief or value which that person holds. It is a disease which runs the person's life in the pursuit of intoxication. It has no respect for the age of the host. (See Nakken, 1988 for a useful construct of the process of the development of addiction.) Adolescents and adults who are chemically dependent are victims of the same disease.

We cannot, however, observe the presence of this disease in a client—we can only see behaviors which indicate that it exists. When the behavioral symptoms fit our criteria for diagnosis, we say the person is chemically dependent. The current criteria for determining whether a person is diagnosed chemically dependent according to the standards in the *Diagnostic and Statistical Manual of Mental Disorders, Third Edition, Revised* [DSM-IIIR] (1987) is the same for adolescents as for adults. But even though chemical dependency is the same disease in adolescents as in adults, it is more difficult to assess.

Difficulties in Assessing Behavior as Symptoms

The kinds of behavioral symptoms which we look for to meet the criteria are somewhat different in adolescents than in adults. This is certainly no surprise, as the behavior we expect from normal adolescents is, in general, different from adult behavior. Any clinician assessing an adolescent must be aware of the influences of developmental issues and tasks of adolescence as discussed in previous chapters. Because so much of our diagnostic information comes from looking at behavioral and lifestyle changes, we must have a good understanding of what is normal for our clients when assessing whether they are chemically dependent. We must learn what we can about each adolescent as an individual and as a person going through a particular life stage when normal changes are dramatic in themselves.

Even when we are sure that the behavior of an adolescent is symptomatic of serious problems, we must take care to distinguish whether it signifies chemical dependency. Behaviors which we consider symptoms of dependency in youth can also be symptomatic of many other conditions: emotional or mental health problems; learning disabilities and related low frustration tolerance; effects of physical, emotional or sexual abuse; dysfunctional learning due to a stressful home life; involvement with a cult or the occult; and grief, to name some of the possibilities. Adolescents often act out to fulfill their role assigned in a system of troubled family dynamics. Kids with any of these problems are likely to use mood-altering chemicals, but are not necessarily chemically dependent. On the other hand, a majority of kids who are chemically dependent also have one or more of the above problems, and we must identify the treatment implications of such predisposing factors.

Most of the criteria for diagnosis can be successfully applied by a determined assessor to many adolescent chemical abusers whose lives are certainly sidetracked and damaged by their chemical use. We cannot afford, however, to be determined to apply a diagnosis. Rather, we must be determined to help the client recognize their problem and define it as something they can successfully confront. How do we know when this problem is chemical dependency? The complicated constellation of issues we see in kids referred for chemical dependency assessment means that we need input from a multi-disciplinary team. The bottom line questions for this team regarding the diagnosis question are:

1. Is compulsive chemical use directly causing or preventing recovery from the problems and consequences which are ruining this kid's life?
2. Has the adolescent tried to control or quit using chemicals, and failed?

Assessment Tools

Adult assessment tools, modified in-house by the diagnosticians using them, are still used for the most part in assessing adolescents for dependency (Owen & Nyberg, 1983). While assessment tools designed for adolescents have been found to be helpful by many, these suffer from limitations such as addressing only alcohol use or only drug use, or lacking research which shows them to be any more valid and reliable than "home-cooked" questionnaires. There is, as yet, no accepted standard for assessment.

A 1983 survey of seventy programs treating adolescents found general agreement that such a standardized assessment tool was desirable, and most programs willing to participate in research to develop such a tool (Owen & Nyberg). Since that time, promising work has been done by several researchers toward development of empirically validated assessment protocols, though none has as yet been available on a widespread basis for clinical use. A tool developed by the Chemical Dependency Adolescent Assessment Project in St. Paul, Minnesota appears to be backed by the most research testing, and promises to make a significant contribution. Another tool being field tested with encouraging results is being marketed by PerCen of Minneapolis. These tools as well as others will be entering the market within the coming year.

Whatever progress is made in providing us empirically tested standardized assessment tools, none can hope to answer all our questions. A tool could tell us about a client's chemical use, its consequences, what other kinds of problems are present, personality characteristics, how that person compares on specific factors to adolescents being treated at various levels in our continuum of care. This is extremely valuable information. Standard tools are a first step in developing research designs that may one day tell us much more about what approaches to treatment work, and with which adolescents.

Standardized criteria for diagnosis and assignment to appropriate levels of care for treatment must come from the treatment field. While our initial and worst fears are that kids who need treatment won't always fit a system with uniform standards, we must face the fact that such criteria are already being set by insurers and HMOs, with cost interests underlying their guidelines. Informed decision-makers can set such guidelines in much more appropriate ways, but we need information to give them. This is where standardization of diagnostic and gatekeeping criteria can help.

Besides providing more reasonable guidelines within which to provide treatment, such an approach cannot fail to point out the need for a better continuum of counseling and treatment services for youth.

AN APPROACH TO ASSESSMENT INTERVIEWING

As standardized tools become available, are refined, validated and become trusted, clinicians will rely on them with more assurance for diagnostic decisions and level of care recommendations. But the third major function of assessment — motivating the adolescent for treatment — still remains the function of personal interview. While the impersonal aspect of the person-to-object relationship involved in an adolescent taking a test may avoid some defensiveness and distrust, making the determination of diagnosis clearer, it will do nothing to reduce the client's anxiety about treatment. This will continue to depend on the personal interchange with a clinician who is willing to listen, to dialogue, to establish a relationship which conveys respect and dignity, and concern for the adolescent as an individual.

The role of the assessment clinician differs in significant respects according to the setting. The example format described here is written from the point of view of a gatekeeper in a treatment program. While assessors work in many other situations, it is the counselor in this situation who is most often accused of inappropriate assessment motivated by the need to fill treatment beds. In many communities, these counselors may be the only available experts in adolescent chemical dependency.

I will outline some of the biases and beliefs which are reflected in this approach. The primary client is the adolescent. The client has the right to refuse treatment, and should be locked up only in situations which would allow such treatment for an adult, such as: (1) for detoxification; (2) for short-term emergency hold to protect the person from critical danger of harm to self or others; (3) under civil commitment through the court; (4) when adjudicated and incarcerated for committing a crime.

Counseling and treatment should be delivered with respect for the dignity of the client. Old "break them down so we can build them up" models of treatment are abusive and unnecessary, and in fact contrary to the principles implicit in the Alcoholics Anonymous program of recovery, upon which the majority of treatment centers claim to base their approaches. The skill required to work with a chemically dependent person in denial is not to break the addictive defense system, but to empower the person to face the painful addiction over which they have been powerless.

Assessment is a problem-solving process. Someone — a parent, school official, judge, psychologist, perhaps the adolescent — has determined that an adolescent has a serious problem, and thinks it might be chemical dependency. It is helpful to realize that when our client is an adolescent, there are often interested adults who wish to participate in the assessment process, and setting guidelines about their participation is sometimes difficult. Referents, whether they are parents or helping professionals, are invested in the assessment.

They often have in mind the outcome they want, both in terms of diagnosis and treatment recommendations. Parents, for example, may prefer to define their child's problem as drugs rather than face the possibility that a family situation is to blame. It is all too easy for the clinician to respond to the interested adults as if they were the persons for whom we are conducting the assessment, forgetting that the primary client is the adolescent. (For some counselors, the primary client may *not* be the adolescent. A quick way to determine who the real client is, is to ask, "To whom are my recommendations expected to be helpful?") It is helpful to look at the referent as a secondary client in most situations.

Beginning the Interview: Engaging the Client in the Problem-Solving Process

Teenagers don't willingly see a counselor for a chemical use assessment. They almost always come because of external pressure. Most often they are frightened, angry, and blaming. Typically, they are in denial of any possible chemical dependency, resistant to assessment, and unwilling to enter treatment. How can this negative posture be changed to one of cooperation with the assessment process?

Meeting the client. Make it clear from the beginning, to the adolescent and the accompanying adults, that the adolescent is the primary client. Approach the group in the waiting area of your agency, addressing the adolescent while offering a handshake. "Hi, are you Tom Smith? I'm Ken Counselor, the Clinical Supervisor here, and I do the admission assessment interviews. Are these people your parents? . . . Will you introduce me? . . . (Greet parents, shake hands, comment briefly on their long drive, the weather, etc.) Well, we'd better get to work. Tom, I understand that you are here for possible admission to our treatment program. You and I need to talk about what is going on with you and decide whether we can work together. Then we'll get back with your parents and discuss what should happen. (Provide an orientation session, if possible, or coffee and reading material for the parents.) Tom, please come to my office with me."

The Balk. A high percent of kids will say, at this point, something like, "Well, if I have a choice, I've made it. I'm getting out of here *now*."

If possible, deal with this one to one in your office. The general line of response can be. "That's up to you, but if you walk out now, what are you walking into? . . . Obviously, things are not going to be the same as before. If you leave here without cooperating, what will be the next move? . . . If the problem isn't you, let's talk about what *is* the problem. There's obviously some kind of major problem, if you're being brought here against your wishes. Let's nail it down and talk to your parents about it . . .

"We won't keep you here against your will—look at the place, it's not locked. In fact, even if you decide you want to stay, I need to make sure we're the right place. We only treat chemical dependency, you know. When we have somebody in treatment here, we want to make sure we're treating the right thing, or treatment won't help. That's a waste of time and money, and it makes us look bad if people are just as bad off after treatment as they were before."

The Confidentiality Contract. Assure the client of confidentiality. "I'll be telling your parents (or the referent) what I see as the problem, and probably recommending some ways to work on it. But I won't tell them the specific things you tell me in this meeting. What you tell me is confidential, unless it involves child abuse or preventing someone's death (including any other exceptions to confidentiality). I won't tell them how often you've used drugs or what you stole or whether you're a virgin. I might need your help later, though, if they need to know some specific things in order to decide whether to do what I recommend. But that's up to you."

Setting the Agenda. Make the purposes of the assessment clear. "I'm being asked for my opinion about whether you are a chemically dependent person. (Explain chemical dependency. Example: 'Many people who use alcohol and other drugs find that the chemicals have become way too powerful, causing problems in their lives. Some people who realize this can control their use or quit by themselves. Others need help. Chemically dependent persons have a disease in which they can't always control their chemical use. Even though they get in trouble, they can't seem to get control of their behavior and their lives. They need help, just like people with any other disease.')

"I have a little information from your parents (probation officer, social worker, etc.), but it's not enough to go on. I can't tell from this if you have a chemical use problem, a parent problem, a mental illness problem, are a criminal, or just made some bad choices. If you are chemically dependent, I might recommend treatment here, if you are willing to work with us. But we don't want you in treatment if it's not going to help; then you're left in the same jam. We need to figure out what makes sense here. I'd like you to tell me about the problem as you see it, and we'll try to get to the bottom of this. Then we can figure out what to do from here to get some of this pressure off you. What happened that brought you here?" (Often, by now, the client is a bit puzzled at the idea that they will have a choice about treatment, and elated because they will clearly have the opportunity to "run their con.")

Overview. Listen carefully to the explanation and the client's feelings and rationalizations. Check out with the client whether you understand correctly. Follow any obvious loose ends for your own information. Often, blame will be laid on the adult(s) responsible for the assessment referral or for catching them in illegal activity; ask the client to give you the concerned person's side of the story. (—"After all, they won't accept any recommendations from me if they think you've conned me. Then I'm no help and you walk out of here into the same mess. I've got to have the whole story.")

Get to Know Your Client. Who was this person prior to being involved with chemical use, and has chemical use caused changes? Explain that in order to understand what might be causing the current problems, you need to understand what the client is like as a person, to get a whole picture.

This portion of the interview can easily be started with current information on basics such as age, school status, part-time job, friends, boyfriend/girlfriend, favorite activities, future plans. Go to the area of family situation: who is in the family now? What's your Mom like? Dad? Siblings? Other significant persons?

Move back to childhood, looking for early social learning and memories related to formation of self-concept. This information is useful in a number of ways: it helps us establish a baseline of normality for this individual so we can recognize changes that may be the result of chemical dependency (diagnostic information); it helps us learn about the individual's pre-drug personality and functioning—the "sanity" level we can expect to see when the kid is sober, with strengths and blocks to recovery (treatment plan information); and clues as to what might motivate the client toward a decision to change (the "hook").

Perhaps just as important, it changes the affect and attitude of the client. The defensiveness of the situation dissipates as the client sees no threat to his/her current situation. (Another way to say this, in light of Nakken's construct of Self and Addict [1988], is that we call out the Self to talk to us, and the client becomes much more emotionally available as the guarded Addict is not interested in this part of the conversation.) The opportunity increases to ally with the needs of the child, reinforcing the strengths of the child who was previously "a winner" or empathizing with the difficulties faced by those in difficult childhood situations.

"Remember when you were about five? (Help establish points of reference such as age of siblings at that time, what house the family lived in then, whether it was before or after the parents' divorce, etc.) Were you a happy kid? Sad? Noisy? Quiet? When you got in trouble, what kinds of things had you done? What did your Mom say when she was pleased with you? What did she say to you when she was angry? What did your Dad say when he was happy with you? When he was angry? Did you feel safe and secure at home? Who did you play with? How did you like kindergarten? First grade? Second? Third grade? Anything important happen in your life during this time—births, deaths, divorces, moves? Did you play sports or join clubs? Did your family do church-related things? What did you do for fun? Did you follow rules or break them? What did you want to be when you grew up?"

(This is a time to develop your interest in this client as a person, and show it. How does this person approach life on a thinking and feeling level? What was life like? Interaction during this section of the interview can help build rapport, as the client often moves to a more emotionally open and vulnerable stance. "Did you believe

your Dad when he said you were good for nothing? . . . Really?
How many 'good for nothing' four-year-olds do you know?"
"Sounds like you were a smart little girl . . .")

Consequences of Chemical Use. Questions should become more
specific as the conversation enters the time when chemical use most
likely started. This is when changes start to emerge, as reported in
friendships, activities, grades, problems with authorities, hassles
with parents, frequency of acting out behavior (or of getting caught,
if the acting out predates the chemical use). Ask about first use, and
begin to entwine use-related questions with the rest of the client's
"story." "How were your school grades in fourth grade? Fifth
grade? What were your friends like? What did you do for fun?
When did you first try drinking or using another chemical? What
happened? When did you try it next? What happened in sixth grade?
The next summer? Seventh grade?"

Questions covering the using years (or months) should be more
thorough, covering both chronological pattern of chemical use and
consequences. We are looking for change in the client's life that
resulted from a pattern of increasing frequency and quantity of
chemical use — in other words, evidence that progression of chemical dependency is present.

"Any trouble with school authorities in ninth grade? Skip
classes? Grades holding or sliding? Were you using in the morning
before school? During the school day? After school? How about
weekends? How much time would you say you were high during an
average day that year? How much time did you spend thinking
about using and/or getting chemicals? Did you have to be careful
about covering your tracks from parents, people you owe money to,
or friends who are 'on your case'? How did you get your money?
Your chemicals? Any troubles on the job? Did you deal? Steal? Get
caught? 'Borrow' your parents car? Any accidents? Riding with a
'loaded' driver? Other dangerous behavior? Picked up by the police
for anything? Were you high when you did these things? Trouble
with parents, friends, or girlfriend/boyfriend?

"Have you done things you wouldn't do sober, like double-cross
your best friend or have sex with someone you wish you hadn't
been sexual with? Any problems with pregnancy, abortion, sexually transmitted disease? Ever been raped when you were too intoxi-

cated to take care of yourself? Ever raped anyone? A blackout is when you did something when you were high that you couldn't remember later. What happened, that you know of, during your last blackout? Did you ever think your using was getting you in trouble? Did you ever decide to quit, cut down, or change chemicals? What happened?'' Lead the client through "telling their story" up to the current crisis.

Assessing Diagnostic Criteria

Explain that problems with chemicals are not always dependency, and there are some specific symptoms you must ask about. Diagnosis is usually based on specific criteria, such as that set out by DSM-IIIR (1987). As chemical dependency counselors, we know how to probe for information which applies to diagnosis. We will have been looking for this information as we listened to the chronology described above. As we go through the symptoms with the adolescent, we can ask for more information, and point out what we've already uncovered. Some commonly used criteria and symptoms are discussed below.

Using in larger amounts or over a longer period of time than intended. Ask about this symptom with these questions: "Have you ever set a limit for the evening, and then used more than you originally planned? How often have you bought a stash planning it would last a certain amount of time, but you used it up faster? How many times have you planned to get someplace on time, like home or to a friend's house, but you got to using and didn't make it?"

Persistent desire or unsuccessful attempts to control use. This is an extremely important criteria with adolescents. It is the key factor in making a differential judgement of diagnosing abuse or dependency. Access to self-control is a key in sorting out those who can "grow out of it" from those who have the disease of chemical dependency and will need to abstain from chemical use indefinitely. Look for indications that the adolescent has at some time recognized chemical use as a problem, and made a personal resolution or a promise to someone else that they would quit or cut down their use. A nondependent user, upon recognizing that his/her use causes problems, will change it. A dependent user will almost always want to change it, and will either successfully quit (in which case we would not be seeing him/her), fail in the effort to stop or modify use, or "change his/her mind."

If this is the first time an adolescent has become aware of the severity of the problem, and has not tried to quit, a less intrusive recommendation than inpatient or residential treatment should be tried. A no-use contract along with supportive outpatient counseling or treatment may avert the need for inpatient. If the adolescent's chemical use problems continue under such a plan, we will have established a firmer basis for a dependency diagnosis, and more likely acceptance of that diagnosis by the client.

Uses knowing it causes other problems or makes them worse. This criteria is related to the above in that it requires an awareness of the seriousness of the chemical use. Is the adolescent aware of the relationship between his/her legal, school, family, social, health and emotional problems and his/her chemical use? Kids who have this awareness and continue to use, like those who have made attempts to control their use, are likely to internalize acceptance of the disease concept of chemical dependency more readily, because they have felt and struggled with the power of the dependency. (There is an interesting dynamic with the adolescent who uses knowing it causes other problems and does not attempt to control use: this client, while often appearing sullen, defensive and defiant, is likely to suffer from real spiritual emptiness, and have little experience of love, trust, or hope. This client has so little self-worth that he/she is prepared to let the addiction win.)

A great deal of time is spent in activities necessary to get the substance (e.g., theft), using chemicals, or recovering from intoxication. Add to this list preoccupation with planning the next opportunity to get high, fabricating lies and excuses to cover one's tracks, and rumination over what happened during one's last blackout. It is not uncommon for a chemically dependent youth to find almost all their waking hours centering their energy on the dependency. ("You're not too excited about school these days. What do you think about during classes? . . . First hour? . . . Second hour? . . .")

Activities that are important to the adolescent have been given up or reduced because of substance use. We found clues to what is, or was, important to the client in their "story." Favorite relatives may be ignored, hobbies unattended, sports or clubs dropped, studying ceases, and old friends and pasttimes dropped. We see a marked lifestyle change. Career plans are abandoned as preparation becomes too much work.

Use interferes with responsibilities or leads to hazardous behavior. This is usually an easy criteria to satisfy, as it is often these factors that result in the referral for assessment. It is also one in which kids typically see little problem, given their natural self-centeredness and tendency to take risks. The client goes to school hung over or high, uses on the job, comes home late or stays out all night due to use. Risks such as driving while intoxicated or riding with an intoxicated driver are routinely taken; motorcycles, bikes, snowmobiles, all-terrain vehicles, skateboards and skis all become dangerous when the operator is intoxicated. While this symptom denotes a chemical use problem, it is not very useful for distinguishing between abuse and dependency.

Increased tolerance. Marked increase in the amount of the substance needed for the desired effect (described in DSM-IIIR [1987] as at least a 50% increase) is a key symptom of dependency. Because this symptom is complicated by a couple of factors when applied to youth, it is sometimes misidentified.

1. We must take into account that teenage chemical use coincides with a period of very significant physical growth. Ability to "hold one's liquor" or other chemicals increases simply because of this physical growth. When we learn, for example, that a seventeen-year-old male who now drinks seven beers to feel his desired high started out getting the same effect from three beers at age twelve, we must take into account that this kid has added 60 pounds to the 100 he weighed just five years ago? In such a case, the illustrated increase in tolerance is not enough to indicate dependency.
2. Adolescents mix chemicals. If the young man mentioned above now accompanies his drinking by smoking marijuana, snorting cocaine, or otherwise enhancing the intoxicating effect of his seven beers, we may indeed be seeing evidence of significant tolerance development.

The essential issue to consider in evaluating tolerances increase is: Is the change in the amount and potency of combined chemicals this person now takes to get high so markedly different from past use level that it can in no way be attributed to either the client's physical growth, or to simply learning to handle the experience of intoxication?

Withdrawal symptoms. While the majority of chemically dependent adolescents have not had withdrawal which manifested in physical symptoms, this must not be overlooked. Shakes, tremors, and morning use to avert them are not uncommon. A small percentage of adolescents will require a medically supervised withdrawal regime.

Secretive use. This includes sneaking consumption and hiding a supply of alcohol or drugs. While not DSM III-R criteria, these are useful indicators identified by Heilman (1973). For adolescents, these behaviors are normal when applied to hiding use-related activity from parents and authority figures. They become very significant, however, when an adolescent hides the extent of their use from friends, or hides a stash so as to prevent having to share it with others, or in an attempt to keep oneself from using it up too quickly. This last reason is actually an attempt to control use — "I thought if I put it in a place where it was hard to get at, it might last longer." In this case, the next question should be, "Did it work that way?"

Laying It Out: Conclusions and Recommendations

Discuss with the client what you have learned during the session, stressing the current situation. This may be the first time the client has seriously thought through what his/her life was like and what happened to bring on the present situation. Often a clear picture emerges to both counselor and client that chemical use is a significant factor in causing the current pressures in the client's life.

Presenting the diagnosis of dependency. Even the most cooperative adolescent is likely to balk when told, "You have the symptoms of chemical dependency. That's bad news and good news, Tom. It means that things in your life aren't like to get better, and will probably continue to get worse, unless you are willing to make some changes. That will be hard at first. Your life is in a pretty deep rut, and it will take some work to change that around.

"The good news is, now we know what's wrong that's been making such a mess in your life. You can get back on track and be the competent person you really are by learning to deal with your chemical dependency. (Or, 'There's sure a lot you've had going against you besides your chemical dependency, but you couldn't learn how to handle that stuff when you were a little kid, and you've been high since then. The first step in getting some things going for yourself is to get this disease under control.' We have treatment that works."

The client will need assurance that the diagnosis will be checked out more thoroughly during the assessment phase of treatment, and, in fact, if he doesn't come to agree that chemical dependency is a problem, then treatment won't work anyway. The question is, "Are you willing to come into treatment to learn about chemical dependency and decide for yourself what you want to do about it? You can't do it alone; you've tried that. Here you'll have the help of professionals and other young people. If it turns out to be the wrong thing for you, we'll say so and find another plan."

If the client agrees to continue with the next phase (as often as not because the alternatives are unattractive), then it is time to agree on a treatment contract. "Tom, we need to know you're serious about coming in for treatment. Will you work with us, and participate fully in the daily program activities? Do you agree to stay until you and the staff agree it's time for you to go? Will you work with your counselor to plan your aftercare? . . . We have expectations here. Some of them we take very seriously, because this has to be a healthy and safe place for everyone here. The most serious rules are: no chemical use or possession, no sex with anyone in treatment, no violence, and no leaving the grounds without a pass. If you break these rules, you will be asked to leave. Will you agree to follow these expectations?"

Informing the parents and referent of the assessment outcome. Whether the interview has gone well or poorly, the news must be shared. "Tom, why don't you go bring your parents in, and we can tell them what we've come up with." Ask Tom to share both your recommendation and his decision with his parents, then follow up:

"Tom shared a lot of information, and he certainly meets the criteria for admission here. We would like to admit him for treatment. The first phase of treatment is a very thorough multidisciplinary assessment, and we will be double-checking my diagnosis as well as looking for the best approaches to helping Tom use his strengths in approaching life without chemicals after treatment. We will be asking you to participate in treatment, too."

But what if the assessment leads to a different conclusion? Perhaps the problem is something other than chemical dependency, or the data is inconclusive. "The information that Tom shared with me leads me to believe . . . No, I can't tell you what he told me because of our confidentiality agreement. Why don't we ask Tom? . . . Do you have information that Tom might have left out? . . . There just isn't enough information here today to diagnose Tom as chemically dependent, but I do (or do not) have some recommendations on what might happen from here." If Tom is cooperative, suggest a no-use contract along with family counseling, outpatient treatment, or other appropriate services. If Tom is not cooperative, outline the family's other options. These will often be dependent on the structure of local juvenile law and social services policies. In addition, parents should be encouraged to deal with their own stress through self-help groups and counseling, when appropriate.

A key operating principle is that *assessment is a process*. Explained that way to a family, they can often see that there are intermediate steps for change that are appropriate. Whether an adolescent is admitted for treatment, referred elsewhere, or refuses treatment, it is useful for the family to see the current situation as part of a process in which options will remain open as the situation changes. "If more information comes to light about the seriousness of Tom's chemical use, or he doesn't keep his no-use contract, give me a call and we'll get together again. Meanwhile, family counseling and setting some ground rules may help everyone in the family begin to feel better."

Our goal as counselors should be to recommend a plan for recovery, and to provide encouragement and hope that recovery is possible. When a client or family chooses to reject our suggestions, we had best sincerely wish them luck, leaving the door open for them to come back. *Never* send an adolescent away with a "curse" such as, "Your drug use will kill you unless you come into treatment today!" or "Come back when you fall on your face!"

DETERMINATION OF APPROPRIATE
LEVEL OF CARE

For most adolescents who are chemically dependent, residential treatment will be the treatment mode of choice. Why?

1. By the time an adolescent reaches the level of serious drug problem that can be diagnosed as dependency, it is very often true that their whole lifestyle supports the practice and progression of their disease. School class schedule, between-class hangouts and friends, after school activities, job — all are chosen in one way or another to enable chemical use. Just attending school is, for most chemically dependent kids, like walking into a bar where they are a "regular." Numerous friends will slide up to them in a day and ask, "The usual?"

2. Outpatient treatment for the chemically dependent adolescent requires that the family be an active and responsible part of the treatment team. Is the family willing and able to be part of the treatment team? Are they also willing to change? Young people come from three kinds of families: those who will recover with them, those who will encourage recovery but not join in, and those who will sabotage recovery. Which kind of family does the person you are working with come from? If the client does not live in a family that will nurture, change with, and protect the adolescent, the success of outpatient treatment will be doubtful. What are other strengths and liabilities for recovery? How much protection, structure and assistance will this person need to change his/her life? The client will always underestimate the amount of changing he/she will need to do in his/her lifestyle, and the amount of resistance he/she will encounter.

3. Finding appropriately structured outpatient treatment that is accessible to the adolescent and the family is currently impossible in many areas.

Refer to High Quality Programs

While measuring the quality of treatment is a complex issue, it is one that is important in evaluating our own programs and those to whom we refer clients. In addition to knowing basic information about accreditation and licensing, philosophy regarding treatment approaches, length of client stays and staffing patterns, and costs, there are some additional criteria to address when evaluating quality:

1. Assessments done by any clinician or treatment gatekeeper should result in a variety of recommendations, since no one treatment approach or program meets every client's needs. Of the persons referred for assessment or admission, how many are referred for treatment elsewhere for reasons other than inability to pay?
2. Does the program contact clients after discharge to evaluate outcomes of treatment? What are the results of their post-treatment outcome studies? How do outcomes compare among the available programs? In comparing outcome studies from different programs, be sure to note which clients are included in the follow-up group. Some programs follow all clients admitted, while others include only those who complete treatment plus a specified period of aftercare.
3. What do the clients say about the services they received? Were they treated with respect and dignity? Were they well-prepared to begin a new lifestyle after treatment?

REFERENCES

Adolescent 'state of the art' humbling. (1985, June). *U.S. Journal of Drug and Alcohol Dependence, 9* (6), 15.

Diagnostic and Statistical Manual of Mental Disorders, Third Edition, Revised. (1987). Washington, DC: American Psychiatric Association.

Donahue. (1985, May 31). (Television program.) *Donahue* transcript No. 05315. Cincinnati: Multimedia Entertainment, Inc.

Heilman, R. (1973). *Early recognition of alcoholism and other drug dependencies*. Center City, MN: Hazelden Foundation.

Insight. (1986, May 20). (Television program.) New York: CBS Television Network.

Jackson-Beeck, M. (1985, September). *Institutionalizing juveniles for psychiatric and chemical dependency in Minnesota; ten year's experience*. Paper presented at the meeting of the Minnesota Coalition on Health Care Costs, Minneapolis, MN.

National Institute on Drug Abuse. (1986). Drug use among American high school students, college students, and other young adults: National trends through 1985. (DHHS Publication No. ADM 86-1450). Washington, DC: U.S. Government Printing Office.

Nakken, C. (1988). *The addictive personality: roots, rituals, and recovery*. Center City, MN: Hazelden Foundation.

Newlund, S. (1985, May 5). Are rights trampled when juveniles are put into treatment? *Minneapolis Star and Tribune*, pp. 1A, 6A.

Newlund, S. (1985, June 7). Hearing focuses on state use of lock-up programs for youths. *Minneapolis Star and Tribune*, pp. 1A, 11A.

Newlund, S. (1985, May 5). Proposed changes would limit parents' right to commit child. *Minneapolis Star and Tribune*, p. 7A.

Owen, P. & Nyberg, L. (1983). Assessing alcohol and drug problems among adolescents: current practices. *Journal of Drug Education, 3*(13).

Schwartz, I., Jackson-Beeck, M. & Anderson, R. (1984). The "hidden" system of juvenile control. *Crime and Delinquency, 30*, 371-385.

Smith, D. (1985, June 7). Too many teen-agers locked up, panel told. *St. Paul Pioneer Press and Dispatch*, pp. 1A, 8A.

Worden, M. Adolescent treatment on the hot seat. (1985, June). *The U.S. Journal of Alcohol and Drug Dependence, 9*(6), pp. 1, 14.

Therapy
for the Chemically Dependent Family

Emily Schroeder, MA, CAC

OVERVIEW

The decision to marry and have children is a major commitment made by two individuals and an investment that can involve many years. At any point in the life of a family there can be crises in the marriage. Some couples "stay together for the sake of the children." Others make the decision to separate which may bring added pressure on them as parents. In troubled families it is not unusual to find that there are unresolved issues between spouses which they avoid by their involvement in raising the children.

There are times when a marriage ends because of death of a partner or because of separation or divorce. All family members feel the loss. Whether the family is forced to reorganize because of death or divorce, the parents sometimes form new relationships and the children are caught between the old loyalties and the expectations of those relationships (Boszormenyi-Nagy and Krasner, 1986).

Parents of adolescents are frequently confused by the stresses involved with the developing adolescent and in addition to this, they could be going through their own personal struggles as their children grow more independent. They may be in denial about what all this means for them and make attempts to hold on even tighter to the child (Ackerman, 1980).

Sometimes the problem is that they are feeling uncertain about

Emily Schroeder is Executive Director, The Family Systems Network, 316 Summit Avenue, Summit, NJ.

what is appropriate limit setting for their adolescent children; by contrast, the young person vacillates between needing guidance and being independent. These two forces create struggles between the generations. Although this "generation gap" is not a new situation, the increased use of alcohol and drugs has offered yet another means for adolescents to feel a separateness from their parents, and to feel powerful and more connected with their peers. This as a choice for many adolescents has created a generational crisis.

There are those young people whose use of drugs goes beyond the experimental stage and who become dependent and/or addicted to chemicals. The counselor needs to make a decision about the extent of the use, and whether it suggests experimenting, dependence or addiction. The helping professional must also assist the parents in establishing rules in their home about the use of alcohol or drugs. Most families have attitudes about drugs but are unclear about what they expect when it comes to their child's drinking. Their expectations need to be explicit, as do the consequences for violation of these rules in their family.

We have developed adolescent programs for alcohol and drug abuse to habilitate the chemically dependent child but a good assessment is necessary to determine what the presenting problem is and whether it is related to alcohol or drugs. If chemicals are involved, does the extent of the use indicate the need for a treatment program?

This article will present one way of doing that assessment, within the framework of family counseling, to determine whether the adolescent's behavior is because of an alcohol/drug problem or some other disturbance in that child. Looking at the child within the context of a system, it will also show whether there are unusual stresses in the life of the family and drugs are being used to bring relief or some other "gratification" to the individual. At the same time this behavior provides the family with a scapegoat and distracts from their other problems, thus serving a function for the family.

It will also discuss some of the issues for the counselor in working with dysfunctional families and present some guidelines for the family therapist if the adolescent needs a treatment program.

Finally, considerations for working with the family in the recovery process will be presented in as clear and concise a manner as possible. Although it is not the intent of this article to focus on single parent or reconstituted families, included will be a few comments about the problems unique to this population.

Family therapy is a method of intervening in a system that is out of control. One of the basic premises of systems is that for every action there is a reaction (Foley, 1974). Thus, for every reaction of a parent to a child's behavior there is another reaction on the part of the child. Behaviors escalate on both sides and before long the system is out of control.

When the adolescent is using chemicals and acting out, the parent(s), in an effort to control the child, begins to develop patterns of reacting around that behavior. A goal of working with the family would be to empower the parents, getting them to act appropriately and to get the adolescent back as part of the family, living under the family rules.

If the adolescent is not dependent or addicted, he/she will then live in accordance with family expectations because the parents are again managing the family. If the parents work together and take an appropriate leadership role and the drinking or drugging behavior continues, this would indicate a need for treatment.

Another premise of family systems is that symptomatic behavior serves a homeostatic function for the family (Minuchin, 1974). If there are stresses within the family and dysfunctional patterns are already present, the adolescent's behavior draws attention away from the existing problems. It may be protective of a parent, a marriage, or another sibling or conversely, it's function may be that of calling attention to the need for help.

Families are organized in such a way that they "fit together" and exhibit predictable behavior in times of crisis. In dysfunctional families everyone knows what his role is; without the crisis, family members often do not know how to appropriately connect with one another. Where there is alcoholism in one or both parents, this is even more apparent. This has been described by David Berenson (Berenson, 1976) as the "wet" and "dry" system.

My experience has been that, no matter how disturbing the circumstances are that are being described by a member of an alcoholic family, they do not say that life was "boring." They feel useful in crisis; they flounder in non-stress periods. Is it any wonder that they are often confused or controlling and trust only themselves (Black, 1982)? Is it really a surprise to find that the children at times have not gone through some of their own developmental issues, or that parents feel that they have "missed" or blocked out a lot of their own childhood? Although children in most families learn expected roles that stabilize the system, the more dysfunctional the family, the more rigidly they carry out those roles.

Children of alcoholics and children from dysfunctional families sacrifice themselves for the survival of the system. They grow up to be parents who do not want their children to go through the pain that they recall, but in trying to avoid this, frequently repeat the very same behaviors that they saw in their parents (Karpl, 1983). It is not unusual to find when there is abuse of chemicals in an adolescent that there is an alcohol problem with one or both parents which needs to be addressed. Approaches to this will be discussed in this article.

Included also will be some thoughts on using the halfway house for the child from a dysfunctional family rather than sending him/her home to self-help programs and continued family therapy. What are the criteria for that decision? When working in an adolescent rehabilitation program, one sees how the adolescent sometimes finds ways to get back home rather than going to a halfway house and the collusion that takes place between the child and his parents for this to happen. In spite of what is seen as the problem at home, the child feels an unspoken responsibility as a member of the family.

All behavior is somehow protective to the system and is frequently "sacrificing" on the part of the adolescent. The hierarchies are out of order and boundaries unclear in any family with dysfunction. We also have to consider the stage of the family life cycle when looking at adolescent problems. What is going on in the family at this time?

What seems "abnormal" to the outsider is the "norm" for them. For this reason there is likely to be a reluctance to change. Dysfunctional families generally reach out for help (voluntary or otherwise) when the stress of what is happening is greater than the system can handle. Taking advantage of that crisis and reframing it as an opportunity for growth is the challenge for the helping professional.

PREPARATION FOR THE FIRST INTERVIEW

Even before the first session the family therapist can make an "hypothesis," or educated guess, about what might be going on in the family. Whenever possible it is helpful to get information from the referral source and for the therapist to talk with the family member who is making the call. This sometimes involves the therapist having contact with that person after the appointment has been made. Although it takes added time and effort, it does provide data to make the hypothesis around which he will ask his questions.

The informant from the family is usually the parent most concerned and who, because of the stress of the situation at that time, will give out information from his/her viewpoint and will be cooperative and helpful. That parent is often in a close, protective relationship with the child and the other parent is more distant. Added information about what else is happening in the family will come during the interviews.

It is best to confine one's questions to the problem the informant is describing rather than deviating too far in other directions. The therapist can form his or her thoughts about the problem by what is volunteered or by what is avoided!

Whether the contact has been made because of internal family stress or external pressures from the social environment (court, school, police, etc.), the distress of the person has precipitated the call at this time. Being too sympathetic and understanding might lower the anxiety to the point where the parent becomes comfortable and feels that the problem can be solved without help. In contrast, however, asking too many "personal" questions (about a marriage, for example) could create anxiety that would frighten him/her and prevent following through with counseling unless there is other outside pressure for the family to get help.

GOALS FOR THERAPY

Family Goals versus Therapist Goals

In making an assessment of what the problem is, it is important to remember that in most instances the members of the family have already defined a certain person as "the problem," in this case the adolescent. It is then up to the therapist to gather information from everyone's perspective in order to confirm, amend, or completely reject the original hypothesis. This needs to include more than just information about use of alcohol and drugs.

The therapist and the family often have different goals for therapy. Simply stated, the family wants the problem "fixed." Parents frequently do not want to have to make changes in themselves and already have guilt and feelings of failure as parents because of the problem. Although marital stress might be part of the therapist's unstated hypothesis, it is unwise to delve into a marital problem too soon even when it is apparent. It is important to remember that their *stated* goal is to change the child's unacceptable behavior.

The therapist's goals are: first, to get the parents back in charge of the family if they are out of control; second, to assess the drinking and drugging of the adolescent in question; and third, to make a decision as to whether that child needs treatment for the problem.

Family Assessment

There are several reasons for the inclusion of the whole family in the assessment.

(1) The adolescent who has been "labeled" the problem in the family exhibits behavior that may justify that label but it is not unusual to find that he has had problems that predate the use of drugs and alcohol. Frequently the schools have defined that child in early grades as having learning disabilities, being emotionally disturbed, hyperactive, etc. and the patterns of interaction around these problems are established but the present problem has escalated the anxiety. The question is whether he has at this time lost control over his use of chemicals.

(2) If one person in the family is having a problem, it affects everyone and the viewpoint of others need to be heard. The adolescent whose chemical use is in question has generally been taking a lot of the parents' time and other family members may have experienced a variety of reactions to the demands this child has put on the family. What are their feelings; what are their needs? Who do they turn to for help? If the other children are not part of the discussion,

they feel left out, and they may already be thinking that the problem sibling is getting all the attention.

(3) The therapist is looking for how the family has organized itself around the present situation and what part the different family members play in protecting the adolescent *or* the parents when the family is in crisis (Wegscheider, 1981). This begins systemic thinking about what the benefits might be (because of familiarity) for the family to continue coping in this manner.

Since the behavior of the adolescent identified as "the problem" is also useful to the system in some way, it is important to think about what would happen in this family if the behavior stopped. The homeostatic balance is maintained by the behavior until the system can correct itself. In the alcoholic marriage, for example, difficulty in reorganizing without the active alcoholism is one of the explanations for the high rate of separation in recovery. Drinking is what is "normal" for the family and although they may not like it, they know how to connect around the crises; without it the system is unstable and the members more isolated (Davis, Berenson, Steinglass, and Davis, 1974).

The dependency of families on crises is illustrated by the following example:

> One bright young 18-year old in our practice was not successful in his first year of college and was drinking, partying and frequently cutting his classes. The school suggested that he take a leave of absence and it certainly looked at the time as though he was addicted. His parents *seemed* to agree that he should not use any alcohol or drugs, but there was collusion between him and his father who would "buy him a beer" if they went out to dinner.
>
> Since his return home, he has been given some limits by his parents and has controlled his use and managed his life in a responsible way. He says now that he could not handle the freedom of making decisions completely on his own.
>
> Although his mother reports that he has matured in his behavior over the summer, she is now looking for "another chemical problem, other than alcohol . . . maybe pot" that would be more difficult to detect! This allows her to avoid

looking at her child-centered life, the state of her marriage, and her husband's possible alcohol problem. Without the knowledge of the family's history, it would be difficult to comprehend the mother's need to find an addiction problem to "explain" his behavior. Her father is an active alcoholic.

With no alcohol in the house, the father is complaining that he is also being deprived of drinking at home. The therapists feel that he might have a problem, but no one else in the family seems to want to deal with it. When reframing the son's behavior and seeing it as serving a protective function, one could say that he is regulating the father's drinking!

There is not sufficient evidence to label the son chemically dependent at this point. However, there is no denying that having a family history of alcoholism makes the children high risk for the disease. Children of alcoholics tend to marry alcoholics, become alcoholics, or both. There is the likelihood that her husband is alcoholic, but she is not ready to look at this. Without an understanding of the protective nature of family members, one could not see clearly what is happening elsewhere in the system.

(4) A counselor needs to look at how open or closed the system is, and whether, if closed, it has been so for a long period, possibly generations, or if the presenting problem has moved the family in this direction (Bowen, 1976). Being in a closed family system means that the members are either enmeshed, with little sense of self, or disengaged with a "pseudo-sense of self." By contrast an open system exists when the members can share feelings and thoughts and can live in the family in a healthy manner without getting caught up in issues of other members.

(5) With families in crisis, it is a given assumption that the hierarchies are out of order and the parental balance is somehow skewed, with boundaries unclear (Haley, 1987). Where is the power in the family? It is more common than otherwise to find that the child with the problem is unusually close to one parent, frequently the mother. What other coalitions make up the organization of the family? Are there grandparents in the area? If so, what role do they play in the way the family is organized? It is not unusual to see a grandmother

who is in close alliance with a child and as a result the parents are ineffective in their discipline.

(6) The stage of the family life cycle is a significant factor in any family assessment (Carter and McGoldrick, 1980). With adolescents as the primary focus, the family may be "stuck" at the transitional point of the approaching "empty nest," a time when the adolescent needs to begin to individuate and prepare for developing a life outside the family. The rules that previously governed the family may need renegotiating and the threat of change for the parents creates anxiety from which a "symptom" emerges.

As much as possible, the *adolescent* needs to work through this developmental stage leading to individuation while living at home. This is different from the *young adult addict* who is struggling with how to leave home and get on with his life and for whom guidance with this can be an appropriate therapeutic goal.

(7) Birth order of the identified patient is often a consideration for the therapist. In this an oldest who is struggling for independence while feeling the restraints of home, or a youngest who feels an obligation to be there for the parents but has the same adolescent needs to grow up? These are but a few of the issues that could be involved in the struggle to grow and mature.

There are similarities between some adolescent behaviors and the behaviors of the chemically dependent person. In both cases the adolescent is out of control. The counselor needs to determine through the assessment what goals are appropriate and whether addiction is present.

THE INITIAL INTERVIEW

The Social Stage

In the first interview it is important to spend time helping the family feel comfortable with the therapist. Asking for help or being pressured by other agencies and institutions to get help is frightening and embarrassing to many families. Most people want to solve their problems within the family. In attempting to do so, they have frequently established dysfunctional patterns of interaction. The family would not be there if they knew how to eliminate their suffering. They are looking to the therapist to be an "expert," even though it might be evident in subsequent sessions that they do not easily make changes.

In establishing one person as a symptom bearer who is the "cause" of the problem, parents often believe that if this was resolved everything would be all right. It is the task of the therapist to stick to the family's agenda, but somehow also to "reframe" the situation in such a way that it allows them to see a "new map." Reframing involves looking at behaviors in a positive way and seeing that somehow they serve the family's needs at the time (Minuchin and Fishman, 1981). Pride and guilt may make it difficult for the parents to alter their behavior so that their role is more affective.

The acting out of the adolescent has often created responses from the parents that vacillate between the extremes of holding on rigidly to the rules or giving up and throwing all discipline away. Beneath this are feelings of failure and guilt. It is of importance to make it clear to them that it is the therapist's belief that they have done the best they could in their parenting efforts, given their "training" from their family of origin and their own personal life stresses, but that it may be beneficial to change some of their approaches because their child is having difficulties.

After socially "meeting" each one of them individually while going around the family circle, it is sometimes useful to find out how they knew they were coming to the session. The therapist then knows who communicates such matters to them. It is generally the mother, but this is not to be taken for granted. Because I suspect that it is true, I also ask who did not want to be present, and compliment the family on their ability to get together to help the child with the problem.

Generally speaking, children do not want to go to therapy and I expect them to be resistant to being there. Often this needs to be made as an overt statement, followed by the view that their feelings and perceptions are important and valid, and that everyone in the family has a helpful contribution to make for their own development as well as the growth of the family. I add, however, that first we will get the parents' view of the problem, thus beginning early in the session to establish boundaries and acknowledge hierarchies.

One must always note who is missing and get information about that. I often ask who "should" be here but was for some reason omitted. Sometimes it is a grandparent who lives near by; often an adult child who is away at school or married, and it was not thought to include that person. The chances are that the missing person is aware of the problems and could be helpful. Arrangements can be made for a session that would include them. It also becomes more clear during this process who is missing and perhaps is not wanted in the session by some member. Part of the hypothesis might include speculating about this. All families have "secrets," and that person not there might be the most informative and for that reason discouraged from being present.

After the initial stage of getting acquainted, I ask if there are any questions they have about me, thus making the statement that I am going to be open with them (and covertly suggesting that I hope for the same). It is important not to lose sight of the fact that the family comes to a "stranger" and can be expected to exhibit their best manners in order to give the impression that the family is OK. There is much that they will omit in the beginning of therapy. I don't push too hard for this, rather deferring more information in some areas until a later date when there might be more trust.

Noting where everyone sits in the session also can be a clue to who is close to whom. Generally this will be confirmed (or denied) by the way they communicate with each other as the interview proceeds.

Identifying the Problem

When the family and the therapist become more comfortable, the counselor can then throw out the question of why they are present. Although there are different views about to whom this question should be addressed (Haley, 1987), I am of the opinion that it needs to be directed to the parents, thus establishing a boundary that defines them as the leaders of the family. This is particularly true when the presenting problem is an adolescent.

Initially questions need to focus in some detail on the parents view of the problem. When did they first notice the change in behavior, what were the changes, and what did they try to do to resolve them? Although I will be speaking directly to the parents at this point, the therapist needs to note what is happening with the others who are present. If there are interruptions, it may be necessary to block the interference by letting them know that they will have their turn to give their perceptions. Are they restless? Are they silent? Do they send out nonverbal messages through facial expressions or body language? Are they in any way trying to take over or distract from the problem? Facts such as these are clues to family dynamics.

I will ask each of the children how they see the problem, thus giving the message that I also value what they think. There may be remarks that suggest other problems in the family, particularly tension and disagreements between the parents. These are noted by the counselor, but it is not necessary to comment on them. One of my "hidden agendas" is to find out what is going on in the system that it might need to have a child in trouble. I know that ultimately that must be resolved, but for the present it is important to stay with the presenting problem (Haley, 1987).

As stated earlier, systems organize in such a way that members do what they must in order to keep the homeostatic balance, or in short, to keep the family from "falling apart." Behavior usually protects in some way the marital dyad, even if it is addictive behavior. One is not exclusive of the other. Therapists sometimes make the mistake of thinking that the family wants change, rather than that they want the problem "fixed." Actually, this balance is what they know and are therefore more comfortable with, and it is unstable at this point.

When there is an alcoholic parent, everyone has learned roles to play in crises, and the therapist perceives the family's ability to organize around the drinking. When the problem is with an adolescent's use or abuse, the same principle applies: the parents organize in some way to try to stop the problem but have little success when there is addiction.

If there is an addicted parent and child who is using alcohol or drugs, the situation becomes more complicated because the adolescent's use may be a way to get high or feel relief from pain, and it may be the illness of chemical dependency, but from a systems perspective it could also be protecting someone or an attempt to get help from the outside world.

I did one family session where the adolescent in question, an only son, second child, was not present at the first session.

>It was apparent to me early on by behaviors observed, not by words expressed, that there were coalitions in the family. The oldest daughter, a high school senior, was her mother's confidant, a good student and parentified child. The third sibling seemed to be the one who brought fun and humor to the family, and the youngest, a seven-year-old daughter, was the "darling of them all."
>It was clear from the start that there was a problem between the parents and that the mother was protective and overly close to her son. This protective relationship was evident through the sessions in spite of efforts on my part to alter that dynamic.
>When I commented in the first session that he seemed to have the most "power" in the family, I explained it by saying that he was the only one they were not able to get to the session. Although he was not close to the father, much of his behavior mirrored the father's problems.
>The parents continued to disagree about what was needed and he continued to drink and act out. Eventually he was sent to treatment. After his discharge he continued using and was in and out of programs. The father was also an alcoholic, in denial, and the mother in time divorced him. The family began to develop some stability and the father eventually was sent to treatment by his company for his poor job performance.

Taking a Drug and Alcohol History

Most counselors, when getting a referral to assess an adolescent's chemical use, take the child and talk to him alone to determine the extent of his use or abuse of alcohol or drugs. Since the rules of confidentiality make it private information to the counselor, it certainly is acceptable practice to talk to the adolescent in this way, making the statement that he might be able to be more honest and less fearful of consequences. The family therapist could incorporate this as part of the session. However, I have never been certain that the child at this point would be as trusting and "honest" as one might think.

Our experience in family therapy is that the adolescents are likely to exaggerate or minimize their use, depending upon which seems more beneficial to them or the family. One of the differences we have noted between the young and the older population of users/abusers is that the older alcoholic tends to minimize or deny the problem and the adolescent population is more likely to exaggerate. It fits in with the need to find "acceptance" with one's peers in a chemically oriented society.

Because of this, some of us who are doing family therapy are inclined to think that chemical dependency counselors can always find an abuse problem if they are looking for it. Parents are feeling like failures and filled with guilt and they need to find some reason why they are out of control as parents. Chemical dependency as an "explanation" could be arrived at through the collusion of these two groups. It does not resolve the issue of whether there is chemical dependency nor whether the problem warrants treatment in an adolescent facility.

Family therapists tend to focus on the use of alcohol and/or drugs in a more behavioral way. Although it is important not to ignore the adolescent, we include it as part of a history of the use of all family members. The intent is not to ignore the problem but to put it into a perspective that fits/does not fit with the family values. The therapist approaches this nonjudgmentally by saying that we live in a society where a high percentage of adults use some kind of mood changers, and that we need to look at how this family and all of its members fit into this pattern.

Each family that comes to therapy because of an adolescent behavior problem has a code about drinking that is unique to them. It might come from a religious conviction, from a bad experience with alcohol in the parent's past, or it might be a very liberal attitude which is cultural. They might also have much more rigid views about use of other drugs. There might be alcoholism in one of the parents or another sibling. Without knowledge of the "cultural" attitudes that are unique to them as a family, it is difficult to evaluate the problem in the adolescent (McGoldrick et al., 1982; Kaufman, 1985).

What has worked for us in family therapy has been to question each member, even to the youngest, about their drinking and their drug use. We ask what constitutes "a lot" of drinking versus "a little," and what they drink, since alcoholic beverages have different alcohol content. We ask what drugs they have tried even once and what they would choose if they could have any substance that they wanted. This tends to detoxify the subject of usage. In addition, if there is exaggeration or minimizing from any member, it may bring a reaction from others in the family, thus also giving added information about attitudes towards drinking and the use of drugs.

It is important, however, to keep *your* concern with the identified adolescent about whom the family is acknowledging problems without getting distracted by what is reported about the use of others in the family. A good family therapist ends an interview with a confirmed or revised hypothesis from all the information subtly gathered from everyone.

I recall one fourteen-year old who was referred to us by the school counselor. He so exaggerated the extent of his use that we wondered what the truth was.

It became apparent after a few sessions, when he was abstaining and living up to the rules laid out for him, that the family was still in great pain, and that the father was possibly an alcoholic in denial. This was not the stress, however, that unbalanced the system; the "problem" in the marriage at that point was that the father was having an affair. The pressure in the marital dyad became greater than the family could bear and the son had a "crisis."

The son "confessed" to a guidance counselor that he was abusing alcohol; the parents took him to a facility that did an assessment (where he made exaggerated statements) and made the recommendation that he be sent to a rehabilitation facility. This was not acceptable to the parents and family therapy was offered as an alternative.

There was also a younger sister, very charming, bright, and "good." Although the siblings did not know what was happening in the marriage, they felt the sadness of their mother and had acted accordingly: the daughter made an even greater effort to please the parents and the son, more belligerent, acted out. For each of them it was their attempt to re-establish the homeostatic balance.

It was the wife who came to me individually to tell me the "secret" and that she was going to leave when she finished her graduate studies. Although her husband was drinking excessively at this time, arriving home on the last train from the city where he worked, she could "handle" this, but would not tolerate another in his series of affairs.

The family dropped out of treatment when the husband ended the relationship with the other woman. The signal that this had happened for the therapists was that the wife received a mink coat for Christmas and resumed her willingness to meet his train, stopping with him on occasion for "a few drinks" on their return to their home.

Collusion was involved in the continued drinking once the affair was resolved. Further evidence of this was the wife stating that her husband had ordered a beer for the 16-year-old son on a ski trip, thus denying even to the boy that he thought his son had an alcohol problem.

Issue of Parental Alcoholism

What are the options for the therapist if there is suspicion that there is a drinking or drug problem in the parent? Too often, counselors want to confront that head-on which usually results in alienating the person who appears to be chemically dependent. Generally speaking, that parent will come for help for his child, but does not want to be challenged about his own drinking and will protect it at all costs. This certainly was the situation in the above cited family.

It makes more sense to go around it in another way, one which also brings about discussion and reactions from the family. The counselor can attempt to get a "contract" from everyone to agree to abstain from use during the time of therapy in order to "help" the adolescent get his life in order. This frequently generates more information for the therapist and brings out in the open what may have been covert until this time. The major "rule" in the alcoholic system is "Let's not talk about it." Getting feedback from other members gives the therapist added information for the assessment of the family situation. Other options will be discussed later in the article.

It is important, however, that this information come up but not become a distraction from the problem of the adolescent. He bears the symptom because of his behavior, and from a systems perspective, could be protecting a parent or the marriage. Children who act out in an alcoholic family are not only destructive to themselves but could also be reaching out for help for the families. Loyalty prohibits that they "talk" about the issues at home, but unconsciously they can act out what the problem is by using chemicals.

Ending the First Interview

In summarizing to the family what I think has occurred in the session, I am setting the stage for change. The goals at this point are to unbalance the system by beginning the process which empowers the parents and at the same time allows the troubled adolescent and other siblings to have some input about what they see and feel as family members. Just having an "outsider" involved is change, and this in itself is threatening.

To move too quickly would be a mistake. It is important to recognize that the system has been organizing around this problem and that they need help in defining more clearly what it is and how they can better work towards a solution (Haley, 1987). There are other issues that will have surfaced during the interview. These need to be acknowledged and postponed until the parents can again become the family's managers and the child who is the identified patient resumes an appropriate place with the other siblings.

I want the adolescent to have the chance to "show" his parents that he can be responsible. Sometimes I will give him the task of writing out what he considers is the problem that brought them to therapy and his plan for correcting it. This is to be delivered by the parents in a sealed envelope, which again forms a boundary between the adolescent and the parents. My plan as therapist is to see them together without the children at the next session. I explain that we will have different kinds of meetings, sometimes with parents alone, sometimes with the child or children by themselves, and the rest of the time together.

By having the parental subsystem come alone for the next session, I am making a statement that is defining the parents as the heads of the family who will join together with me from time to time to gain some new insights. It is important for counselors to remember that most parents are not "bad" parents; rather, they are "stuck" at this point in their lives.

I will get signed releases to talk to other individuals and agencies with whom the child is involved. My verbal statement is that we need to touch base with all the significant people who might be helpful. In doing this, I am also "tightening up the system" so that the child sees that we can use all the resources that are available to help solve the problem.

In closing, the family should be told that the adolescent will stop using if he doesn't have a problem. If he continues using, we have to decide why he has not stopped and that perhaps he is not able to because he does, in fact, have an addiction. The adolescent and the other siblings need to hear this.

SESSION TWO

Having the parents comes together without the children serves several purposes. In addition to drawing a boundary around the parents, it gives them the opportunity to work on some of their parenting differences and determine how they can form a united front. During a stressful time with their child, it is not unusual to see parents sticking rigidly to their views. Sometimes they are fighting out their personal issues in this manner (Stanton, 1982).

It is a time when they can be told that they need to put their spousal differences to one side for the time being to help their child. This could work paradoxically. Their "secret" is distracted by their child's acting out behavior, but in working successfully as parents, they are learning indirectly to live more cooperatively together (Haley, 1980). Concentrating on rules, how they are going to carry them out, limit setting and consequences for infractions gets them interacting with an agenda. An added suggestion could be random drug screening of the adolescent for the parents to be assured of their child's abstinence.

Getting them to agree in order to empower them as parents,

thereby restructuring the system's hierarchical order, is probably the single most difficult thing that needs to be accomplished. In this session one begins to have a sense of the function of the child's behavior in the system. The distance/closeness between the parents becomes more apparent as well as the enmeshed position of one parent towards the child.

If there was no clear contract regarding their own use of alcohol or drugs, talking more to the parents about this might be appropriate at this time, reframing it in the context of being "helpful" as parents rather than as a problem they might have with alcohol or drugs. Most parents will respond to the statement from a counselor, kindly stated, "Wouldn't you want to do the best you could for your child?" If they present arguments about why they should not be asked to do this, the question at least may make them uncomfortable about their continued use during this period.

SUBSEQUENT SESSIONS

Continuation of the sessions to include the whole family becomes a review of the family's week, with the therapist noting the parent's ability to begin to join together to manage the family, looking at the adolescent's "plan" for change and his behavior in school and at home. With guidance from the therapist, the parents start to talk with their children about rules and consequences.

Through this process begins the work of restructuring the hierarchies that are skewed when the family first comes for help. Parents need to learn to work together. Putting the less involved parent in charge of the adolescent is an effort to break up the close relationship with the other parent, thus empowering the parent who in some sense (perhaps because of an alcohol problem) has been "disqualified" by his/her partner.

Although the spouse (and/or children) may believe that one parent has an alcohol or drug problem, this will become more apparent if he/she is unable to take the responsibilities that the counselor is giving to that spouse. Confronting it head on, as stated earlier, seldom works. The therapist needs to take the positive position that the parent can function more effectively and then get his view when he is unable to do so by asking, "How come? What kept you from doing this because I know you care about your child." When he does get involved, give affirmation and praise. This puts the responsibility for his/her own functioning on the parent with the alcohol problem.

Being in therapy implies change and is threatening. Disqualifying a parent because of a drinking problem is not productive and often would be duplicating what the family has been doing. Getting him to talk about his drinking may help him to decide for himself what would be "reasonable drinking."

Thus a dialogue can begin with the parent about drinking: what does that person think constitutes a little; a lot? The subject of alcohol which has not been talked about thus surfaces and puts the parent himself in charge of his belief about drinking. The family, and the spouse in particular, might disagree with his interpretations, but this too is information that was covert prior to this. Conversely, a spouse of an alcoholic can in time make his/her own decisions based on what is acceptable or not acceptable about the relationship (Treadway, 1987).

What is important, however, is that the counselor pursue the drinking, gently but clearly, little by little, not judging the parent with the problem. At the same time the spouse needs to feel that you are not disqualifying him or her! Emotionally it involves "holding the hand" of the spouse while at the same time getting the alcoholic to begin to explore his use (Treadway, 1987). This involves working little by little in sessions, never to the point of alienation of the parent. This requires that the therapist be sensitive to the fine line that exists between creating an awareness of one's drinking and feeling threatened.

Pursuing the drinking problem in a parent cannot be the main focus in sessions. The therapist needs to warn the family that if the anxiety level gets to be more than they can tolerate, the adolescent who is the problem may have to act out to get the focus back on himself.

Use of drugs or alcohol in an adolescent when the parent is a recovering alcoholic makes a different statement than with the parent with active abuse (Bepko and Krestan, 1985). Asking the right questions will reveal what is happening in the family. Is the behavior an attempt on the part of the adolescent to get the parents' attention when all else has failed? In recovery the alcoholic must focus on himself, but the child also has needs for recognition. Conversely, the parent may be trying to play "catch up" as a parent, and the children do not know how to handle this change. I remember reading in a local newspaper the comment of a recovering alcoholic woman who was a counselor in a nearby rehabilitation program. "I was more devastated by finding out that my child was an alcoholic than I was about learning about my own disease." No child deliberately overdoses, but it certainly does get the attention of the parents and often brings them back together when they are unable to connect with each other without drinking being an issue.

In families where the parent is in early recovery, the system is unstable without alcohol as the focus and at times the adolescent provides that focus. The professional needs to determine whether this family is having difficulty relating without having alcohol at the center of their lives. Hating the drinking is not the problem; the issue is that the members know what to expect and know how to act in crisis. Unlike many other families, crises are often "normal" in the alcoholic system. Relating as family members without playing the roles is the beginning of what change is all about.

If the adolescent's acting out continues to escalate, it could mean that he is unable to control his use and rehabilitation may be indicated. At this time, an appropriate referral can be made. The therapist needs to be familiar with programs for rehabilitation, and can make the arrangements for admission. The parents will be more "ready" to deal with this alternative and the child will not be as powerful as he once thought. Getting the parents to cooperate with each other to get the necessary help is an important step since the changes in the family dynamics will create even more manipulative behavior as a result of the stress of the adolescent's need for treatment.

Position of Family Therapist When Adolescent Is in Residential Treatment

Once arrangements are made for the chemically dependent child to enter a treatment program for adolescents, the role of the family therapist is to cooperate with the program. They will have education groups about chemical dependency for all family members and offer sharing groups for parents to give them contacts with others who have been struggling with the same problems. Identification with one's peers is part of the healing process and often assists parents to give themselves permission to change. No longer do they have to "hide" as they learn that they are not alone.

The dysfunctions that occur in chemically dependent families have developed over time and parents are not always aware of what changes have occurred for all the members. Often it is a situation with intergenerational alcoholism, a common occurrence, and it is even more difficult for them to "let go." Families with this long history of alcoholism offer a real challenge to the helping professional. Telling people to stop doing what they have been taught to do as a loyal family member sets up uncomfortable conflicts for parents.

The 12-Step programs of Al-Anon and Families Anonymous also begin to teach parents the concept of letting go of what they cannot control, and beginning to look at what they can do about themselves. It provides another support group that gives families permission to make changes.

When the adolescent enters a treatment program that is accessible to the parents for visiting and family groups, the therapist needs to "let go" of the family after the initial contacts with the family counselor in the program. They can make themselves available to that person by offering their services for any special problems that may arise.

If the treatment program is at a greater distance, it might be advisable to see the family at regular intervals. Discussion of what is happening with their adolescent out of the home, how other members are feeling about the attention that is being given to the adolescent, what other problems are coming up for them without their sibling at home creating "crises" are among the topics for discussion. Who misses the adolescent most? Least? What is better or what is more difficult not having him/her at home? These are examples of areas to explore.

The family needs to be referred to self-help groups for themselves. Education about chemical dependency as a "family disease" can be given during this time. It is important for the family therapist to encourage them to go to the "family week" that is offered by most programs.

Particular attention needs to be given to how the parents are feeling about having a chemically dependent child. There is overwhelming guilt and a feeling of failure (often covered by anger) that emanates from many parents in facing this, and at the same time "relief" that the child is getting help. Often anger masks their hurt and disappointment. A sensitive counselor can help with such feelings when they surface and encourage discussion with the other family members in the program.

Referral to a Halfway House

When is a halfway house indicated for the adolescent? Many times the counselor sees this as the "solution" when there is alcoholism in a parent and a disruptive environment in that home. There are times when this may be the most appropriate referral, but my experience has been that it is sometimes a decision that is made without considering family therapy as an option. The implied message is that if the adolescent changes he can then return to a home where there may have been little or no change, and that he will then function in a sober manner. It also suggests paradoxically that he is both the problem and the solution.

Because of the loyalty that exists in families, there are many young people who will not go to a recommended halfway house. As much as they complain about their parents, they are like "homing pigeons" and find a way to return there. There is sometimes collusion with the parent and everyone "cooperates to make it happen." Frequently the adolescent breaks a major rule in the treatment program and is discharged.

As one young adolescent from a very dysfunctional family said in one of our sessions:

> "I have to be at home to help my family." He was labeled the problem child because of his drugs, alcohol and disruptive behavior but saw himself as the "hero" who needed to hold the family together.

He had gotten himself kicked out of the first program that he was sent to and went AWOL and hitchhiked a hundred miles to get home from the second. He again got into trouble and the courts sent him to yet another treatment center and while there he threatened suicide and was discharged to his parents' care. He later overdosed on drugs at the bus terminal in NYC and called his mother. She made arrangements for him to be hospitalized in a psychiatric unit. Looking at him in one way, one could say that he was the "bad kid;" or a "mental case." Reframing it, he was sacrificing himself even to the degree that he would attempt suicide to help his parents stay together.

The other "bad guy" in the family was the father. His wife felt he was an active alcoholic, in denial. We were able to involve him in a session following one of the son's crises, and he opened up and spoke very honestly of his concerns about the family.

The wife showed up at the next session with just her young daughter, and was filled with excuses as to why the males in the family were not present. It appeared that she, too needed him to be the problem. Keeping his mother "busy" certainly kept her from pursuing the divorce that she thought that she wanted.

These situations are never that simple.

Referral Back to the Family Counselor

Keeping in touch with the counselors at the rehabilitation program and cooperating with them is one way to assure coordination of services for the family with an adolescent who is chemically dependent. The counselors in the program can usually tell when the family therapist understands addiction. It is essential that this be the case when there is a family with chemical dependency.

Unfortunately, there is still resistance on the part of some chemical dependency counselors to making the referral back to the family therapist as part of the plan for on-going care. Those of us who are family therapists with a background in alcoholism counseling have pondered this, and one of the possible explanations has been that the "successful" programs for alcoholism have been modeled on the individual approaches of the 12-Step programs of AA, Al-Anon, NA, and Families Anonymous.

In treatment, their focus tends to be largely on the individual rather than the role of that individual as part of the system. Too often one senses that adolescent counselors seem nonverbally to "blame" the parents. This attitude is transmitted to the adolescent and to the parents. At times the counselor has unresolved issues of his/her own that interfere with an open attitude about working with the whole family.

On other occasions, there is a lack of understanding of family therapy and systems thinking, and it is seen as something for the "family" rather than for the individuation and recovery of all family members.

Most dysfunctional families are from "closed" systems where the rule is not to talk about it, not to feel or think differently than the rest of the members. It is the goal of the 12-Step programs to help members of a family to go from this position to one of being more "open," with freedom to grow.

This is also the goal of family therapists. Loyalty is a key factor in keeping the family "stuck" in their old ways. Education alone is not enough to alter old values, old ways of interacting; it takes a caring therapist to help them make changes. A goal in recovery is for everyone to learn to make appropriate choices for themselves. This requires that the family gradually become organized into new patterns of interaction.

I see family therapy as the "bridge" that helps members cross over into new ways of relating that are more appropriate to their personal growth. The 12-Step programs help individuals make changes. The family therapist, simply stated, helps them to see when to take an "I" position and when to be part of the "we-ness" in their relationships, and to know their "bottom line." Their rebellion and the pull of their loyalty to the family often keeps them in a confused state and they cannot be objective.

The Serenity Prayer says, "Grant me the serenity to accept the things I cannot change, the courage to change the things I can, and the wisdom to know the difference." I believe that the family therapist helps them to make that distinction.

Continuing Family Therapy

Whenever possible, it works well to have the family therapist involved in the final session while at the treatment program. Frequently distance or time prohibits this, but it is important to review the on-going care contract so that this can be openly discussed and supported. Family therapy can be correlated with group sessions for the parents and the adolescent. The two are not mutually exclusive. What is essential, as in earlier sessions with the family, is that the therapist have a clear understanding of alcoholism and family dynamics and the connection that exists between the two.

In early recovery, the fears from the past experiences often bring back the anxiety of the parents when the adolescent comes home. The family therapist should expect that they will be "walking on eggs" and work with this as an early recovery issue.

The counselor needs to give encouragement for the family to go to their respective self-help groups. These are also complementary supports for the therapist, whose practice often cannot give the frequent daily support that is needed for the members to individuate and begin the separation process that is appropriate to families with an adolescent.

Letting go is a hard concept for parents to grasp. Sometimes they revert back to the extreme of "throwing their rules out the window" or covertly checking the activities of their child. Changing to new ways of parenting is not easy.

Parents, and in particular the one who has been overly close to the adolescent, may find it difficult to let the 12-Step program sponsor guide their child. This is a problem that needs to be explored and clarified in the sessions. It is helpful if the sponsor meets the parents, but initially the adolescent may not agree to this. It is sometimes a good idea to suggest that the parents might do the driving to meetings the first week until they find people in the program who will give them rides. Whatever makes the family members more comfortable during this transition period can be an acceptable option in early recovery. Getting into their child's program for sobriety, however, is not appropriate and if this seems to be happening, it needs to be dealt with in therapy.

It is important to keep the system "cool" in early recovery, not bringing up toxic issues that could raise the family's emotional level to its former state. Basically, this is the primary function of the sessions. They are not giving up parenting when they stop enabling their children; they are finding new and more appropriate ways to parent. They need to explore the difference between "enabling" and "parenting."

Chemical dependency is a disease which affects the individual and those around him. Parents tend to focus on the adolescent before, during and after treatment. They, who at one time were upset with their child's behavior, often continue to have a need to keep him the center of attention in the early recovery stages. In many of the aftercare groups parents seem to talk about what he is doing now: "He can't get up in the morning." "He isn't talking to us." "He isn't being a member of the family." "He's never home." These are some of the statements one hears from parents who are still struggling with change. The child continues to play the same distracting role as before even though he is not using alcohol or drugs.

This is early recovery! As long as he is sober there is the chance that he will find new options for himself. People do not change that quickly! As with the adult recovering alcoholic, the adolescent needs to concentrate on not using, and in the beginning there may not be many other changes. A family therapist can reframe this as "his continuing to do his job in the family without the use of chemicals," and when the family begins to make healthy changes, he won't need to play this role of scapegoat. The adolescent's recovery for him must come first. He has enough problems staying straight in a peer situation where using is commonplace. For this he needs his own on-going care program.

Relapse

If the tension escalates in his family, particularly with his parents, the recovery adolescent knows on some unconscious level that relapse will put the focus back on him, thus relieving the other stresses in the family. Relapse is an issue that must have consequences. This is one of the primary uses of the home contract and being consistent in carrying it out is the job of the parents. If the chemically dependent child knows that he is going to "lose" something by using, it is an inhibitor that can help him to stay straight. If the parents do not uphold their end, he then knows that there is no great cost, so why not use.

LATER STAGES OF FAMILY THERAPY

In the middle and more advanced stages of therapy the therapist can begin to work with helping the parents and adolescent negotiate with each other. This gives the young adult the opportunity to be more responsible for himself. The parents have the final say, however, and can go back to old or revised rules if he is not ready or able to handle certain responsibilities.

This approach allows gradual and appropriate lessening of parental control and fills the needs of adolescents to be both independent and dependent. If a child cannot handle a situation, he needs to know that he can have help from his parents. They need to learn when to let go and when their adolescent needs them. Standing by and being available is not easy for many parents. Getting on with their own lives lessens the tensions between the adolescent and his parents, but many of the population that are in therapy for chemical dependency are stuck in the stage of the family life cycle which leads to the "empty nest." The "excitement" of problems keeps them otherwise occupied as a way to avoid this process in the progression through the lifecycle.

If the system still needs a "symptom bearer," I sometimes "help" the child to find a new way to keep the focus on himself because of the toxic issues between the husband and wife. How many times in on-going care groups in an adolescent program I heard parents complaining about relatively minor problems, but speaking with the same vehemence that they had months before about his erratic behavior when using chemicals. It is as if they still need a "problem." Far better to substitute something else to keep them involved than to have the child relapse and use again. Actually, planning this in a "playful" and paradoxical way often brings about changes. Even if the task is taken literally there is no great harm done. Nothing is forever! Using this as a technique can be an effective way to paradox the family and get their attention regarding the need to change (Madanes, 1984).

Anyone who understands the dynamics of the chemically dependent family knows that relapse returns the family to its familiar homeostatic balance, in this case with the focus on the adolescent who has "slipped." Parents who need a problem in one of the children as a way to avoid dealing with their own issues do not easily give up their old roles of over/underfunctioning as parents.

ENDING FAMILY THERAPY

Therapy with the child centered alcohol problem can continue for many months, even extending into a time frame of one to two years. The time between sessions is gradually increased. As the therapy progresses and the individuals make changes, the system slowly reorganizes in a new way and abuse of chemicals is no longer the function of helping parents relate to each other.

Signs that treatment is near completion are that the child seems to be coping well with his life, is functioning without chemicals and that there is a new respect between the generations. Parents are getting on with their own issues. If they desire marital therapy, working with them as a couple can begin at this time.

Many families do not stay in therapy for the length of time that would be most helpful, and stop treatment when the child seems to be functioning in an acceptable manner. If the family therapist has been effective in joining with them as they make changes, they will contact that person again if the need arises.

It is also not unusual for dysfunctional families to "drop out" of treatment without having a final session that allows for closure. It is helpful to write them a letter suggesting that if they are finished with the counseling it would be appropriate to have a closing session. Families that have lived on crises as a way of organizing their lives are familiar with "rescuing" and "survival." Their history does not often include "ending" relationships, and they can benefit from this as a learning experience.

Therapists can not expect that recovery will go smoothly because families' roles are changing and change is always traumatic. When we are working with a family that has had alcoholism in its members for many generations, we are talking about families where the alcoholism is only "the tip of an iceberg."

Choices for the Co-Dependent Parent

Doing therapy with a parent who is an active abuser is difficult but not impossible if the system is organized around helping the child. It is not unusual, however, for the alcoholic parent to become less and less involved and for the overfunctioning spouse to continue the sessions. Working with the motivated parent can be productive and may be interpreted as a statement to the alcoholic about the need for change.

In the family where there is chemical dependency in one of the parents, there may be other changes at a later point. Prior to therapy the spouse saw no alternatives for problem solving. The therapist can offer the following as choices: (1) to continue their present way of coping and not make changes; (2) to emotionally detach from the drinking or (3) to leave the situation (Berenson, 1979). Working through the option they see for themselves can be productive in therapy. If this occurs in the early sobriety, however, the adolescent could revert back to his scapegoat role and thus protect the marriage. The family therapist needs to be aware of this in working with the family.

Growing and changing over time helps the spouse make decisions about living with alcoholism; it must be recognized the alcoholic also has choices about using. It usually creates a crisis if the spouse chooses not to live with the alcoholism. The alcoholic can then stop using and get help or continue using and expect separation. Not many who live with alcoholic partners get to the point of "either-or . . . the drinking or the marriage." Having this "crisis" later in therapy when the chemically dependent child is more secure in his recovery lessens the need on his part to relapse or create a crisis of his own.

Single Parent Families

Single parent families are in the process of reorganizing their lives to live without one member in residence. This can be a result of divorce, separation or death of a partner. There are times when the parent is despondent or stressed to the point of functioning inadequately and children step in and "parent."

In situations of separation or divorce, when one of the children abuses drugs or begins drinking, this often will get the attention of both parents and they are forced to talk with each other about his behavior. This is a way to stay connected. It is not unusual, however, for the child to have some fantasy that the parents will get back together.

I remember one such situation:

> A 17-year old came to our rehabilitation program for an assessment of his drinking problem. His parents had divorced several years before and the father had new young children by a second marriage. The son lived with his mother and a younger sister but he had been allowed to shuttle between the parents' homes.
>
> When his behavior was more than the mother could handle, he went with his father for a period; life there would get tough and he would return to his mother's home. Nothing except alcohol and drugs seemed to change the pain he was feeling about his life situation. Help came when he arrived home drunk and hurt his sister. The mother called the father and said, "Something has to be done," thereby beginning a new effort to solve the problem. They went through the juvenile court system which sent him to an alcoholism recovery unit for an evaluation. He got help with his drinking problem, and the family got help. For the first time both parents were involved together in solving the problem.
>
> One of the results was that he finally began to accept that his parents were not going to reunite (he admitted that this was his wish), and that he had to take responsibility for what he was doing. He got better and got on with his life. The family system changed and operated differently with the parents cooperating together. With all his "power" to move back and forth, he had been "stuck" on a life event that he was not able to accept.

Whenever possible professionals need to work with the parents in these situations. It should be made clear from the beginning, however, that the intent is not to change their marriage, but to help with the co-parenting of their child. A divorce or separation means a marital relationship is ending, but not that parenting is no longer a role.

SUMMARY

In all life situations, approaching the completion of the task of child rearing can raise questions for parents about their own relationships. Having new experiences is part of the development of the teenager, along with the need for peer acceptance. In a time when drugs and alcohol use are increasingly prevalent, the curiosity to try drugs has become of crisis proportion.

One of the basic differences I sense in attitudes between the generations is that while young people may see drugs as "exciting," their parents tend to see them as "frightening." In years to come, however, this may be less apparent because the present generation of drug users will become tomorrow's parents.

The treatment of addiction in our young people is in its infancy. We need constantly to evaluate our experiences and be open to all effective models of treatment. Since children are not adults and must in most cases return to their homes, we cannot be satisfied only with the residential and outpatient programs of rehabilitation that work with them apart from their families, and give education and group support to parents as part of treatment. We also need to include the ongoing help that family therapy offers.

Systems theory states that change in one person in a system affects everyone. This approach to chemical dependency takes into consideration that alcoholism or chemical dependency is a disease that organizes the family in some manner to solve the problems it creates. Those efforts at solution form the patterns of interaction, the skewed hierarchies and the weakened boundaries within the family that allow the problem to continue without treating the illness. It becomes the "glue" that holds the system together.

All behavior serves a function in a system. The question is not why a behavior occurs, but what happens when it does. Looking at it from this perspective gives the professional a chance to intervene with suggestions. Even though the family life may seem chaotic to the outsider, what happens when there are crises is usually predictable behavior.

The major rule in a closed system is, "Let's not talk about it," Because of feelings of guilt and betrayal, it is difficult to tell outsiders what is going on in one's family. Acting out what the problem is, however, is not unusual and therapists need to "listen" to what the behavior is saying.

Many kinds of situations with children create dysfunctional patterns. If there are already other difficulties in the family the adolescent's behavior draws attention away from the existing problems and the focus is put on him. Whether the child has the disease of alcoholism or is abusing drugs and alcohol, the behavior can serve many purposes. For example, from the standpoint of the individual it can be an attempt at self-gratification and peer acceptance. Systematically, its function can be protective or an effort behaviorally to reach outside the system and get help for the family.

When the child is living in a family where there has been separation, divorce or death, the behavior may be somehow an attempt at connecting the parents or it could be a distraction from the pain of abandonment and loss both for himself and the other family members.

One approach to doing an assessment that determines whether a child's problem seems to be addiction or dependency is to have sessions with him and his family. We need to be sure that we are not taking him out of the home, putting him in an adolescent program for habilitation and labelling him chemically dependent if the problem can be solved at home with therapy. If placement is appropriate, professionals in the program can provide support and education about chemical dependency.

It is not unusual to find an alcohol problem in one or both parents. This can not be disregarded but initially it is unwise to make it the prime focus of the therapy since confronting the drinking of a parent in a direct way seldom works. In addition to this, if the anxiety level in the family rises too much, it is possible that the adolescent will act out in some way to get the focus back on himself. Use of drugs or alcohol in an adolescent when the parent is actively drinking is treated differently in therapy than if the parent is in recovery.

When working with adolescents, it is suggested that the therapy continue after treatment in order for the system to attain a new balance. Twelve-Step programs help the individual focus on himself; family therapy is the bridge that reconnects them in a more appropriate way as a family.

Getting parents to agree on a course of action, and to "let go" of the child is probably the single most difficult task for the family counselor. Almost universally the child with the problem has been overly close with one parent. If this is the case, it is essential to help the family to reorganize the way they live together so that drugs or alcohol are no longer useful. Drugs both keep one dependent and give one space.

If there are marital problems parents must be persuaded that they need to put them temporarily to one side to help the child. Paradoxically, if they do this successfully it can give them rewards and awareness of new skills for working together. If not, they can later focus on their own issues in marital therapy when the system can handle separation if reconciliation of their issues does not seem possible.

REFERENCES

Ackerman, Norman J., M.D. "The Family with Adolescents." In *The Family Life Cycle, a Framework for Family Therapy*. Carter, Elizabeth A, and McGoldrick, Monica (eds), New York: Gardner Press, Inc. 1980.

Bepko, Claudia and Krestan, Jo Ann. *The Responsibility Trap. A Blueprint for Treating the Alcoholic Family*. New York: The Free Press, a Div. of Macmillan, Inc., 1985, pgs. 219-224.

Berenson, David. "Alcohol and the Family System." In *Family Therapy: Theory and Practice*, edited by P. Guerin. New York: Gardner Press, 1976, pgs. 288-289.

———. "The Therapist's Relationship with Couples with an Alcoholic Member." In Kaufman, Edward and Kaufmann, Pauline. *Family Therapy of Drug and Alcohol Abuse*. New York: Gardner Press, 1979, p. 238.

Black, Claudia. *It Will Never Happen to Me*. Denver, Colo.: M.A.C., 1982.

Boszormenyi-Nagy, Ivan and Krasner, Barbara. *Between Give and Take. A Guide to Contextual Therapy*. New York: Brunner/Mazel, Inc., 1986, p. 191.

Bowen, Murray, M.D., "Theory in the Practice of Psychotherapy." In *Family Therapy, Theory and Practice*, edited by P. Guerin, N.Y.: Gardner Press, 1976, p. 68-87.

Carter, Elizabeth and McGoldrick, Monica. *The Family Life Cycle, a Framework for Family Therapy*. New York: Gardner Press, 1980.

Davis, Berenson, Steinglass, and Davis, 1974, studies quoted in Paolino, Thomas, M.D., and McCrady, Barbara, Ph.D. *The Alcoholic Marriage; Alternative Perspectives*. New York: Grune & Stratton, 1977, pgs. 124-126.

Foley, Vincent D., *An Introduction to Family Therapy*. New York: Grune & Stratton, 1974, pgs. 39-44.

Haley, Jay. *Problem-Solving Therapy, Second Edition*. San Francisco: Jossey-Bass, 1987, pgs. 107-111.

_____, *Problem-Solving Therapy. Second Edition*. San Francisco: Jossey-Bass, 1987, pgs. 25-34.

_____, *Problem-Solving Therapy. Second Edition*. San Francisco: Jossey-Bass, 1987, p. 20.

_____, *Leaving Home: the Therapy of Disturbed Young People*. New York: McGraw Hill, 1980, p. 45.

Karpl, Mark. *Family Evaluation*. New York: Gardner Press, 1983, p. 37.

Kaufman, Edward, M.D. *Substance Abuse and Family Therapy*. New York: Grune & Stratton, 1985, pgs. 159-164.

Madanes, Cloe. *Behind the One Way Mirror*. San Francisco: Jossey-Bass, 1984.

McGoldrick, M. et al. *Ethnicity and Family Therapy*. New York: Guilford Press, 1982.

Minuchin, Salvadore. *Families and Family Therapy*. Cambridge, Mass.: The Harvard University Press, 1974, p. 110.

Minuchin, Salvador and Fishman, H. Charles. *Family Therapy Techniques*. Cambridge, Mass.: Harvard University Press, 1981, pgs. 73-77.

Stanton, M. Duncan, Todd, Thomas C. and Associates. *The Family Therapy of Drug Abuse and Addiction*. New York: Guilford Press, 1982, p. 346.

Treadway, David. Workshop in New York City, sponsored by Lifecycle Center, Newton, Mass., April 10, 1987.

_____, Workshop on Adolescents, New Jersey College of Medicine and Dentistry, 1987.

Wegscheider, Sharon. *Another Chance: Hope and Health for the Alcoholic Family*. Palo Alto: Science and Behavior Books, Inc., 1981.

Strategies of Intervention – A Community Network

Matt Green, MEd, CAC

INTRODUCTION

Intervention strategies with adolescents involve recognition of a problem and initiation of treatment. This definition is frequently used when discussing the distinction between primary prevention, that is, preventing misuse from occurring, and secondary prevention or "intervention" (Johnson Institute, 1984). Whatever label one wishes to use the concept remains the same. It involves the recognition of a problem, encouraging help, and supporting the sufferer while he/she receives that help.

There has been a major shift in emphasis in adolescent drug abuse over the last two decades. It was in the 1960s when we, in Newton, first began dealing with these young people and their drug/alcohol problems. The first year twelve teens were hospitalized with serum hepatitis. School staff were frightened by the number of teenagers using drugs and alcohol. By the early 70s, illicit drug use waned and alcohol became the drug of choice among these adolescents. Information that warned of the dangers of L.S.D., the high price of other illegal drugs, and easy access to alcohol were probably partially responsible for this switch (Stutman, 1985). The problem of drug abuse seems to have once again intensified during the 1980s; thus, there has been a great deal of attention focused on how school and community agencies are dealing with this issue (Green, 1986a).

Since teenagers are required by law in most states to participate

---

Matt Green is co-founder and co-director of the Newton Youth Drug/Alcohol Program, 100 Walnut St., Newtonville, MA 02160.

in some kind of formal educational process, schools have a large stake in the drug issue. Teens bring their troubles to the school house door, forcing the school to deal with their problems. Others in the community have also seen increasing numbers of adolescents with drug and alcohol problems. These professionals, as well as parents, rarely have adequate training or experience in treating substance abuse to feel comfortable and competent in helping teens (Green, 1986a).

Models of secondary prevention are not without their share of specific difficulties. The selection of attainable goals, and development of strategies that are socially, economically and politically feasible are just two of many problem areas (Krivanek, 1982). Added to these is the difficulty of adolescence. The feelings of invincibility but insecurity, coupled with a relatively short history of illicit use, makes the task of working with teens appear impossible.

A model operated by an intervention program through the public schools, has been successful in dealing with these drug using adolescents. The implementation of this program educates, evaluates and confronts teens through a cooperative network of school and community agencies. The schools are not exclusively responsible. The goals are to provide information and education about the lifestyle of the drug abuser and to monitor the abuser's behavior throughout the day. Cooperation between the school and other community agencies such as the court, police, and social service is essential. These are the institutions most important in the life of the drug and alcohol abusing teen. The public school staff works together with the community to provide a program that can meet that teenager's needs. The program then becomes a mandatory part of court probation conditions or of school participation. The aim is to have clear communication, so that consistency of treatment is maintained. This unusual alliance has been established in Newton, Massachusetts — The Newton Youth Drug/Alcohol Program (Green, 1982a, 1987).

The concept of drug/alcohol intervention operated through the public schools, is one questioned by many school administrators (Green, 1986b). Arguments made stress that schools are for education not medical or mental health treatment. School does not own the responsibility for the student's emotional and physical problems

(The Johnson Institute, 1984). Since school is the only constant in an adolescent's life, and children of all ages bring their problems (e.g., drug and alcohol abuse) to the educational environment, the school does have the obligation to try and implement change. It is for these reasons the Newton Public Schools have taken it upon themselves to do just that.

The following is a brief background on the reasons for adolescent alcohol abuse in Newton.

ADOLESCENT ALCOHOL ABUSE — THE REASONS WHY

The issue of alcohol misuse by teens is hardly confined to low income youth. Many middle and upper-middle class youth also misuse. Newton is a city with the reputation of attracting upper-middle class professionals. There are, however, also pockets of poverty that affect about 10% of the population (Executive Department — Newton City Hall).

Clinicians have traditionally identified children of low income families as experiencing a particular sense of powerlessness and frustration when they contrast their own means with that of others.

This is hardly confined to the low income group. The tensions and pressures which are the fallout of professional achievement among upper-middle class adults are reflected among children, in an early felt need to prove their worth (Jorge & Masur, 1985). Increasing parental divorce rates, pressures to achieve, combined with lack of direction and support from family and community, all contribute to the inability to cope found in large numbers of middle and upper-middle class youth. Within this setting, alcohol use by teens is accepted and even encouraged (Huberty & Malmquist, 1978).

Although the statistics can be elusive, youth workers and professionals in the field are in agreement on the existence of four trends in alcohol use patterns occurring among adolescents.

1. Alcohol is becoming the preferred drug among teens.
2. Drinking and driving problems are occurring among younger adolescents of junior high school age.

3. The incidence of chemical dependency and related dysfunctional behaviors needing intervention and treatment is increasing.
4. Parents tend to look the other way or even to encourage drinking by their children in the belief that alcohol is preferable to other types of drugs. (National Council on Alcoholism, 1984)

BEGINNING THE INTERVENTION PROCESS

In order to begin the intervention process, one needs to decide if the teen has early chemical dependency, with loss of ability to regulate drinking (The Johnson Institute, 1984). If dependency were indicated, a more comprehensive approach might be appropriate. This would include a treatment program and the development of an abstinent lifestyle. The following case will illustrate our approach to these youth.

Case 1

Dan, an 18-year-old high school senior was identified by his guidance counselor as possibly having an alcohol problem. The counselor received information from the basketball coach that the student had been drinking during the school day. Discussions with the counselor, illuminated the facts that: Dan had frequently needed places to sleep other than home, there were family disputes, and his father had died from alcoholism.

Dan was well-liked, had achieved academic honors and was the captain of the basketball team. His friends admitted that his social life consisted of heavy drinking. He had also suffered from frequent blackouts (alcoholic amnesia). He had been suspended from athletics for a two-week period because of the school drinking episode. Upon interview Dan did not perceive any problem as a result of his drinking. He did admit to feeling remorse after missing 2 foul shots at the end of a game, that resulted in a loss for the team. Dan had been drinking during the course of that game (Newton Youth Drug/Alcohol Program, 1986).

What should be done for such a young man? There are four parts to Dan's case that help determine how to proceed. The first is that his father had died of alcoholism. This points directly to a family history of chemical dependency. The second is that Dan's friends characterize his social life as consisting of heavy drinking. The third points to the frequency of his alcoholic blackouts. The final piece seems to bring together the previous three. As a result of his drinking behavior, Dan's life was seriously disrupted through a suspension of his athletic eligibility. Intervention is recommended.

His drinking needs to be discussed with him as a source of two kinds of problems: consequences of heavy drinking, and risk of later alcoholism. He needs basic knowledge and supportive education in order to see how alcohol might be causing his school athletic problem and social difficulties. Qualifying him as a problem drinker or alcoholic is of no consequence at this stage. What is important is that the school and athletic department understand his "at risk" behavior and be supportive of the need for intervention and confrontation of his problem.

Teenagers with drinking problems rarely recognize that they exist. They do not seek help complaining of "alcohol dependence" or "a drinking problem." What they or significant others complain of are symptoms that are negative consequences of drunkenness (The Johnson Institute, 1984).

Chemical dependency in adolescence manifests rapid development with severe symptoms. There is no period of social usage. The young person's inability to control use is much like what is seen with heavy smokers; they can stop completely but cannot smoke moderately. Serious consequences that may develop within a few years of the onset of drinking may include: trembling in the morning, withdrawal hallucinations, and abnormal liver function. There is often evidence of a strong family history of chemical dependency or alcoholism (Huberty & Malmquist, 1978).

An alcoholic cannot control what he drinks, so the treatment must include abstinence. Inpatient treatment in an adolescent population is indicated due to the severe nature of the problem. The following case illustrates this profile.

Case 2

Bill, a 17-year-old high school junior was referred to the intervention program from court, after a D.U.I. (driving under the influence of alcohol) conviction. He was mandated to participate in the program for the duration of his probation (one year).

At the time of referral, Bill was drinking daily. He was also being treated for depression at an outpatient mental health clinic. The attending psychiatrist felt that the drinking was episodic. His conclusion was based on the fact that drinking alcohol in combination with anti-depressive medication can produce adverse reactions e.g., coma or possible death. The teen was defensive and frightened about his drinking.

A review of his academic records indicated that his grades had shown a rapid deterioration from all As to failing grades. Also he had recently been dismissed from the hockey team for frequent intoxication.

A review of his family history showed an upwardly mobile, wealthy family. He reported that both grandfathers were alcoholic and that his mother frequently drank to excess.

A rapid behavior decline took place within 8 months. Bill finally ended up as a patient in the hospital intensive care unit after he collided with a telephone pole, driving at excessive speed while intoxicated. In the hospital Bill admitted to daily drinking and not taking his medication. He asked for treatment for his alcohol problem (Newton Youth Drug/Alcohol Program, 1983).

INTERVENTION –
A MODEL OF RECOVERY FOR ADOLESCENTS

Exploration

Upon referral into the intervention program, the adolescent begins to explore his pattern of drug/alcohol use. Attendance is generally made a requirement or a condition of an individual's obligation to school, court or the police. The program then provides the student with a conceptual framework for understanding his drug/alcohol abusive behavior. This framework is similar to a behavioral contract. It must be simple to understand, easily explained and consistently carried out. The contract states that:

1. Court referred teens remain in the program either for the duration of the probation period (1-3 years on average) or until failure to comply with program requirements.
2. School and police referred students register themselves for at least 1 academic year.
3. Satisfactory completion of the program results in earned high school credit; the amount of credits is determined by the length of stay.
4. Unsatisfactory performance means no school credits are given and the student is returned to the referral source for further disposition to court or jail. (Green, 1987b)

All program participants are required to attend either Alcoholics Anonymous and/or Narcotics Anonymous at least twice weekly. These meetings are local open public meetings and are monitored by program staff to guarantee participant attendance. The purposes of this requirement is to provide education about the disease of chemical dependency and to provide an experience which encapsulates various life situations. Finally, it provides a resource for those who decide at some later time, that treatment is necessary.

Participants must attend group and individual counseling weekly. The commitment to the program of a year provides the opportunity for youth to focus upon a variety of problems. The group process encourages a nonthreatening consistent environment for the development of trust. Groups are highly structured and confrontive, in an attempt to guide individuals through the process of becoming honest about the consequence of their drinking and/or drug use behavior.

Group sessions are a four phase process. The session opens by asking each participant to share "old business." This might be a complaint about program policy or an update on the progression of a personal dilemma previously discussed. This initial phase forces each participant to talk, thus encouraging participation in later discussion. Typically, participants use this time to complain about rigid program policy.

The second phase requires participants to share "new business." This is the point when the educational process begins. Participants will often inform program staff of conflicts they are experiencing with what they interpret to be program time taken from job or recreation. For example: Tom informs the staff that he has purchased $25 tickets to a concert on the evening of a program meeting. Staff response is that it's Tom's decision to go to the concert or to the meeting. Of course, if Tom is not in attendance at the meeting he will be returned to his referral source as a consequence. If Tom was referred from court, his decision may ultimately decide his freedom or imprisonment. In group, Tom is presented with his alternatives and consequences of his decision. The group helps to guide Tom in the decision.

Phase three of group process requires each participant to verbalize the type and quantity of substances used over the last week. This strategy forces the individual to think about the substances they use on a regular basis. Very much like chain cigarette smokers, teens often use substances so regularly that it becomes an unconscious part of their existence. It also sets up the group to be a "watch dog" for individuals who are being dishonest or for those whose use seems to be accelerating.

Finally the group engages in open discussion. A word or phrase is written on the room's blackboard to be the basis for discussion. The words must be used to correlate how an individual became a member of the program. Examples of words used are: "honesty," "guilt," "trust," "relationship." Sometimes slogans found at Alcoholics Anonymous or Narcotics Anonymous are used such as: "Easy Does It," "Live and Let Live," "One Day At A Time."

Vocational assistance, court liaison and interpretation of events are also available to each individual. Participants are required to attend all meetings on time without exception. Absence and tardiness are not tolerated, and result in immediate termination from the program. As a result, time becomes an important concept in a teens participation. For example; group meetings take place on Wednesday evenings at 7:00 pm. Program staff inform participants that they are required to be seated in the group room by 7 pm according to the clock in that room. At 6:59 pm a staff member walks to the door of the group room and watches the clock's second hand make it's last minute sweep before closing and locking the door at 7 pm. Anyone found outside the room as little as 5 seconds after the hour is considered in noncompliance with program requirements and thus terminated. This strategy teaches responsible behavior and provides a highly structured atmosphere. The strategy remains successful as long as it is consistently carried out. Group members must know that program policy is consistent. This particular rule has produced so much discussion over the years, that a high percentage of newly referred students are aware of the rule before joining the program. Furthermore, students must attend all program meetings free of mind altering chemicals. Failure to achieve this requirement also means termination from the program.

The strong limits placed on individuals help to provide a mechanism for the school, court, police or other referral sources to monitor the behavior of the teens. In addition, high school credits are granted for successful participation. The promise of credit becomes added incentive for success or as a road back for those who have dropped out of school.

Therapeutic/Intervention

As the individual progresses, a change in thought process develops. Through the group modality, program staff teach participants the meaning of "response" and "reaction." "Reaction" is the primitive method of dealing with a situation. Its meaning is similar to what happens when an animal feels it's being attacked. An animal will strike back without thought process. "Response" to a situation requires thinking before acting.

These two concepts are illustrated repeatedly during group discussion. Example: If a court referred program member engages in an illegal activity like drinking alcohol in a public park with some friends, that would be a reaction to a situation. A response in this situation would be that the student might suggest that they move their drinking to someone's home or perhaps postpone the activity until more carefully made plans could take shape. This would show that the student has thought about the consequences of the illicit activity thus following the road of least risk.

Upon completion of the teen's commitment to the program, he/she is able to: state thoughts and feelings which lead to abusive drinking and/or drug use, and identify moments of out of control usage. They can list alternatives to use at such moments, and implement them in their lives. Argument, conflict, tension and boredom which can take control are handled by describing specific actions in his/her plan for future development (Green, 1987).

Compliance

When change takes place, participants begin to adopt program philosophy and goals as their own. Individual's with drug/alcohol problems continually have unrealistic expectations. Examples of these during the teenage years might be; expecting to perform well on the athletic field with a hangover or the expectation of no consequence for continual absenteeism from class. Students who are never confronted for their behavior, are allowed by the community to continue their illusion.

Our students learn through discussion the type of risks they usually take. The effect of consistently taking high risks is discussed in the context of resolving family disputes, work, athletic activities, driving, and abusive drinking and drug use. These teens are encouraged to seek help from other professionals, and to view it as a way of using resources, rather than as a weakness or character defect. We emphasize seeking realistic personal change, and to have benchmarks for testing progress periodically. For many students, plans for maintaining "sobriety" and continued treatment become an essential part of their future. The program has extensive contact with inpatient detoxification and treatment/rehabilitation facilities, making referrals as well as to be used as an aftercare placement for patients coming back (Green, 1987).

Treatment versus Intervention

In our minds, intervention and treatment are closely allied. We consider this model not only intervention but treatment, and a method of secondary prevention that cannot be ignored. If a student of ours seeks formalized treatment and becomes "straight," he/she is a staunch advocate of abstinence and an evangelist in his approach to his drug using friends. So here we have young people aged 17-22, who are teachers by example to their peers. These young people participate in a "recovery" group during the school day. This group, led by program staff, is housed in the city's high schools. It becomes a sanctuary of support for these students who wish to remain drug/alcohol free in the same environment where they once used drugs (Green, 1987).

THE PROGRAM MODEL

By coordinating the community and the school, the Newton Youth Drug/Alcohol Program design accomplishes the following: (1) Receives and evaluates adolescents with behavioral problems, specifically drug/alcohol related and addresses them through counseling, and education from the school. Referrals are made by special programs, guidance personnel, school psychologists, administrators, and other support staff. (2) Receives and evaluates adolescents based on referrals from the police department. This is a means of diversion for first time offenders. After an arrest, an alternative is presented to the offender and his parents — 1 year of program participation or criminal court proceedings. (3) Receives and evaluates adolescents based on referrals from the court system. (4) Receives and evaluates adolescents based on referrals from city human service departments. (5) Makes available counseling, education, and support services for adolescents reintegrating from residential drug treatment. (6) Makes available support services for parents of students, through groups. (7) Provides teacher training in the identification of adolescent substance abuse, before the problem becomes a crisis.

All referrals coming from the various community agencies are the same adolescents who are also having difficulties in school (Green, 1986b). It is in this way the program is able to coordinate these community groups to provide appropriate services for the adolescent.

INTERVENTION—A MODEL OF TREATMENT
FOR THE ADOLESCENT

It was generally agreed on, more than a quarter century ago, that the alcoholic had to "hit bottom" and voluntarily seek help before it could be effective. That generally happened too late to salvage much of his life. We now know, that it is unrealistic to expect that an alcoholic will seek help on his own—though a few do (Wegscheider, 1981). As for an adolescent, too many say that those years are a time to experiment, have fun, and discover one's identity. This developmental expectation together with the denial, delusion, and compulsion characteristics of the disease of chemical dependency seldom allows adolescents to deal with what is real—addiction. Fortunately, we have also discovered that there are other ways. We have learned that "hitting bottom" is just another way of saying that the alcoholic has found himself in a crisis, so painful and so frightening that he will do anything to escape from it—even stop drinking. Further we know that such crises can often be created. This is the intervention process (Wegscheider, 1981).

Intervention for the adolescent combines three important processes. The first is a confrontation of the individual's behavior. This strategy is implemented initially, for a teen, by being referred to a "drug program." The referral step is an overt recognition that a drug/alcohol problem exists. The confrontation strategy is then employed in group process, discussing the link between drug use and aberrant behavior. Then finally, it is utilized through forced attendance at Alcoholics Anonymous or Narcotics Anonymous. Attendance at these meetings gives a clear message to the teen that the problem is severe enough to warrant an association with self-admitted "alcoholics" and "drug addicts."

The second strategy involves networking with other community agencies. These agencies, in all likelihood, have been involved with the teen at some point in time. Agencies such as the court, social service, public treatment clinics and the police, all monitor the adolescent's behavior. These agencies must give a consistent and clear message to the teen that they will not tolerate chemical use. The same consistent message coming from these agencies, creates an atmosphere that the adolescent perceives as tough and unbending. This can "raise the bottom" for the individual so that he/ she surrenders to his/her dependency sooner.

Finally, the teen must understand that what he has been doing e.g., chemical use, isn't working anymore. If that is the case, it is time to put some trust in someone who might be able to make his/ her life work better. Establishing trust for an adolescent happens over time. Time also becomes important when attempting to break down denial, a by-product of chemical dependency. Intervention for the adolescent therefore, must extend over a long period of time to give the process a chance to work. The required time commitment of a year or more in an adolescent intervention program enables denial to break down, and trust to work its way into the confused mind of the chemically dependent teen.

As individuals work the various phases of intervention, they are routinely confronted with some basic principles. (1) They are brought to the realization that chemical dependency is their primary problem. (2) They learn how the disease of chemical dependency affects it's victims at various stages. (3) They learn that taking care of oneself means assuming responsibility, and facing the consequences for their behavior. (4) They learn how their chemical dependency behavior affects the rest of their family and the community.

Sometimes, of course, the program fails. What then? Certainly matters are no worse than before, and probably they are better. Much has been learned. The seed has been planted. In some cases, 6 months down the road we get a call from a former participant. He needs treatment. We are available to him. Minimally, these individuals know where to go when they finally decide they want help.

The most effective recovery programs combine professional treatment with membership in a 12-step program like Alcoholics Anonymous or Narcotics Anonymous (The Johnson Institute, 1984). Our program of intervention introduces these individuals to recovery.

Responsible behavior and decision making by youth requires that they be presented with all the facts, and consistent consequences for their behavior. Programs that link education, adjudication and rehabilitation can accomplish this task. If the problem of adolescent alcoholism and chemical addiction is to be managed in the future, it will be a result of the community's efforts to ally it's resources and teach youth to adapt a responsible attitude (Green & Green, 1985a, 1986c).

REFERENCES

Green, Matthew (1982). Courts and Schools: An Alliance to Combat Adolescent Alcohol Abuse. *Counseling and Human Development*, 15 (No. 3), Denver: LOVE.

Green, Matthew, & Green, Joan (1985). Testimony delivered before the United States House of Representatives Select Committee on Narcotics Abuse and Control: The Newton Youth Drug/Alcohol Program, *the Congressional Record*. Boston: Sept. 21, 1985.

Green, Matthew (1986a). Interviews conducted with school case workers, The Youth Development Program: Newton Public Schools – Newton Baker Project, Judge Baker Guidance Clinic (1968), Newton, Massachusetts.

Green, Matthew (1986b). Interviews conducted with school administrators in Massachusetts: Newton, Brookline, Woburn, Canton, Sharon, Hull, Dedham, Westwood, Wayland, Concord, Waltham, Plymouth, Franklin, Whitman, Hansen.

Green, Matthew (1986c). The School – An Avenue of Change for Drug Using Teenagers. *The Brown University Human Development Letter*, 2 (No. 6): 1-4. Providence: Manisses.

Green, Matthew (1987). Intervention Strategies with Adolescents: The Newton Model. *ERIC Reports*, U.S. Dept. of Education Office of Educational Research and Improvement, ED 284 142, Washington, D.C.

Huberty, D.J., & Malmquist, J. (1978). Perspectives in Psychiatric Care. *Adolescent Chemical Dependency*. XVI. Clarke.

Johnson Institute (1984). Looking at Adolescents with Alcohol and Drug Problems. *Digest of Alcoholism Theory and Application*. 2 (No. 1) 7-9. C. Peter Brock.

Jorge, M.R., & Masur, J. (1985). An Attempt to Improve the Identification of Alcohol Dependent Patients in a teaching General Hospital. *Drug and Alcohol Dependence*, 16: 67-73.

Krivanek, Jara A. (1982). Drug Problems People Problems – Causes, Treatment, and Prevention, Chapters 8-9, New York: Allen and Urwin.

National Council on Alcoholism (1984). Survey, New York.

Newton Youth Drug/Alcohol Program (1983, 1986). Pre-admission interview. Newton, Massachusetts.

Stutman, Robert M. (1985). Taken from context of speech delivered before Massachusetts School Superintendents at Pine Manor College; representing U.S. Dept. of Justice, Drug Enforcement Administration: Chestnut Hill, Massachusetts.

Wegscheider, Sharon (1981). Another Chance – Hope and Health for the Alcoholic Family, Chapter 11. Science and Behavior Book Inc.

Intervention and Student Assistance: The Pennsylvania Model

Lawrence Newman, BS
Paul B. Henry, MDiv, AAMFT
Patricia DiRenzo, EdD
Thomas Stecher, MEd

INTRODUCTION

Public schools are increasingly being asked to perform tasks which are beyond the traditional role of educating students. Nowhere is this more apparent than in the area of dealing with the epidemic of adolescent alcohol and drug usage of the past two decades. Repeatedly, we have turned to the schools to assist in coping with this surge in the self-destructive behavior of our young people.

This change in roles has presented the educational community with a variety of problems and challenges. School personnel are not trained to effectively counteract the negative impact alcohol and drug usage has on the learner. They have questioned how schools can take it upon themselves to work with issues such as the misuse of chemical substances, addiction and suicide.

Until recently there seemed to be no clear answers as to how a school might proactively respond to these concerns. Over the last decade a new concept, the Student Assistance Program, has emerged as a viable option for schools. "SAP" has been modeled after the Employee Assistance Program which has become widely recog-

Lawrence Newman is President of Comprehensive Student Assistance Programs in Chester, PA. Patricia DiRenzo is Regional Coordinator of Student Assistance Programs for The Pennsylvania Department of Education in Allentown, PA. Thomas Stecher is the Southeast Regional Coordinator for Student Assistance Programming for the Pennsylvania Department of Education in Haverford, PA.

nized in business and industry as contributing significantly to reductions in work-site related alcohol and drug related problems.

Alcohol and drug problems exist in all educational settings regardless of their rural, urban or suburban environment. These conditions have a significant impact on the learning climate of the school. Young people harmfully involved with alcohol or other drugs tend to be disruptive in class or not participate at all; they are frequently absent or late to class; and generally they are considered a negative influence on the student body as a whole.

In 1984, as a result of the need expressed by numerous local school districts for the development of an intervention program for high risk youth, the Drug and Alcohol Education Section of the Pennsylvania Department of Education, launched a pilot Student Assistance Project. In the initial phase a review of existing programs from around the country was conducted and the best features of each were incorporated into a systematic training model. The model combined both content and process (didactic information on high-risk topics as well as group process, simulations, group process analysis, and action planning). Four school districts representing urban, suburban and rural Pennsylvania were selected to participate in the inaugural training of the Pennsylvania Student Assistance Program.

Since this initial effort numerous refinements have been made to the model. Because of concern for other dysfunctional behaviors segments on depression and suicide have been added, as well as, a more detailed group process design. The overall training agenda covers five days, with 37.5 hours devoted to essential content and group process.

However, training alone will not make a Student Assistance Program successful. There must be a firm commitment from the entire school district: school board, superintendent, building administrators, teachers, auxiliary staff, parents, and students if the program is to have an impact. This commitment is expressed in release time for Core Team members to meet, developing in-service programs to involve all faculty and staff in the effort, and by the institutionalizing of the Student Assistance Program. This effort can not be considered "another new program." It must be seen by all as an essential component of the school's or school district's proactive response to high risk issues and concerns.

The Student Assistance Program process, as developed and implemented in over one hundred Pennsylvania schools, would not be possible without the involvement and commitment of several state agencies. The Pennsylvania Departments of Health, Education, and Welfare contributed extensive resources towards the establishment of this effective intervention program.

A similar commitment was made by local drug and alcohol programs and mental health agencies in order to make this program a practical option for school districts. Another group who has contributed significantly to the Student Assistance Program effort is the Grand Lodge of Free and Accepted Masons of Pennsylvania. Currently more than half of all Pennsylvania state-sponsored residential trainings take place at their youth facility, Patton Campus, in Elizabethtown, Pennsylvania. All costs for training (rooms, meals, etc.) are being funded by this most generous organization.

The Student Assistance Program is a way of coming between or interfering in the high risk behavior of a student in a school setting. It is a process for early identification of young people who are having school-related difficulties because of drug and alcohol use or who are at risk of suicide or other mental health problems. The key to the Student Assistance Program is the identification and referral of these young people to appropriate community services. It is not a treatment program.

STATEMENT OF THE PROBLEM

The primary impetus for implementing Student Assistance Programs lies in the epidemic of high risk behaviors among adolescents. National and Pennsylvania-specific data shows that alcohol and drug use is now commonplace among teenagers and for many this usage begins as early as preadolescence.

However, these are not the only problems affecting young people. The need for a "broad brush" Student Assistance Program is magnified by the growing concern for adolescent depression and suicide in our society today. Add to this an assortment of mental health issues and the need becomes ever greater.

THE RESPONSE

Essential Elements of a Successful Student Assistance Program

In light of these statistics something must be done. School districts must enact a proactive response to the increasing number of students who are displaying high risk behaviors. Below are listed the essential elements of a successful Student Assistance Program.

A. District Policy

When a school district begins a Student Assistance Program, a critical element is to review and revise School Board approved policies and administrative guidelines for chemical use/abuse and suicide prevention/intervention/postvention. The Student Assistance Program functions as an adjunct to a district's disciplinary system; and, as such, must be so reflected in a policy in order to clearly spell out procedures, provide a necessary support to rehabilitative efforts, and protect those school personnel involved.

A district's drug and alcohol policy needs to be comprehensive, fair, and consistently enforced. It needs to deal with suspected use as well as actual use. It needs to deal with disciplinary as well as rehabilitative actions. It needs to include parent and police involvement.

If any response to alcohol or drug use is to be effective, it must be reasonable and positive in its intent. The following are some basic ideas to be considered by school administrators before responding to alcohol or drug situations.

1. Alcohol and drug use occurs to a significant degree within every school district's student body. Much of this use may be unseen during the school day. However it persists and instances of student use are being identified frequently.
2. There are positive steps that can be taken to help prevent, intervene in, and reduce the abuse of alcohol and drugs. These steps can be effective in helping the student while protecting the school population.
3. Due to the complex nature of alcohol and drug use, tough dis-

ciplinary action alone may be limited in its ability to modify a student's drug using behavior.

4. Discipline policies can be more effective in alcohol and drug situations when they are not limited to punishment, but include opportunities for counseling as part of a school's balanced response.

5. Extreme punishment, such as automatic expulsion for all alcohol or drug offenses, may encourage alcohol and drug usage during the school day. An expulsion that results in an unsupervised absence of a student has the potential of intensifying the alcohol or drug use of the student involved.

6. Clear understanding and expectations on the part of all members of the school population is possibly the foremost factor that can affect the success of a school's policy.

7. There is a complex relationship between the role of the school in its care and education of a child and the laws that affect that relationship. Within the framework of current law, there exists room for schools to design policies that are best suited to their circumstances and resources.

Given these basic considerations the next step would be the development of an effective policy. Listed next are nine simple rules for policy development.

1. Sound and defensible policy begins with consensus. This would include schoolboard, administration (central and building level), faculty and staff, community members, students and parents.

2. Good policy should set clear expectations for behavior and explicit action which follows if these expectations are not met.

3. Congruence should be sought between the seriousness of the offense and the punishment sought.

4. Equity, consistency, fairness, and reasonableness are the cornerstones of a legally sound policy.

5. Policy should not be written in a way that prejudges but rather specifies how guilt will be determined.

6. Good policy contemplates a variety of situations, but does not try to cover all contingencies.

7. The best policy is predicated on protecting the safety and welfare of most students rather than punishing a few.
8. Effective policy must take into account appropriate legislation, case law, and regulation but should not act as a juvenile justice code.
9. Legal review and board approval are prerequisites for the adoption of a conduct review.

School personnel are likely to encounter students who are involved with drug and alcohol use at some time during a school year. Realizing this probability, it is reassuring that current laws provide schools with a foundation as well as the flexibility to develop effective responses to such situations. By working within the framework of existing laws and by employing practical extensions of governing laws and regulations, schools have available the basic elements and safeguards necessary for a useful school drug and alcohol policy. This section will present seven elements for consideration:

1. The functions of the school in drug and alcohol situations
2. The role of school staff involved in drug and alcohol situations
3. Conducting searches
4. Confiscation of a substance
5. Confidentiality
6. Due process
7. Police involvement

This material is advisory only and general in nature. It is not intended or designed to provide binding legal advice. In each case, facts in a local district will impact on the specific decision to be made. Cases at the local court of common pleas may require different legal resolution in different school districts. The law in this area is constantly changing and school districts should always discuss the specific instances in their district with their local school solicitor.

1. *The function of schools in drug and alcohol situations.* The foremost function of schools in drug and alcohol situations is to protect the health, safety and welfare of students and staff. At the same time, consideration must be given to safeguard school property and the overall process of education.

A key component of this effort should be the development of clear procedures for staff to use when faced with drug and alcohol related situations. Procedures or administrative guidelines help to clarify the function of the school as distinct from that of law enforcement officials in drug and alcohol situations. The difference is important due to its bearing on the actions of school personnel.

2. *The role of school staff in drug and alcohol situations.* School professional staff operate under the concept of "in loco parentis" during regular operations of the school. This concept provides school personnel with certain rights and responsibilities similar to that of the parent. For practical reasons, this allows administrators and teachers to take those actions necessary to both protect and educate each student on a day-to-day basis.

The role of school staff in drug and alcohol situations can be vital in helping students face drug and alcohol related problems. As individuals in contact with large numbers of students on a long-term basis, teachers are in a position to encounter and recognize possible symptoms of drug and alcohol problems as they emerge. From this vantage point, teachers can identify clear cut student behavior that warrants disciplinary action as well as the more subtle symptoms that indicate the need for intervention. School staff should be aware of the responsibilities associated with this role in terms of both the confidentiality of drug and alcohol related information and the governing school policy and expectations. In many circumstances, school personnel may be called on both in their capacity as advisors protecting the rights of a particular student and in their capacity as representatives of the whole school population as distinct from a particular student. This dual role requires sound use of professional judgment on the part of all school personnel. A distinct written policy on the part of the local district can be an important and effective tool in defining these roles.

3. *Conducting searches.* The concept of "in loco parentis" clearly sets school personnel apart from the law enforcement officials. School personnel are not usually encumbered by the laws and procedures established for law enforcement personnel, particularly in regard to the conduct of searches. However, some case law suggests that the rules for conducting searches by school personnel are affected by whether police involvement and criminal charges are

the basis for a search or are incidental to a search undertaken for other reasons.

It is clear that schools and school staff have the right to conduct searches in certain circumstances. A search may be conducted based on considerably less evidence than required by the police, especially when the search is to protect the health, safety, and welfare of the children and the educational process. School officials fulfilling their duties will not be held to the same standards as law enforcement officials.

Much confusion and uncertainty exists as to the meaning of the many laws that govern schools, students, and drugs. The laws in this area frequently change and continue to evolve as they are explained and elaborated upon by the cases affecting local districts. However, it is clear that the school must act carefully, out of concern for the student population, under the doctrine of "in loco parentis" and not as a law enforcement agent. As school staff work more closely with law enforcement authorities, the rules governing such actions become more strict.

4. *What to do if you confiscate a substance.* In our various contacts with school personnel, we have become aware of questions regarding the proper procedure for drug confiscations within a school or district.

We would recommend the following procedures to protect the administrator and the school, as well as the particular student and his/her rights:

a. Never accuse a student of possession or use of any drug.
b. Place any confiscated sample in an envelope (a witness should be present).
c. Note the following on the outside of the envelope:
   • date and time
   • school name
   • description of contents (i.e. leafy vegetable material, pill, capsule — do not guess at labeling)
   • signature of both parties (administrator and witness)
d. SEAL THE ENVELOPE — to insure proper sealing, use tape.
e. Call a local law enforcement agency, such as State Police (juvenile officer) or local police. This call should be made by a school official.

f. Indicate at the time of the call that there is a sample to be analyzed and the proper authorities should pick it up (always turn it over to someone who is authorized to dispose of the substance).

g. Have the official receiving the sample open it in your presence and witness that you did indeed deliver the indicated sample. It would be helpful to have the officer sign the envelope too.

h. Request that they advise you of the results of the sample analysis.

i. Should you decide to take action — whether legal or administrative — you will have followed a procedure that protects your rights as well as those of the student.

5. *Confidentiality*. The issue of confidentiality and its application to school personnel can be a complex legal issue. Differing legal interpretations can be drawn describing how laws and regulations affect school personnel and their actions. The school employees for whom specific laws dictate confidentiality requirements due to the nature of their work are school psychologists, school nurses, and school counselors. For other staff, the law is less specific. However, practical extensions of existing laws provide direction for schools to follow in their policies and procedures.

It is extremely important that school districts distinguish between educational records and records on treatment for drug and/or alcohol abuse. Different laws govern the confidentiality of different records; they should not be confused. Similarly, confidentiality of health records maintained by local school districts are governed by the School Code.

6. *Steps in due process*. There is no extensive case law available regarding schools and due process proceedings. However, that which is available has supported the actions of schools provided such action is reasonable. It is important to remember that school disciplinary proceedings are not legal proceedings in the same sense as a court trial and do not place students in "double jeopardy" should students be involved in subsequent criminal proceedings.

7. *Police involvement*. Available case law indicates that police involvement does affect the procedures schools should follow in school searches as well as how to handle students suspected of drug and alcohol involvement. It is important to develop an effective

relationship with the law enforcement officials who hold jurisdiction in the location of the school. A cooperative approach can greatly improve both effectiveness and consistency in the handling of drug and alcohol situations. Such a combined effort can help both schools and law enforcement personnel understand each other's abilities and limitations in handling specific situations.

Key Things to Remember:

1. Know the facts; do not act upon hearsay and vague suspicion.
2. The confidentiality of students' records is governed by law.
3. Schools should have a working relationship with local police. This relationship may dictate the effectiveness of a school policy.
4. Individual rights are balanced in regard to the general welfare. Every effort should be exerted to maintain this balance.
5. Schools may conduct warrantless searches but only according to specific guidelines, and under very defined circumstances. See your solicitor for guidance and binding legal advice.
6. Regulations on student rights and responsibilities provide important information regarding school discipline procedures.

A sample policy is included in the Appendix for review.

B. In-School Suspension Program

If a school district has an in-school suspension program, it must work directly with the Student Assistance Program because it affords an opportunity to closely observe students. When a student is confined to the highly structured environment of an in-school suspension program, the staff can monitor attitude and behavior changes that classroom teachers often cannot. They interact with students one-on-one, and may be able to provide valuable behavioral data for the "Core Team."

The in-school suspension staff needs training in the following areas: crisis management, intervention, mental health concerns such as suicide and depression, and recordkeeping related to high risk behaviors. They must also understand the Student Assistance Program concept and see they are an integral part of its success.

C. *Student Assistance Team*

The heart of the Student Assistance Program is the Core Team. In order to be most effective we find the following personnel to be essential team members: a Central Office Administrator (Superintendent, Assistant Superintendent or Pupil Services Director), a building administrator (Principal or Assistant Principal), at least one counselor, at least two teachers, and one staff person from auxiliary services such as a nurse, psychologist, special education instructor or in-school suspension coordinator. In addition, staff appointed by county mental health and drug and alcohol programs serve as ad hoc members of the Core Team and attend the initial Core Team Training.

The Core Team serves many key functions. Primarily, they are responsible for the early identification and referral of students. This is accomplished by gathering behavior-performance data on a student suspected of being harmfully involved with chemicals or demonstrating other high risk behaviors. Data comes from all professional and auxiliary staff who come in contact with the young person during the course of the day.

Once sufficient information is obtained the Core Team discusses the options available for the student. The first step may be a parent conference, or if the young person has come to the attention of the Core Team through a policy violation they will work along with the administrator responsible for the disciplinary action to get the student the help he/she needs. Each case is different and each young person is handled as an individual using the school policy as the guidepost.

The Core Team also assists in in-servicing all faculty and staff as to their role and responsibilities. They must attempt early on to engage the entire school community if this effort is to work.

D. *Key Personnel Workshop*

Members of the Core Team, district administration and Board of School Directors need to have a common base of knowledge about Student Assistance Programs. The Key Personnel Workshop is a short meeting prior to the residential off-site training or nonresidential local training that seeks to pre-service all key district personnel as to what Student Assistance is (an identification, intervention and referral process) and what it is not (an in-school treatment program). It provides an opportunity for potential Core Team members to have questions answered and misconceptions addressed. Trainers meet the teams and begin to form the ongoing relationship that lasts long beyond the initial training.

It is pointed out during this session and emphasized throughout the early preparation for Student Assistance programming that Core Team members must have released time to meet. School districts in Pennsylvania guarantee their Core Teams at least two common planning periods per week. Many districts have gone beyond this suggestion. The formula is simple – the more common meeting times for the Core Team, the more young people who are served.

E. Core Team Training

The Pennsylvania Model consists of one full week of residential training. It has been our experience that this time is essential to cover all material necessary to successfully implement a Student Assistance Program. Members of the Core Team must have a common knowledge base regarding adolescent chemical dependency, suicide, and other mental health concerns to apply to this early intervention concept.

The actual training is divided into several key segments. Days one and two focus on providing Core Team members with needed content. The topics mentioned above serve as the base with additional components added to complete the puzzle. Topics such as family dynamics, children of dysfunctional families, treatment and continuity of care are presented using large group instruction techniques, audio-visual materials, and small group interaction.

Throughout days three and four, Core Teams begin to address the issue of group process – how are we working together? This is accomplished through a variety of nonacademic and simulated experiences aimed at having Core Team members carefully examine the intricate balance of task and maintenance issues. It is our belief that these two days are equal in importance to the content of days one and two. Without a knowledge of group process and an opportunity to address existing group questions and concerns, the Core Team will be less effective.

An additional day of training is devoted to the development of a team-specific Action Plan. The Core Team completes a planning booklet which serves as a blueprint for the early operation of this Student Assistance Team. This process enables the Core Team to anticipate potential roadblocks to program success, as well as listing specific needs the team has in order to function effectively.

As a result of this intensive week of training, the Core Team returns to school armed with new information about high risk young people, a true sense of being part of a team, and an action plan to enable the program to be implemented and move forward.

F. Group Facilitators' Training

Following the initial Core Team Training and the implementation of the Student Assistance Program, it is necessary to establish a variety of student support groups. These groups differ from those associated with treatment agencies in their purpose. School-based support groups focus on school-based issues, e.g., getting to class on time, doing assignments, establishing a new peer group, etc. They do not focus on treatment issues.

In order to set up these groups, additional training for Core Team members who will lead the group is essential. There are general facilitation skills appropriate to all groups, but each support group has specific needs. Training must be set up to accomplish both tasks. An intensive training design is recommended to provide necessary content for group facilitators in conjunction with simulated group sessions to allow practice and feedback in a safe, controlled, setting.

Some school districts use only Core Team members as group facilitators. Others draw on the support and expertise of their ad hoc drug and alcohol and mental health agency personnel to co-facilitate groups. In either case, it is recommended that group facilitators have attended basic Core Team training in order to (1) understand the Student Assistance Program Concept; (2) understand that an intervention is a process, not an event; (3) understand why the groups need to be educational and not therapeutic; and (4) facilitate the information flow to and from groups to the Core Team.

G. Faculty In-Service

In examining the need for comprehensive training to make a Student Assistance Program work, we must not overlook the general faculty and staff. Without their cooperation and support, the Core Team would not be able to function. It should be noted here that "staff" in a school consists of all personnel who come in contact with students. Therefore support personnel such as secretaries, custodians, cafeteria workers, and bus drivers, must not be overlooked.

A minimum of one full day of in-service training for all staff prior to the implementation of a Student Assistance Program is needed. The staff inservice should have a dual focus: (1) general awareness sessions on high-risk topics such as chemical dependency, depression and suicide, (2) the specifics of the district's program—including an introduction of the Core Team members, how to make a referral, what do the various forms mean, legal liabilities for staff and faculty, etc.

H. Central Referral Point

Strong linkages between the Student Assistance Program and community agencies are essential in order to help high-risk students and their families receive needed services. A county drug and alcohol staff person and a county mental health staff person serving as ad hoc Team members begin to forge these links. Another mechanism for establishing these links is through the creation of a Central Referral Point.

Since Core Team members are not clinical diagnosticians, the county drug and alcohol and mental health systems should agree upon one person or agency to serve as the Central Referral Point to either system for a Student Assistance referral. A clinical assessment will be performed by a licensed practitioner, and further referrals will be made as needed to public or private agencies.

The Central Referral Point concept aids in (1) getting students seen by a professional fairly quickly; (2) relieving any diagnostic implications from a Core Team; and (3) preventing a student from "falling between the cracks" until an appropriate treatment plan is in place.

The Pennsylvania Results

In the 1986-1987 school year, approximately 2,923 students have been identified by Core Teams in 64 school districts implementing Student Assistance Programs. This has resulted in approximately 893 referrals to local community agencies.

Student Assistance Programming is the most effective, proactive method for dealing with our at-risk population. Based on the results achieved in Pennsylvania thus far, Student Assistance Programming is a feasible and workable process for all school districts. However, no one can do it for individual school districts. School Boards must make an honest commitment of time, resources, and dollars. Anything less results in a sub-par program, which may do more harm than good. Who suffers when the program fails? It is the at-risk young person. We cannot afford to allow that to occur.

For further information about this program, please contact:

Lawrence Newman
President, ComSAP
Comprehensive Student Assistance Program
415 East 22nd Street, Chester, PA 19013

(215) 876-5500

APPENDIX

SAMPLE SCHOOL DISTRICT
Anytown, PA 10000-0000
DRUG AND ALCOHOL POLICY
and ADMINISTRATIVE GUIDELINES

Preface

This policy, including the rules, regulations, and guidelines, is a concerted effort by the "Sample School District" to openly and effectively respond to the current uses and abuses of drugs, alcohol, and mood-altering substances by the members of our entire student population.

Statement of Policy

Through the use of an up-to-date curriculum, classroom activities, community support and resources, a strong and consistent administrative and faculty effort, and rehabilitative and disciplinary procedures, the "Sample School District" will work to educate, prevent, and intervene in the use and abuse of all drug, alcohol, and mood-altering substances by the entire student population.

Definition of Terms

Drug/Mood-Altering Substance/Alcohol—shall include any alcohol or malt beverage, any drug listed in Act 64 (1972) as a controlled substance, chemical, abused substance or medication for which a prescription is required under the law and/or any substance which is intended to alter mood.

Examples of the above include but are not limited to beer, wine, liquor, marijuana, cocaine, crack, hashish, chemical solvents, glue, look-alike substances, and any capsules or pills not registered with the nurse, annotated within the student's health record and given in accordance with the school district's policy for the administration of medication to students in school.

Crisis Intervention Counselor — is a certified program specialist with an expertise in the area of social restoration and student high-risk behaviors.

Distributing — deliver, sell, pass, share, or give any alcohol, drug, or mood-altering substance, as defined by this policy, from one person to another or to aid therein.

Possession — possess or hold without any attempt to distribute any alcohol, drug, or mood-altering substance determined to be illegal or as defined in this policy.

Cooperative Behavior — shall be defined as the willingness of a student to work with staff and school personnel in a reasonable and helpful manner, complying with requests and recommendations of the staff and school personnel.

Uncooperative Behavior — is resistance or refusal, either verbal, physical, or passive, on the part of the student to comply with the reasonable request or recommendations of school personnel. Defiance, assault, deceit, and truancy shall constitute examples of uncooperative behavior. Uncooperative behavior shall also include the refusal to comply with the recommendations of a licensed drug and alcohol facility.

Drug Paraphernalia — includes any utensil or item which in the school's judgment can be associated with the use of drugs, alcohol, or mood-altering substances. Examples include but are not limited to roach clips, pipes and bowls.

Rules and Regulations

A student who on school grounds, during a school session, or anywhere at a school-sponsored activity is under the influence of alcohol, drugs, or mood-altering substances or possesses, uses, dispenses, sells or aids in the procurement of alcohol, narcotics, restricted drugs, mood-altering substances, or any substance purported to be a restricted substance or over the counter drug shall be subject to discipline pursuant to the provisions and procedures outlined in "Sample School District's" Discipline Code.

School Guidelines

As an integral part of the "Sample School District" Drug and Alcohol Prevention Program, these guidelines represent one component in a districtwide effort to respond effectively to drug, mood-altering substance, and alcohol related situations that may occur at school or at school-sponsored activities. These guidelines are intended to provide a consistent minimum disciplinary means to respond to drug, mood-altering substance, and alcohol related events. The "Sample School District" will provide a safe and healthy environment for students with due consideration for their legal rights and responsibilities. The board reserves the right to use any extraordinary measures deemed necessary to control substance abuse even if the same is not provided for specifically in any rule or regulation enumerated herein.

Adolescent Inpatient Treatment

George E. Obermeier, MS
Paul B. Henry, MDiv, AAMFT

One only has to examine the characteristics of the sixteen- or seventeen-year-old chemically dependent patient to understand why adolescent inpatient treatment must be "habilitative" and not rehabilitative as has been the case for adults. Habilitation encompasses the teaching and internalization of necessary coping and decision making mechanisms needed for continued maintenance of a drug-free lifestyle.

The primary goal of inpatient treatment for the chemically dependent adolescent is to get the adolescent to internalize a commitment in taking responsibility for abstaining from alcohol and other chemicals. The abuse of alcohol and other drugs must be treated as the primary problem, even though there are problems with other destructive behaviors. Adolescent treatment must focus on sobriety and developmental tasks as well, due to the conditions of socioemotional developmental arrest (Jones 1985). For example, requiring abstinence, in effect, threatens loss of identity and personal security for the youth. The developmental issues are tied directly to the dependency. An effective adolescent drug/alcohol inpatient program must address the entire range of developmental tasks, so that motivation of the adolescent will occur, permitting maintenance of a sober lifestyle. In a comprehensive assessment of adolescents involved with alcohol, it was concluded that taken as a group, these patients exhibit a wide range of problem behaviors much more frequently than those observed in a randomly selected group of youth in the same community (Winters 1985). This study also indicated

---

George Obermeier is Executive Director of New Beginnings at Cove Forge in Williamsburg, PA.

that these behaviors extended to psychological and emotional problems with family and peers. Other studies have noted that this group is more likely to be experiencing academic and social difficulties in school, and a significant number will have been involved with the juvenile justice system (Yamaguchi and Kandel 1984). Based on the complexity of the illness, it only seems natural that the treatment approach should be a multi-disciplinary "Holistic" model.

THE THERAPEUTIC COMMUNITY

The therapeutic community movement used in psychiatric hospitals and popularized by a number of adult drug treatment programs, when "modified," works effectively with chemically dependent adolescents. For more information, the authors recommend reading the book by Almond and Arson (Almond and Arson 1974). The following, however, will provide some general insight into how they are modified relative to treatment philosophy.

A treatment community model approaches individuals as a part of a group, working to develop a trusting relationship so that it might be used as a catalyst for affecting change and monitoring behavior. Negative peer pressure was one of their primary influences prior to treatment, conversely; positive peer pressure can be as effective during and after inpatient treatment. Recall earlier data which showed the support offered to the group of nonusers by having friends who were nonusers. The community provides a forum for identity, to crystalize a sense of belonging and norms for expected behaviors. The newly admitted adolescent is given very little status of authority while ample nurturance and demonstrations of caring are consistently offered by peers and staff. The assignment of big brothers or big sisters, with peers, who take the responsibility to acclimate the new member to the community, eases the initial transition and aids in the coping to the uncomfortable new surroundings. The big brother explains the rules and provides a role model for appropriate behavior.

Before entering the program, most patients were not monitored with clear, consistent, age appropriate and behavioral expectations. Without a consistent framework to use as a guideline, they found it difficult to adjust and cope with the complexities of maturation. In this sense, adolescent chemical abuse may be a thrust toward independence and autonomy. However, as chemical dependency progresses, destructive behaviors ensue, arresting maturation and true independence. Therefore, an essential element within the community is control, which is first established by the staff and ultimately turned over to the recovering group to monitor and maintain. Levels of responsibility are established by the staff and progression is based upon the individual growth in accomplishing his individualized treatment goals. With earned responsibility, the patient gains privileges and status within the community.

The structured therapeutic community provides membership in a peer group where acceptance is based upon the desire to maximize one's individual potential and fulfill one's need to "belong." Many patients have perceived themselves as failures, not fitting in with the "jocks" or the "academic group" or other status giving groups. The user group, however, readily provided what they had not experienced elsewhere — a sense of excitement, as well as belonging to a family without constraints. Inpatient treatment provides an alternate peer group which reinforces desired behavior. Responsible behavior is rewarded with status and privileges. Negative behaviors are confronted and dealt with using expected behaviors as the standard for comparison. This provides the adolescent with a way to learn essential life skills in preparation for re-entry into the world outside the therapeutic community.

COMPONENTS OF INPATIENT TREATMENT

Family Therapy

An essential part of any inpatient treatment model must be the family component. Follow-up statistics at New Beginnings at Cove Forge show a very high correlation in the success of treatment and family involvement. Families must be educated about the effects of alcohol and other drugs to provide a foundation for their own treatment. Frequently, parents are unaware that the behaviors they have endured are symptomatic of the illness. They also need a ground floor orientation to realize the fact that other families have also gone through this, and they now have the opportunity to interact and share with families experiencing similar trauma. Often, this group is most effective in alleviating the guilt, shame, and anger involved with the chemically dependent adolescent.

Adolescents are still an integral part of their family of origin and most will return home following the course of inpatient treatment. In order for the behavioral changes achieved during treatment to continue successfully, support and involvement of the family is mandatory. Family counseling can be accomplished through several different modes, i.e., individual family sessions with and without the patient, family groups and residential family programming. We have found residential family programming to be the most beneficial. It provides the family an opportunity to experience the helping community environment, as well as, other methods of family therapy. Families are able to reduce their fears of relapse while getting assistance in developing new expectations and communication patterns. This component should also assist the family in the development of a family contract geared toward addressing the issues of reintegration and continued sobriety.

The substance use and abuse on the part of all other primary family members must be thoroughly scrutinized and discussed. Habits may require change in order to assist the adolescent in recovery and keep from sabotaging the treatment processes. Where active alcoholism or drug abuse is present in the family systems, the patient is offered staff support in confronting these areas which will only prove unproductive in the recovery of the patient. The task to remain sober will, otherwise, be exceedingly difficult if not next to impossible. The patient must avoid being set up for failure and the opportunity to live in a halfway house or group home setting where the internal pressure of substance use from the primary group is absent, might prove more productive. The family must support the process of continued abstinence.

Continuing Care

To ensure inpatient treatment success, next to family involvement in importance, is the need for structured continuing care. In referring to the post inpatient phase of treatment, we prefer the phrase "continuing care," rather than the traditional term "aftercare'' because we think that ''continuing care'' more appropriately describes the process necessary for adolescents post patient treatment. It is our experience that inpatient treatment often begins a long-term process of care. There will always be individual needs, which due to time constraints, will not be resolved during the inpatient treatment experience. Issues of sexual abuse or incest are examples of those areas which need to be properly addressed in continuing care. The adolescent will need a continual outlet to communicate those problems in attempting to follow the discharge plan which should be carefully prepared during the treatment experience. Individual differences in geographic location of return and service availability are examples of those areas of concern addressed in the continuing care plan. The location of the inpatient center will determine what type of follow-up will be possible and whether continuing care group and individual sessions can be conducted on site or at designated sites convenient to the patient. Many times, schools have aftercare programs for returning students. All options of possible support for the patient should be explored.

Alcoholics Anonymous and/or Narcotics Anonymous (AA/NA) are self-help groups that can provide support and guidance for continued work in recovery. As part of the discharge planning procedure, a patient should be hooked up with a recovering person to ensure that appropriate meetings are attended by the patient. AA/NA are also the most effective resources for providing information about the physical effects of continued use, reinforcing the negative consequences of such use. Therefore, AA/NA meetings, both in-house and off grounds, will expose the patient to the real world process of step issues and minimize individual stresses. Getting in touch with one's own conscience and higher power are part of the spiritual maturation process leading to recovery. It is the belief of the authors that healthy recovery is attained by achieving and maintaining a BALANCE of physical, mental/emotional, and spiritual well-being for the individual.

Other self-help groups may be necessary for the family and primary support group as part of the continuing care plan. Families Anonymous, Al-Anon and Al-Ateen are the most widely available groups. Specific geographic areas have special groups which may prove invaluable to the continuing care of the patient.

As part of continuing care, the treatment program should have some method of follow-up to check on the progress of the patient whether it be with agencies, schools, or the juvenile justice system. Such follow-up can curtail problems encountered after the inpatient treatment process, and help correlate information with others as to how well the adolescent is actually doing. All treatment programs have an ethical responsibility to continue to help patients after the inpatient experience.

Group and Individual Counseling

In an inpatient unit, counselors should only have caseloads of six to eight clients because adolescents tend to be more crisis oriented than adults. The out of control behaviors of adolescents in treatment continually stress counselors and other program staff. This behavior manifests itself in taking risks. When these adolescents were using, they were always taking risks, because in adolescence, use of any substance is illegal. Early on in treatment, they exhibit inappropriate behaviors which require the attention of so many staff. This is especially true in the first seven to ten days while the young person is so deeply entrenched in denial, and therefore, acts out in resistance. Counselors need to be flexible and responsive to patients as well as to attempt to sort out regular adolescent development issues and how chemical use has influenced them.

When one takes into account that approximately sixty-five percent of our adolescent population has been either physically or sexually abused, a greater number of resulting issues are going to be intensely magnified. Issues of anger and trust are two very tenuous areas that often have to be addressed in order to motivate the patient in the recovery process.

Patients are all different and have distinct issues relative to the primary disease of chemical dependency. So many of them need this opportunity to get a "strangle hold" on reality, gain some self-esteem and learn the skills to help them to survive. A milieu of therapeutic skills are needed to work with this age.

Group therapy is the primary modality in an adolescent inpatient unit because group provides many different ways for patients to identify feelings, build trust and operate in a setting where they are comfortable with peers. Group therapy can be instrumental to the adolescent in processing information from a lecture or film relevant to his or her life. Others can then share their experience or offer suggestions.

The chemically dependent adolescent has developed a set of behaviors, which if left unchanged, will lead him back into chemical usage at some point when a crisis occurs following discharge from inpatient rehabilitation. Therefore, it is necessary to effect a lifestyle change and to continually challenge those behaviors in the adolescent that threaten sobriety. The inpatient treatment program is a context where behavioral change can be monitored on a 24 hour basis. Positive changes in behavior can be supported and negative behaviors can be confronted and challenged. Group therapy is an excellent modality to achieve this goal, because the adolescent's group becomes the time when behavioral change is intensely explored.

An inpatient community thrusts the chemically dependent adolescent into a situation where he must continually deal with his peers and with positive responsible adults. This means the adolescent will continually be in an environment where behavioral change is expected. Often this emerges in the daily activities of having forty or more adolescents living and interacting together. When acting our behaviors emerge, the constant message should be to deal with it in group. This allows the adolescent an opportunity to get appropriate feedback on his behavior and by processing it within the group context find new insight and support for change.

The main issue in inpatient treatment is to develop a sober lifestyle. This is a near impossible thought for the chemically dependent adolescent who cannot seem to imagine life without being high. Group therapy needs to be directed to having the adolescent focus upon the specifics of how and when chemicals have been detrimental to his life. By developing some insight into a previously unexamined lifestyle, the adolescent will learn to avoid or change those situations wherein the risk to use can become realized. More importantly though, group therapy must focus upon giving the adolescent concrete means of coping without chemicals. One of the problems faced by adolescents is that every experience is a new experience for them. Their limited life experience leaves them without previously tried solutions to troublesome situations. Groups, therefore, become the context for learning and "trying out" new solutions or coping skills. If the newly recovering adolescent "fails" in a group experience, it can become the context for learning without the potential for harmful or fatal consequences. Group therapy is actually the laboratory where experimentation with a new sober lifestyle begins.

Individual counseling also has its place in the inpatient environment. Just as adolescents need the group experience, they also need the opportunity to be alone to explore issues that are deeply troubling them. Too many of these adolescents have not recently had the experience of having an adult listen to them and accept them for what they are. The inpatient staff must devote much time and energy to listening and responding. These sessions will actually augment the group experience because as the adolescent grows and develops trust and confidence in individual relationships, he will likely feel more confident in interacting and responding in group experiences.

Each group and individual encounter provides an opportunity for an adolescent to give and receive honest feedback, to learn positive communication styles and to realize that people care about who he is and what he does with his life. If this happens, it will be a valuable lesson on the way to recovery.

Medical Component

Prior to entering an inpatient therapeutic community, some few adolescents will need medical detoxification services. Based on our experience, over about a ten-year period, this number should not exceed five to eight percent of the total admissions to the adolescent program. Alcohol remains the primary drug of choice for many adolescents, but because of their age, they have not consumed over a long enough period of time to have experienced the gross physical complications of withdrawal which require medical detoxification. However, the decision to detoxify should always be made by a licensed physician based upon the acute manifestations of withdrawal.

Another group of adolescents will require social detoxification or observation during their withdrawal period. They may experience a variety of physical and emotional complications, but these effects can be monitored within the treatment community. A sensitive and caring staff can assist the adolescent in making the physical and emotional adjustments to a drug-free environment. Within 72 hours, the adolescent can be fully integrated into the treatment community.

A thorough medical assessment will include a complete physical, a medical history and bloodwork. For those youth whose history includes the high risk behaviors of intravenous use of needles and/ or homosexual or multiple sexual partners, there needs to be testing for AIDS.

Chemically dependent adolescents are essentially healthy despite their use of chemicals, yet in treatment, we see a variety of medical needs which need to be treated. Among the most common condition is acute and chronic bronchitis. This is caused by frequent smoking of both cigarettes and marijuana. For this reason, we believe it necessary in adolescent treatment settings to address the issue of cigarette smoking. It is certainly a significant health and addiction issue. Cigarette smoking should, at the least, be restricted in treatment settings. Medical and other treatment personnel should provide these youth with reliable information about the addictive nature and health consequences of smoking nicotine.

Often, chemically dependent youth have had a period of time when they have not paid attention to their diet and nutrition. As a result of their poor diet, we frequently see conditions such as gastritis and irritable bowel syndrome. The latter is caused by excess acid secretion, which causes an irritation of the intestine.

Other health complications which we commonly see in chemically dependent adolescents includes acne (which is stimulated by poor nutrition), urinary tract infections, genital warts, dermatitis, scabies and pediculosis.

The primary effects of chemical usage for adolescents are to the nose, throat, chest, stomach and bowels. The liver and kidneys are not as significantly effected in the adolescent usage.

Education

In an adolescent treatment facility, the patient must be educated about the importance of maintaining academic progress and its subsequent value for the future. For many, their educational careers have often suffered significant deterioration (Kandel 1975). Remedial educational objectives are necessary to assist the adolescent in recovering the time lost due to chemical abuse. The educational aspect needs to motivate growth in everyday learning, exemplifying the positive and lifelong aspects of a continued education.

There are several means by which programs aspire to meet the individual needs of the patient. The ultimate goal, however, is to enhance the likelihood for completion of the high school degree. Local school districts can provide generic junior and/or senior high school classes and are usually reimbursed by the home school district. They may also offer special education classes. In the manuscript by Kandel, it was mentioned that a larger than normal percentage of learning disabled students exist in the population. There may also be a supervised study system, whereby, teachers venture to sustain school work passed along by the home school districts, for it is the home district where school expectancies are clearly defined. The size and type of inpatient facility will determine, to some extent, what kinds of educational opportunities can be offered. An important concern here is that recovery is likely to be hindered if educational deficiencies are ignored during treatment and continuing care.

A final effort should be made for those youth who are technically out of school and not likely to return. A General Equivalency Diploma (G.E.D.) program can be implemented with minimal effort and thus hopefully provide the first successful experience in education these patients can remember. Many patients surprise themselves by completing the requirements with relative ease during treatment, not realizing the potential of achieving the diploma prior to treatment. The self-esteem benefits are far reaching and provide an increased opportunity for employment in the future.

Finally, experiential learning is crucial to the adolescent patient. Adolescents in general have short attention spans, but chemically dependent adolescents have even shorter ones. Therefore, talking to them has limited value. They need to be involved in experiential learning processes in order to develop essential lifetime skills. The most effective tool in educating this population is active participation.

Physical Recovery

When an adolescent enters inpatient treatment, the substance abuse has affected their physical/mental-emotional/spiritual development. The first part of them to respond to the termination of drug use is their physical well-being. Discontinuation of chemical use results in a more energetic, clear thinking, responsive individual. From a "holistic" perspective, it makes sense to initially help that process along in order to provide a solid foundation for the other two areas. Many facilities give inadequate attention to a physical activity component in their program and even less to adherence factors relative to continued participation after treatment.

We have asked kids in juvenile detention facilities, "What do you do for recreation?" Over sixty-five percent of this delinquent population answered, "Get high; Catch a buzz; Party." The negative correlation between recreational activities and drug usage cannot be stressed enough for these patients. Programming geared to enhance continued physical activity in the post-treatment experience is indispensable to effective recovery. Research has shown that a post-treatment activity program has a significant effect on treatment outcome (Hyman 1987).

The benefits of physical activity have been investigated in the treatment of alcoholism (Sinyor et al. 1982). Several important findings from research have emerged. The most important benefits are that physical activity improves self-esteem and self-confidence (Gary and Guthrie 1972; Mobily 1982), reduces stress (Ransford 1982), and depression (Folkins and Amsterdam 1977), and makes physiological improvements on resting heart rates, oxygen intake, blood pressure and muscle tone. These benefits can be initiated and effectively reinforced during the course of treatment. The guarantee for quality recovery lies in the adherence after treatment.

A study conducted by Thompson and Whalsel (Thompson and Whalsel 1980) concerning the "effects of perceived activity choices" reveals that *variety* is one of the key components for continued adherence to physical activity. This substantiates other studies (Wright 1980) that report alcoholics have a lower regard for positive leisure time activities than nonalcoholics. Our experience indicates that these results are magnified with younger age groups due to their preference for risk taking activities. Most treatment programs provide activities geared toward reducing high energy levels in an attempt to promote learning and reduce destructive behavior. However, little effort is spent in developing a program that meets individual needs and is concerned with post-treatment adherence. This is a gross oversight in adolescent treatment, as recreational use is a primary factor in contributing to dependency development. Programming should exhibit a wide range of activities effective in altering moods, and providing natural highs, as well as enhancing physical development and conditioning. Adolescents must be able to perceive the benefits of their behavior in order for them to repeat it. A wide variety of activities ranging from walking and fishing to white water rafting and climbing high elements, accommodates every lifestyle and personal preference. Within the context of treatment goals that are individually specified, beneficial program provides diversity, variety and fun (Gary and Guthrie 1972; Folkins and Amsterdam 1977). Individualized treatment goals would reflect, for example, the use of more aerobics for patients dealing with depression, and more team activities for those patients with problems in socializing or having isolation issues. This area of treatment lends itself to creative counseling that patients are more responsive to in that they are experiential learning opportunities.

One of the major drawbacks of treatment programs has been the standardized scheduling, rather than the exploration of activities which best suits this population of risk takers. Individuals indicate specific preferences by which to alter their states of consciousness—whether by use of chemicals or other more healthy approaches. Unfortunately, our culture promotes changing how you feel with chemicals. One of the most difficult concepts to internalize for patients is that being drugged is not the same as being "high," and that we can bring about "high" states naturally. This is important in that these young people cannot imagine not getting "high" for the rest of their life. The problem lies in the fact that they have lost touch with how to achieve these states free from chemicals, which will be discussed later. What is important is that physical activities provide the perfect medium to teach adolescents how to have fun and recreate without chemicals.

With proper goal setting and record keeping, an effective recreational therapist will demonstrate to the patient their ability to gain control over one aspect of their life, and concurrently, see the physical benefits of healthy living. Establishing control over one aspect of their lives contradicts past "failures" and can be the necessary reinforcement for further development of internal locus of control. Adolescent patients tend to score high in the area of external locus of control (Mobily 1982; Wright 1983). It has been encouraging to note in recent publications such as "Alcohol and Research World" and "AA Grapevine" the promotion of physical well-being to quality recovery.

Wilderness Adventure Program concepts and outdoor initiative courses have been used to expose adolescents to unique endeavors that foster group dynamics and acquaint them with "natural highs." This process is invaluable in providing additional therapeutic tools and placing the adolescent in an environment where street behaviors are ineffective (Cardwell 1980). These activities also provide a noncompetitive environment for counselors to interact with the client to gain trust and insights about the client in a nonauthoritive medium. It enhances the development of teamwork, self-esteem, positive self-image, decision making and coping skills.

Wilderness Adventure Program

The Wilderness Adventure Program is an adjunctive treatment program aimed at supplementing already existing forms of traditional treatment. The distinguishing characteristic of the Wilderness Adventure Program is that active participation is used to facilitate group process. Activities are designed to challenge the individual both physically and mentally. They offer individuals a direct experience which makes concepts learned more immediate and specific. By placing participants in situations which force them to think creatively and use their physical abilities to achieve a goal, certain interactions and feelings emerge. The most important one to be exhibited is cooperation. The working toward a common goal, which cannot be accomplished individually, provides for a sense of togetherness and group responsibility. The success of an individual becomes the success of the group, and the achievement of the group is possible because of combined effort.

The overall objectives of the program are as follows: (A) To increase the participants' sense of self-esteem. The aim of many activities is to allow the participants to see themselves as increasingly capable and competent. By attempting a graduate series of activities, which involve a perceived risk, and success (or sometimes failing) in a supportive atmosphere, a participant begins to develop true self-esteem. A positive self-concept is necessary for the formulation of responsible attitudes, beliefs and values in developing appropriate social interactions. Some of the activities involve initial anxiety. As the person matures, he must learn to be familiar with the anxiety that precedes any new venture, cope with that uncertainty, and dare to enter fully into new situations. (B) To increase group process and encourage support within the group. Children soon recognize that their behavior effects others in the group and so they must learn to respond positively when others in the group act responsible toward them. Trust soon develops within the group. Once a person feels secure in himself and the peer group, he will be willing to seek out challenges he was previously afraid of. Achieving a high level of group involvement and cooperation is necessary for more difficult activity and will often provide an avenue for behavior change in the individual. (C) To develop an increased level of agility and physical confidence. A number of the activities involve the use of balance and coordination of physical movement. They are physically and mentally challenging to the group. Through the successful completion of these tasks, the group and individual members receive feelings of accomplishment and pride. (D) To learn about oneself and learn to enjoy interacting with others. The activities are designed with the element of fun and excitement that appeals to adolescents.

The adolescent will be in the program for six weeks. During that time, he will start with the group activities that foster group spirit and stress cooperation rather than competition. This is achieved through the nine competitive games. In the initial phase of a patient's stay, they will participate in simple tasks on the adventure course. These include trust falls, spotting, or a blind walk. During the time of minimum skill events, the instructor will evaluate the group in terms of what events to move to next. If, in the instructor's judgement, the group cannot safely meet the demands of a particular event that would naturally follow, then that event will be deferred until the group can safely undertake it.

The next step in this process would involve completing high risk activities that require group cooperation, trust, and communication. These would include such activity stations as the wall, the electric fence and the spider web. Once the group has successfully gone through all the elements on the adventure course, they would then proceed to going on an overnight camping trip. The camping trip, by its very nature, necessitates the group to get along and cooperate in order to fulfill such basic needs as eating. The more the individuals have invested in such undertaking, the more responsibility they will take from the outcome of the experience. For this reason, they are also involved in all of the planning that goes along with the trip, such as the menus, work details and activities scheduled.

The goal of the final phase is to foster concern for others. This is accomplished through the leading and teaching skills learned by others, and also through participation of service projects. What this involves is that the participant develops and executes a plan to improve the community in some way. This then enhances an understanding for man's need to contribute to the maintenance of quality habits in nature and provide a better world for others to live in.

Nutritional Concerns

Proper nutrition is necessary to achieve quality recovery and is an adjunct to physical development programming. Extensive information has been developed on the importance of proper nutrition, especially relative to the addict, alcoholic and adolescent (Cardwell 1980; Reed et al. 1983; Pechter 1983). One pitfall of many dietary programs is that the programming is based on the assumption that "junk food" is essentially harmless or that diet should only be discretionary if a nutritional health problem *is* present. It is essential that in doing all that is possible to arrest chemical dependency, one should increase their changes by maintaining a state of optimum health. This should, on a very basic level, address educating clients in some small way about nutrition in order to facilitate proper decision making during post-treatment recovery. Nutrition is one vital factor in the chemical functioning of the human body and overall physical development. Food introduced into the body initiates changes in metabolism. We are biochemical beings and the changes brought about through nutrition can be cumulative and dramatic. Substantial evidence suggests that sugar, caffeine and certain carbohydrates sometimes have devastating cumulative effects on the body (Cardwell 1980; Reed et al 1983; Pechter 1983).

FUTURE DIRECTIONS

The multiple issues of maintaining sobriety and the completion of developmental tasks demand programming relevant to both areas. The incidence of chemical dependency during adolescent growth halts the developmental process, resulting in arrested socio-emotional development and persistent immaturity. During the past several years, significant strides have been made in understanding the unique demands of adolescent treatment, however, continued research and progressive program development are necessary. If any inpatient treatment program believes they have all the answers, it will not take long for them to fall out of step with the rest of the field. Too much effort is being put forth toward helping this adolescent patient population to ignore the strides of improving research and pertinent data relevant to improving the quality and outcome of patient care. Continued development of treatment modalities that foster positive peer pressure, confrontation skills, identity clarification, self-actualization, delay of gratification, problem solving techniques and concepts in physical health and spirituality will be areas of investigation which will provide further direction for adolescent inpatient treatment in the future.

One of the most interesting and recurrent conversations we have had with young people revolves around the idea that even though they know their lives are unmanageable, coupled with a variety of substance abuse related problems, they just cannot imagine not getting high anymore. This is reflective of their concrete thinking patterns and the need to develop techniques to develop abstract cognition. That previous comment reveals some interesting notions about this particular patient population. The first fact is that these adolescents really do want help in gaining control over their lives. They have reached such a point on the continuum of unmanageability that they "don't care" about getting better. Second, this group has assimilated that the only way to get "high" is through the use of chemicals. The third and most devastating portion of that thought process is when you ask them to describe their highest high. The descriptions all reveal a state of "no feeling," i.e., totally wasted, obliviated and annihilated. They have actually re-associated the "high" state with this self-medicated anesthetized state, where in fact, they cannot be high because they cannot perceive. In order to be high, one has to be able to perceive and interpret the state one is in. When we better comprehend how the brain works, there will be many advances in our understanding of dependency and how to deal with it.

As we look at the research which reflects that chemically dependent adolescents are low in self-esteem, lack good coping skills and are deficient in problem solving techniques (Bartin and Dubber 1982), future research relative to family issues and high risk children could lead to some innovative ways in dealing with prevention and early intervention. More research in techniques of dealing with family dysfunction will, also, prove to be essential in improving inpatient treatment. We already know of the high correlation that exists between family involvement in treatment, and how well the adolescent does in recovery. Inpatient treatment centers, therefore, need to develop more resources for working with families. Most families are not aware of their dysfunctional systems of operation and need as much time as possible to interact with other parents in family groups, partake in parenting seminars, and be involved in family therapy with their child. Part of what has to happen in the future is for us to help keep families from labeling and judging themselves "bad," relative to having a dysfunctional system. All families have some dysfunctional qualities; they vary in degrees of impact on the overall family system. Family residential treatment allows families to experience the therapeutic process, thereby gaining better insight into the changes their child is experiencing and preparing themselves as a family unit to resolve those dysfunctional qualities which may hinder their child's recovery. Families often need to continue therapy to stabilize the new balance being achieved after the treatment experience.

For some adolescents, re-entry into the home environment is a critical issue relative to their recovery changes. The family will not only be the primary support group, but must be ready to accept and implement those changes brought about by the treatment process. If parents fail to recognize this or have difficulty coping with new changes, it may negatively impact the recovery process. Therefore, some adolescents may benefit from a transitional living experience such as a halfway house for adolescents, rather than returning home, where chemical abuse or other abusive patterns exist within the family. This creates another problem, as there are few re-entry facilities for adolescents. Most halfway houses are designed for adults and are simply inappropriate for adolescents who need more structure, supervision and direction. We need to develop these types of living environments that would maintain focus on abstinence while providing the supportive structure of the inpatient setting. The adolescents are expected to attend school, maintain a sober lifestyle, develop responsible behavior patterns and appropriately interact with their peers.

Effective aftercare remains a critical issue for future direction, as too few communities have the services available to support the newly recovering adolescent. Having experienced an inpatient treatment process that was devoted to addressing most of their needs, adolescents find little to support their recovery. Too many outpatient facilities are oriented to one hour per week group therapy or individual therapy sessions, rather than a more comprehensive process utilizing previous inpatient components. AA and NA groups are often dominated by adults, and adolescents feel intimidated or left out. Many of the old aftercare ideas relative to "ninety meetings in ninety days," "no relationships for four years," "changing people, places and things" have some unrealistic expectations for young people today. Obviously, adolescents need to work on interpersonal relationship skills, but need to be accepted and belong with groups of other non-using adolescents. This process is necessary for a young person to form a healthy identity. Not enough planning has been developed in planning recreational activities for recovering adolescents with nonabusing peers.

As can be ascertained from the previous discussion on future directions, as well as some earlier comments, the field is now just in the embryonic stages of development. The induction of new ideas and techniques must continue to make this field progress in its endeavor to help the chemically dependent adolescent. As professionals in the field, we are proud to act as contributing factors in such a worthwhile cause, helping our young people and future leaders.

REFERENCES

Ahmond, R., Arnson, J.: *The Healing Community: Dynamics of the Therapeutic Milieu*. 1974.

Bartin, J.E., Dubber, P.M.: Exercise Applications and Promotion in Behavioral Medicine: Current Status and Future Directions. J Consult Clin Psychol 50: 1004-1017, 1982.

Cardwell, G.R.: Research and the Fallacy of Recidivism Studies on Wilderness Programs for Troubled Youth. In Harris, B., Wilson D. (Eds): *Adventure Programs for Human Services*. Denver, Colorado Outward Bound School, 1980.

David, J.: *Endorphines: New Waves in Brain Chemistry*. 1984.

Folkins, C., Amsterdam, E.: Control and Modification of Stress Emotions Through Chronic Exercise. *Exercise in Cardiovascular Health and Disease*. 280-294, 1977.

Gary, V., Guthrie, D.: The Effect of Jogging on Physical Fitness and Self-Concept in Hospitalized Alcoholics. J. Stud Alcohol 33: 1073-1078, 1972.

Herz, A.: Role of Endorphines in Addiction. Mod Prob Pharmaco-Psychiatry 17: 175-180, 1981.

Hyman, G.P.: The Role of Exercise in the Treatment of Substance Abuse. Unpublished Physical Education Thesis, 1987.

Jones, R.: Identification and Management of the Toxic Adolescent in Sherin, R.B., Comerci, G.E., Daniel, W.A., Greydayus, D.E., Jones, R. (Eds): *The Toxic Adolescent: Substance and Alcohol Abuse, Vol 1, Number 4,* 1985. Thieme, Inc. New York, Stuttgart 1985.

Kandel, D.: Stages in Adolescent Involvement in Drug Use. Science 190: 910-912, 1975.

Mobily, K.: Using Physical Activity and Recreation to Cope with Stress and Anxiety: A Review. Counselors J 36: 77-81, 1982.

Pechter, K.: Nutrition: A Better Way to Fight Alcoholism. Prevention 1983.

Ransford, C.: A Role for Aminos in the Antidepressant Effect of Exercise: A Review. Med Sci Sports Exerc 14: 1-10, 1982.

Reed, B., Knickelbine, S., Knickelbine, M.: *Food, Teens and Behavior*. 1983.

Rumbaugh, C.L., Fand, C.H.: The Effects of Drug Abuse on the Brain. Med Times: 37-52, 1980.

Sinyor, D., Brown, T., Rostant, I., Seraganian, P.: The Role of a Physical Fitness Program in the Treatment of Alcoholism J Stud Alcohol 43: 1982.

Thompson, C., Wahlsel, I.: The Effects of Perceived Activity Choice Upon Frequency of Exercise Behavior. J Appl Soc Psychol 10: 436-442, 1980.

Winters, K.: The Adolescent Assessment Project. Minneapolis, Minnesota, 1985.

Wright, A.N.: Therapeutic Potential of the Outward Bound Process: An Evaluation of a Treatment Program for Juvenile Delinquents. Ther Recre J: 33-41, 1983.

Yamaguchi, K., Kandel, D.B.: Patterns of Drug Use from Adolescent to Young Adulthood: III. Predictors of Progression. Am J Public Health 74: 673-681, 1984.

A Self-Help Approach
in a Day Care Model

Frank Edwards
Lou Huston

Because business and professional men in a Southern community are concerned and innovative, adolescent males are breaking free from addiction to alcohol and other drugs, completing their education, and developing positive relationships with their families. Local members of Rotary International, a service organization, established the Rotary Adolescent Treatment Center (RATC) in Gastonia, North Carolina, in 1986. The out-patient facility applies the self-help principles of Alcoholics Anonymous (AA) and Narcotics Anonymous (NA). Its therapy staff consists primarily of former abusers of drugs and alcohol who recovered through the methods of those two self-help Fellowships. This chapter describes the philosophy under which the facility functions, and outlines the operational procedures at RATC.

The program described here may differ — sometimes widely — from that of medically and psychiatrically oriented treatment centers. Each model has its successes and its failures. As an out-patient self-help operation the facility described here puts effective treatment within reach of many who otherwise could not afford help. Perhaps our experience in a program that admittedly is more pragmatic than scientific will be informative to those of more rigorous disciplines, as well as helpful to those who may wish to apply or adapt some of our procedures.

The facility accepts for treatment adolescent males of ages 13 through 20. The determining factor has less to do with the attitude

---

Frank Edwards is Executive Director of the Rotary Treatment Center in Gastonia, NC. Lou Huston is employed by Fellowship Hall in Greensboro, NC.

183

of the prospective patient than the attitude of the boy's parents toward his need for treatment. It is crucial that the parents be willing to go to any possible lengths to obtain treatment for their child — and that includes treatment for themselves. By the time they even consider out-patient treatment for their son, they have tried their own methods repeatedly and have seen them fail. Although the adolescent may be in various kinds of trouble, he usually is not ready to admit that he has a problem with addiction. He is still having fun from drinking, or using marijuana or other mind-altering chemicals. His agreement to accept out-patient treatment may at first be an alternative to what he sees as an even more unfair and unacceptable interference with his life.

"Doug" is a fairly typical example. He began using drugs at age 12. At 16 he was on cocaine as well as alcohol and other addictive substances. Doug hated his parents and terrorized them to the point where *he* controlled *them*. Reported as a runaway, he convinced the police and a judge that his father and mother physically abused him, which was not the case. Later he stole computers to finance his cocaine addiction and got caught.

Instead of sending Doug to a juvenile correction facility, the court granted probation contingent upon his receiving professional treatment for his addiction. The cost of an in-patient program long enough to be effective for Doug was beyond his parents' means. Doug grudgingly agreed to out-patient treatment as being slightly preferable to confinement.

It is fairly usual for adolescent patients to test their parents and the staff, particularly during the early weeks of treatment. Some, weary of the routine, leave treatment against medical advice (AMA), often after confidently expressing to other patients the belief that they have learned enough at the facility either to abstain on their own, or "handle it without getting into trouble."

In most cases they almost immediately resume taking drugs or drinking alcohol. Some drop-outs find they can no longer manipulate their parents into putting up with their behavior and are barred from the family home. Patients who relapse into drinking or use of other drugs are accepted back into treatment when they have stopped the substance use. This voluntary return may occur within two or three days, or four or five months later, under the original enrollment plan. Such a lenient policy would be considered counter-productive in most in-patient facilities with a shorter program. A common practice in such places is not to readmit a dropout while any of his co-patients are still in treatment, lest a "revolving door" atmosphere adversely affect morale.

In a long-term out-patient center, however, tolerance toward dropouts helps the young patient appreciate the accuracy of what he has skeptically heard about compulsion and obsession in addiction. No one ever comes back with a success story. Patients are often startled by the physical change they see in a returnee who has been back in the old life only a week or two.

By sharing his recent experience the errant one helps the others understand better such terms as obsession and compulsion. Too, he may deter some from following through on their own plans to drop out.

When they first enter treatment the adolescent patients are introduced to the concept that their problems stem from addiction to one or more chemicals, that this addiction amounts to a disease that is progressive, incurable, fatal—but *treatable*. The treatment at this facility is based on helping patients apply the 12-Step program of recovery successfully employed in Alcoholics Anonymous and Narcotics Anonymous. Their willingness and ability to apply recovery principles is proportionate to their acceptance of the serious nature of their addiction. In turn, even halfhearted efforts to apply recovery "steps" often result in the stripping away of denial and a more realistic recognition of the problem.

Credibility at RATC is further established through counselors and other staff members who are themselves recovering alcoholics and addicts who apply the same AA/NA principles in their own lives.

Program goals include enabling the patients to discover the fact of their addiction, and to assume personal responsibility for applying recovery principles to maintain abstinence on a life-long basis, one day at a time. Other goals are to end isolation, and improve relationships with parents, peers, and the community.

The out-patient program includes parents and siblings of the adolescent patients. These family members suffer emotionally from their attempts to cope with the attitudes and behavior of the addicted patient. An educational program of lectures, films and video tapes, combined with individual and group counseling, helps these family members abandon misconceptions about addiction and apply their own recovery program.

This is achieved by introducing the parents to the Fellowships of Al-Anon and Nar-Anon. These two independent organizations charge no dues or fees, and are entirely separate from AA and NA but utilize the same 12-Step program to modify negative emotions and behavior.

Adolescent patients attend the RATC out-patient program for a minimum of six months. The four levels of treatment are of about six weeks each, preceded by a two-week orientation period. Patients in Levels I and II attend the center from 8:15 am to 9:30 pm, Monday through Friday; 10:00 am to 6:00 pm, Saturday; and 1:00 to 6:30 pm Sunday. Upper Levels III and IV allow time for school and employment. In the first six weeks that comprise Level I the patients are returning to normal physically and mentally, and focus on the basics of recovery from addiction. During Level II tutors are provided at the center, then the patients attend city schools during the remainder of the program.

After completing Level IV, the patients enter a three-month After-Care Program. Reasons why RATC conducts an overall nine-month program when so many successful, highly-regarded in-patient programs are of much shorter duration are detailed in ensuing pages.

The young patients arrive at RATC by three routes: The Intervention Process (explained in Chapter 5); referral by professionals, and by lay sources. Professional referrals include not only those by physicians, the clergy, Employee Assistance Programs, mental health facilities and personal attorneys, but also, the court system when the juveniles are convicted of law violations. Others are brought in by parents, and by members of AA, NA, Nar-Anon, or of the sponsoring organization, Rotary International.

ORIENTATION

During the two-week Orientation period the new patient receives physical and psychiatric examinations. The physical includes a drug-screening urinalysis and an HIV (AIDS) test. The psychiatric interview, usually an hour and a half in length, is conducted in the doctor's office to provide a freer atmosphere for the frequently confused and agitated adolescent.

The patient's Primary Counselor conducts a psycho-social assessment. Data is obtained on the patient's education, work history, and family relationships. The Counselor asks the patient to describe the extent of alcohol and drug use by his parents and siblings. Such information may prove helpful to the patient in deciding whether his own use imitated a role model, or was in part a means of asserting independence or rebellion. Evidence of hereditary factors may help the patient accept the disease concept, thereby reducing guilt and blame, both of which hinder recovery. The counselor also obtains the patient's recollection of the age he began using alcohol and other drugs. In this Orientation period the patient attends classes explaining what the center expects him to learn and how it expects him to behave.

The counselor obtains his responses to questionnaires probing the patient's use of addictive substances, his resultant behavior and mental emotional reactions to this use. These include diagnostic tests prepared by leading medical centers such as the Mayo Clinic and Johns Hopkins Hospital.

Staffing sessions are held every week, with personnel offering input on the patient's health, attitude, behavior and progress. At the same time the primary counselor and the family counselors maintain close contact with the parents, sharing this information with the rest of the staff.

Between the second and third week the Director, Medical Doctor and Counseling staff meet to address the question, "Can we help this young person?" That is the chief consideration in making the decision whether the patient is appropriate for treatment at RATC.

If judged appropriate, the patient enters, or continues with, Level I. Approximately eighty percent of the cases are deemed appropriate to continue the program.

Those determined to be inappropriate fall into three categories.

(a) Dual diagnosis: If, after being abstinent from alcohol and other drugs for a significant period of time, the patient continues to manifest bizarre thinking and behavior, the presence of underlying psychological problems is suspected. These include inappropriate responses in conversations, counselling sessions, classrooms and group. He may start rationally with a subject, then wander off onto an irrelevant topic. Often it is the other patients who detect such bizarre behavior before staff members do, whether it occurs in group, class, or just among themselves. They appear able to accept a variety of responses normal among adolescents in withdrawal, like sullen aloofness, bursts of anger or talkativeness, but then identify one of their number as somehow "different." Upon confirmation by a psychiatrist of an underlying problem, the patient is transferred to a facility treating psychiatric illness. When discharged from the second facility as cured or improved, it is not unusual for the patient to return to RATC to complete successfully the outpatient program.

(b) Some adolescents, while in treatment, are faced with home conditions deterrent to recovery that the parents are unwilling to change. In one instance the patient's mother brought a teenage girl in the house to live with them. The patient had sex with the girl. From an active participant in group, helpful to the others, he now sat in silence. One day another patient told of extreme guilt feelings about having sex while drinking, behavior contrary to his religious upbringing. The first patient suddenly blurted out in group the guilt tormenting him over having sex with the girl in his home. The mother refused a staff member's suggestion that she remove the girl from the home. In another case, a patient's older brother, in his mid-twenties, drank and used drugs in the home, greatly tempting the patient to relapse. The parents refused to believe that the older son was on drugs, and declined to have him submit to a urine test. In spite of this temptation the younger boy continued in treatment. A year later he was still maintaining abstinence.

(c) Other adolescents are unable to break away from peers who are users, and while in treatment seek out the old haunts and associates. For such patients, in-patient treatment may be the solution.

LEVEL I

For practical reasons and from trial-and-error, RATC imposes a variety of restrictions for admission and for continuing the program. Males only, 13 through 20, are accepted. Married adolescents are excluded. Both parents must agree to participate in the program.

Whether old or young, male or female, addicts are characterized by an aversion to discipline, external and internal. The book *Alcoholics Anonymous* calls this tendency "self-will run riot." With adolescents, rebellion against authority is normal in the transition to adulthood. The teenage patient, even though he came "voluntarily" to treatment, resists the very rules that if revoked would make treatment impossible. His reason is overwhelmed by anger and unrecognized fear: anger at being restricted, fear of losing the relief and euphoria provided by his addictive chemical.

So, until the adolescent patient attains sufficient self-discipline and an understanding that he is in a life-or-death situation, restrictions are necessary at RATC, particularly for those in Orientation and Level I.

Out-patients in Level I are not permitted, while in the facility, to watch TV, listen to the radio or stereo. They may not read literature not approved by the Center. They cannot talk on the telephone or receive mail or packages.

A dress code is in effect. Conceivably it may change, to keep pace with the succession of teenage fads. But at publication the code bans tank tops, sleeveless T-shirts and black T-shirts. Patients cannot wear clothing depicting drugs, drug paraphernalia, or rock and roll bands. Tight-fitting pants are forbidden. Patients must wear shoes, and not flip-flops. Banned also are hats, bandannas and head-bands.

These restrictions elicit protests and grumbling from some teenagers as they test the staff and the program. The rules are not arbitrary, however. The banned apparel, the entertainment diversions and outside contacts are strongly linked to their drug-using lives. They need to be continuously aware they are learning a new way of living. Most of the young patients eventually see that their out-patient program is so demanding that there is little time for their former diversions. Also, as they note their peers in the upper Levels enjoying increased privileges, they are motivated to adapt and earn the rewards.

From 8:30 in the morning into early evening the patients listen to lectures augmented by up-to-date films and video-tapes on the effect of alcohol and various drugs on their bodies and minds. Included are lectures on the principles of recovery. These classes are given by counselors and lecturers whose self-disclosures as former abusers of alcohol and drugs lend credibility to the material.

At RATC the lectures, films and tapes are interladen with classes on recovery principles. The patients learn that recovery involves more than merely not drinking and not using. During the day the adolescents are also attending group sessions, where they learn to apply the principles described in the didactic lectures. Further, they attend daily meetings of AA and NA and receive individual counseling.

The curriculum includes the study and discussion of two main texts, the books *Alcoholics Anonymous* (1939) and *Narcotics Anonymous* (1982). Each book contains the same Twelve Steps of Recovery, and the same basic philosophy along with the individual history of the two Fellowships. The books include several personal recovery stories of alcoholics and drug addicts, to help patients identify.

In this AA-oriented facility, treatment has two main focal points: First, to assist the adolescent to identify, by examining his own behavior and substance use, the symptoms of addiction that constitute the disease, and to recognize his need for help to recover from it. Second, to guide the adolescent in understanding and applying the 12-Step recovery program of AA, so that he may replace negative traits with positive attitudes and behavior conducive to comfortable abstinence and increasing emotional maturity.

Lectures, films and video-tapes explain the disease concept and describe the specific symptoms that distinguish the addict from the nonaddicted person. The patient learns that the chief symptoms include blackouts (memory lapses after a drinking episode), increased tolerance (requiring larger amounts to obtain the original effect), loss of control (getting intoxicated despite intentions not to do so), continuing to drink or use other drugs when the substance has caused problems in any life area (family, job, school, health, finances, the law, social relationships).

On the recovery phase, lectures include descriptions of the 12-Steps and how they are applied. Character defects common to all human beings but which increasingly govern the addict's life are described with examples. The patients learn that mind-altering chemicals, by affecting reasoning and judgment, loosen restraint on such self-defeating traits as pride (ego), self-centeredness, resentment, fear, dishonesty and guilt. Recovery, the adolescent is informed, results from applying the 12 Steps to develop the positive opposites of humility, unselfishness, forgiveness, faith, honesty and self-acceptance.

Many patients at the facility began using alcohol and other chemicals at 10 and 11 years of age, when the capacity for abstract thinking and logical reasoning has not yet developed. On the average, RATC patients started using mind-altering substances at the age of 12. With continued substance abuse they remain immature into their late teens and early twenties. Older alcoholics, whose problem developed after some successful functioning as adults, often show in treatment deterioration in the ability to handle new concepts and ideas. This function usually returns sufficiently for them to absorb recovery principles in a standard 28-day program. Adolescents with long-term substance abuse lack the experience of dealing with concepts, which may explain why longer treatment is frequently required by these young people.

Weekday Schedule

The Monday through Friday schedule starts with a general assembly at 8:30 in the morning. A counselor covers any changes in the day's routine, and invites any volunteer from the patient population to read a brief inspirational message from a center-approved publication. This reinforces recovery principles and also helps the adolescents overcome shyness about speaking before groups.

Interspersed between lectures and film showings are discussion sessions. A morning class called "Moms and Pops" gives the patients the opportunity to tell the others what is going on between themselves and their parents. The issues are usually not serious problems. One boy may report that yesterday's difficulty with his mother has been worked out, while another ventilates frustration over parental criticism about neglecting his chores.

This half-hour session is followed by the same patients participating in group therapy. Each learns how he is seen by the others. All discover how addiction and self-centeredness blind the individual to defects that the group members see clearly. The group process gradually breaks down the assumption of uniqueness that underlies denial and is one of the barriers to recovery. Facilitators at the center observe that the young people tend to be more confrontive than is the case in adult groups. A second group session is held in the afternoon, three days a week, with athletics on the other two days.

A book study session in the afternoon covers assigned chapters from the textbooks of the two Fellowships, Alcoholics Anonymous and Narcotics Anonymous. This study gives the patients the basic recovery principles for alcoholics and users of other drugs, with autobiographical examples to enhance identification by those in treatment.

Each afternoon a class titled "Coping Skills" involves the patients in drills applying abstract concepts such as tolerance, patience, delaying gratification, and honesty. A counselor may present a hypothetical situation and ask for solutions involving the quality under discussion. Role playing is frequently employed in this class.

The patients are served two meals daily at the center, lunch and dinner.

Seven nights a week the patients conclude the long day with an AA or NA meeting. On two nights a week the meetings are held at the center, with talks given by local members of the two Fellowships. On the other five nights patients are taken in the center's van to local AA or NA meetings or to those in nearby communities.

The adolescent patients return to their homes around 9:30 pm.

Weekend Schedule

The weekend regimen is lighter. On Saturday the out-patients assemble at 10:00 am for the community session, followed by a one-hour AA or NA meeting. After lunch the boys enjoy four hours of supervised recreation, including outside trips for bowling, boating, horseback riding and visits to a nearby amusement park. One or more staff members accompany the patients.

This recreation does more than provide a break in an intensive week of treatment and study. It gives the boys and young men a chance to learn how to have fun sober. A frequent statement by the adolescents is that until they came to the center they did not know how to enjoy themselves without being high on some chemical. In group sessions and informally they describe how in early childhood they felt they didn't fit in, and that shyness and feelings of inadequacy kept them on the sidelines. The discovery of alcohol or other mind-altering substance was, they said, a tremendously liberating experience. Reduced inhibitions enabled them to mix with other youths and to be accepted even by peers for whom a chemical boost was not necessary.

The Sunday schedule begins at 1:00 pm with two activity periods separated by an AA or NA meeting. Patients return home on Saturdays at 6:00 pm and on Sundays at 6:30 pm.

Expectation of Patients in Level I

Each patient must complete a test booklet and write a brief paper to demonstrate his understanding of how Step One of the recovery program applies personally to him. AA's Step One reads: We admitted we were powerless over alcohol — that our lives had become unmanageable. (In the NA version the phrase "our addiction" is substituted for the word "alcohol.")

Required to *write* this information, the patient cannot skip mentally over these events and dismiss them. He is forced to be specific about his feelings and actions. Earlier in treatment he has heard fellow patients in group describe their own feelings and behavior. His counselor and other staff members have disclosed instances illustrating their own addiction. These serve as clarifying examples as well as evidence he is not alone in this condition. As the incidents pile up on the page, and perhaps several additional pages, he can see in his own words and his own handwriting the mounting evidence that he is indeed powerless over alcohol. If he *could* manage his own life, he must ask himself, why did he let it get so far out of hand? The more capable he is of self-honesty, the less his compliance and inner reservations, and the more his acceptance of the truth that he is without question powerless over addictive substances and that his life has become unmanageable.

To move up to Level II, patients in Level I must have the approval of the peers in their Group and of the Staff. The consensus of the Group sometimes is more critical than that of the Staff. The patients often are in a better position to spot mere compliance in a member or a skilled bit of conning. Giving the Group a voice in a promotion has a value far more than possible refining of the Staff's evaluation. Approval and endorsement by his peers — peers who for the most part want to be sober and clean of drugs — can be a salutary boost to an adolescent's self-esteem. Even being held back tells the patient that the Group cares enough about him to want him to be prepared, so he can succeed when he reaches the next level.

Usually, patients spend about six weeks in Level I.

LEVEL II

The schedule and structure of Level II are similar to those of the first level. The patient is at the Center from 8:15 am to 9:30 pm Monday through Friday. The Saturday hours are from 10:00 am to 6:00 pm and Sundays 1:00 pm to 6:30 pm.

Patients are able to receive tutoring from the Gaston County Homebound Public School Program. A tutor comes to RATC two or three times a week, enabling patients to regain ground lost in their school work because of their addiction.

In Level II some privileges are restored. In free time they can watch TV and listen to the radio and stereo. They can receive mail and packages from persons on the approved list. When such items arrive at their homes, the patients and parents cooperate for the most part by turning the material over to the staff at the center for approval. By this time most patients have developed such a bond to their group that they monitor themselves, even at home. Those tempted to withhold mail received at home usually become troubled by guilt and find that they can regain comfort by being honest.

Toward the end of Level I their mental faculties have improved. They now share a common background of information, and are comfortable with each other and the staff. Even outside of class and group sessions they are using more of the vocabulary of sobriety than that of the addict. Consequently, the lectures can be more in detail and broader in scope.

Expectations of Patients in Level II

Patients in Level II must complete booklets on Steps 2 and 3 and related papers, and assume a leadership role. Their role models, of course, are the teenagers who preceded them in the higher levels.

Step 2 of both AA and NA reads: "(We) came to believe that a power greater than ourselves could restore us to sanity."

This step requires the Patient to look again at the evidence of his powerlessness over alcohol and drugs and the unmanageability he acknowledged in Step One. It reminds him that acting on his own impulses and desires accelerated his substance abuse, alienated family, created trouble in school, on the job, with the law, and harmed his health. Such repeated use of a substance that harms him, he eventually sees, cannot be termed sane behavior. Step 2 emphasizes the continuing need for rational, experienced guidance to avoid returning to the self-indulgence inherent in addiction.

Step 3 of AA and NA reads: "Made a decision to turn our will and our lives over to the care of God *as we understand Him*." (The emphasis is that of AA in its basic book, *Alcoholics Anonymous* and in all its other literature.) Patients, like members of the two Fellowships, may utilize whatever idea of God makes sense to them. At the center and at AA and NA meetings virtually the only examples of recovery they encounter are those who attain and maintain their abstinence in one or both of the Fellowships. An important part of the philosophy of both organizations is to "Share their experience, strength and hope" with the addict who still suffers. As a beginning, at least, many patients accept the most appropriate Fellowship as their "higher power," and try to follow its principles under the guidance of more experienced members. A goal of treatment is for these patients to continue in AA and/or NA, and in turn help others to achieve comfortable abstinence.

Usually this helping of others begins among the patients themselves, as they encourage newer arrivals in treatment, coach them on the routine, explain lectures and literature to them, and share accounts of their disappointments, frustrations and difficulties. They discover that by helping others they increase their own understanding of the recovery program, and their confidence in it.

For the patient to move on to the next Level he must receive once again approval from his Group of peers and from the Staff.

Level II is also approximately six weeks in length.

LEVEL III

On reaching Level III the adolescent is given "more rope" in regard to time spent at the center, and simultaneously he is urged to assume more responsibility for his life. Consistent with the principles of AA and NA, the RATC program is designed to help the patient return to a normal life. In many cases early use of chemicals made a normal life impossible, so the adolescent must create such a life.

Level III requires the patient to return to public school or to an outside job. The patient makes his decision after discussion and recommendations by his group, parents, and primary counselor. The three Rotary Clubs that sponsor the center are helpful in providing employment for youth in this stage of the out-patient program.

After completing school or work for the day, patients on Level III report to the center by 3:30 pm Monday through Friday. By now the patient has had a minimum of twelve weeks abstinence from mind-altering substances. He is well past the withdrawal stage if he has used alcohol and other sedative drugs. Heavy users of marijuana, cocaine and the hallucinogens may still have occasional flashbacks that include intervals of paranoia. In the afternoon group sessions such patients are urged to talk about these intense fears, and are assured by other members of the group that they are not crazy, but are experiencing a side effect of the drug they formerly used. Upper Level patients may describe *their* past flashbacks, and laugh about them. Laughter by the group at first may startle and mystify the recently frightened drug user, but then, like the upper Level members, his own fearful incidents will eventually cease.

Upper Level patients continue in Group with Level II patients and the more recent arrivals in Level I. To non-users, twelve weeks abstinence may not seem impressive. But to the new arrivals, their fellow patients in Levels III and IV are objects of respect, admiration and even wonder. Consequently they are expected to justify this position by acquiring and demonstrating leadership abilities. Even in the case of older alcoholics coming to AA in their thirties and later, newcomers may be more impressed by a member with a few months sobriety than by veterans with ten or twenty years. Such "eons" of abstinence are beyond conceiving to someone only a few days away from the last drink. Adolescents new in treatment may know intellectually that their Counselor has had several years free from alcohol and drugs, but the presence of a *peer* with twelve to twenty-four weeks abstinence has a more graspable reality.

Acceptance of leadership and responsibility is encouraged beyond their participation at the Center and into *all* their affairs: home, school, work and the community. Not until reaching Levels III and IV do some patients begin to appreciate the cliche they have heard all through the Center and in AA and NA: "There is more to sobriety than just not taking a drink (or a drug)."

Their function in Group includes giving support and encouragement to new patients, who may resent the discipline and what they consider excessively long treatment. Or, the new arrivals may have been branded as hopeless failures for so long that their self-esteem is extremely low. Looking at the upper level patients they despair of ever attaining that much abstinence, let alone such confidence and sense of self-worth.

In Group, those in the two upper levels help reduce rebellion and negativism by sharing their own feelings and experiences when they were new.

Level III schedules for Saturday and Sunday are the same as in Levels I and II.

Patients Expectations on Level III

The Patient must complete a Step 4 Booklet and begin writing his Fourth Step Inventory.

Step 4 of AA and NA reads: "(We) made a thorough and fearless moral inventory of ourselves."

This inventory is much more than a superficial chronology of events in the patient's life. The expanded treatment time available in an out-patient facility is conducive to writing a deeper, more significant inventory than is ordinarily possible for juveniles in a short-term treatment. In group the patient may have revealed tearfully or angrily several distressing events in his life. Yet his first efforts at an inventory may omit any reference to grief over the death of a beloved grandparent, resentment against parents and siblings, humiliations in school, or fear and confusion over his parents' marital conflicts. He may skip lightly over serious consequences of his use of alcohol and hard drugs.

Patient efforts by his primary counselor, plus the continuing group work and lectures, eventually produce an effective self-analysis. Previous omissions may or may not have been conscious. Unconscious suppression is frequently indicated. For example, a counselor may remind the patient of an omitted drunk driving arrest or suspension from school. More surprised than angry or embarrassed, the patient may exclaim, "Oh, yeah! How could I have left *that* out?"

Not easy at best, the inventory eventually becomes a sufficiently thorough account of the patient's life to reveal to him patterns of behavior, and disclose character defects such as anger, resentment, fear, self-centeredness, pride and jealousy. He sees their role in wrecking relationships as well as his use of addictive substances. At the same time the inventory reveals his more positive qualities: his unselfish acts, capacity to love and trust. He becomes aware of past interests and skills that have been replaced by substance abuse.

In group and informally he hears the more advanced patients enthusiastically describe the benefits of completing a thorough, honest inventory—the gained insights, relief, greater self-understanding and a loosening of long-held resentments against people and conditions.

Now nearing the end of Level III, the patient must have the approval of his group and the staff to move up to Level IV. Like the other Levels, Level III is usually completed in six weeks.

LEVEL IV

Patients reaching Level IV have their privileges expanded to require only twelve hours of attendance at the center each week in addition to attending group on Monday, Wednesday, and Friday afternoons.

Probably no phase of the young addict's life is more distorted by alcohol and other mind-altering drugs than his sexual relationships. It is also the area he finds the most difficult to talk about. In the extended out-patient treatment at RATC the adolescent males have an opportunity to deal with these sexually related problems as they occur, as well as to examine those of the past.

The desire for sex and actual sexual relationships are prime triggers for relapse into alcohol and drug use. In his early abstinence his partner is likely to be a user even if only a moderate one — and for an addict moderation is impossible. Just being in the presence of the substance may override his weak resistance, or he may join the girl in the practice to demonstrate his manliness. If rejected he may well find the blow to his ego and the sense of loss so devastating that his short-time acceptance of his addiction and earnest efforts to practice recovery principles are wiped out in a wave of self-pity.

Adolescents in Levels III and IV have an opportunity to discuss their problems in a special Group that convenes on alternate Wednesdays. In the 3:30 pm sessions on Monday, Tuesday, Thursday, and Friday, the Level III patients are in group with the lower level participants. On Mondays and Fridays the Level IV patients are also present, giving the upper levels a chance to offer leadership and encouragement to the new patients.

Every second Wednesday, however, those in Levels III and IV meet together in Group to deal with whatever sexual problem they may have.

Our experience with homosexual adolescents at the facility has been quite limited and with discouraging results. One teenaged male, although admitting his homosexuality, was dishonest in dealing with various aspects of his life, and also made advances to other patients. Having shown no progress after three months, he was given a therapeutic discharge. It is not meant to imply that he could not have been helped at another facility.

The majority of our patients, with at least twelve weeks of treatment free from alcohol and other drugs, are capable of being honest about their thoughts and behavior. They are able to discuss how the Twelve Steps and other recovery principles apply in this important emotional/spiritual area of their lives.

FAMILY PARTICIPATION

Earlier in this article it was stated that parental cooperation and support often are greater determining factors in weighing an adolescent's appropriateness for treatment than the initial attitude and circumstances of the applicant himself. This cooperation extends beyond any contribution toward the treatment fee. It is a basic tenet of RATC that participation by the parents is essential for successful treatment of adolescents.

Since the 1960s, treatment centers for addiction have become increasingly aware that family members become emotionally maladjusted in their efforts to cope with the changing personality and behavior of the addicted member. Parents tend to resist the idea that their child is even *using* drugs, let alone abusing them. The child's withdrawal from family activities, failing grades, truancy, and even problems with the law they attribute to the adverse influence of his associates. Most parents become ready to place their child in treatment only when the problem can no longer be denied, and their own efforts have repeatedly failed.

Experience at RATC is that the adolescent's chance for recovery is vastly improved when both parents take part in the treatment process. At this facility each patient must have two adults participating in the family program, preferably both parents.

The parents attend group and individual counseling sessions, and weekly meetings of Nar-Anon, the self-help Fellowship open to relatives and friends of drug addicts. (The name is derived from the first syllables in the words Narcotics Anonymous.) During the early years of AA (the 1940s) spouses of AA members realized that they, too, were sick, as they expressed it in their literature later. These family members found through trial and error that they could solve their emotional and living problems by applying the same twelve steps of recovery that were helping their alcoholic spouses in AA. Eventually Al-Anon came into being. Later, families of drug addicts found the same to be true of NA's program. In Step One of these family fellowships, the members accept that they are power-less over substance used by the addict with whom they are emotion-ally involved.

Family members at the center and in Nar-Anon meetings face issues common to families of addicts. One of the most prevalent is guilt — blaming themselves for "allowing" or causing the addiction to take hold of their son. At the center they hear lectures and see films and video-tapes explaining the disease concept. In these au-dio-visuals, medical doctors help family members understand that addiction is a physiological reaction to a chemical substance, often with accompanying psychological responses; that it is beyond con-trol by others, and by the addict only through abstinence.

From the experience of regular Nar-Anon members, parents learn the futility of attempts to "reward" the adolescent for promises to change undesirable behavior. Some parents tell of buying their teenager a new car, time after time, when he totals them in acci-dents usually involving alcohol or other drugs. Or, they cover the cost of property theft and damage, pay fines, credit-card debts and cover bad checks. It is unrealistic, they learn, to expect an addict to change behavior out of gratitude. His addiction overwhelms the promise, although it may have been sincere at the time. The actual lesson learned by the adolescent is that his parents will rescue him. They are using "enabling" behavior, preventing the teenager from accepting responsibility for his own actions.

At the center parents hear it is inadvisable to promise the adoles-cent a car, for example, if he will accept treatment, or to give him one just because he completed treatment. Such well-meant gifts, they are told by sadly wise fathers and mothers, only reinforce the adolescent's belief that he must be paid for doing what the majority of people do as a matter of course. To benefit from treatment, the patient needs to see the program as essential for his happiness and survival, not as a parental whim to satisfy in order to get a material reward.

From parents whose sons have successfully remained free from addictive substances, mothers and fathers in treatment are taught a practical Nar-Anon/Al-Anon admonition: "release with love." In blunt terms the phrase means, "Love the kid enough to let him grow up." Practicing such detachment can be compared to the addict's difficulty in achieving abstinence from his drug. Max A. Schneider, MD, in his film, *Medical Aspects of Co-Dependency*[1] (1986) states that the co-dependent (family member) "is addicted to the addict." While simplistic, the phrase helps distressed parents understand their need to apply recovery principles to themselves. It eases their acceptance of Step One: that they are powerless over the addictive substances used by their loved one, and that their own lives have become unmanageable in their confused and futile attempts to manage the life of the addict.

In the RATC program adults learn, practice and share their own recovery process with other adults. From the first, they learn they are not alone in their anger, despair and confusion. They gain hope when they see the serenity and cheerfulness of seasoned Nar-Anon members and hear encouraging accounts from these parents of their own sons' and daughters' recovery.

The parents are involved on a day-to-day basis with their son's recovery, rather than sending him away and expecting him to come home "fixed." He might, in the latter case, come home well started in recovery, but his parents will still be locked in their negative emotions and their unrealistic expectations. At RATC the entire family learns how to get well together.

AFTERCARE

When the Patient has completed the four levels of treatment, he and the adult family members enter the three-month Aftercare Program. They attend meetings at the Center twice a week, enabling the staff to continue assistance and to discover problems encountered in the shifting equilibrium of family relationships. Sometimes the problems are of the kind any family might encounter, but the residue of distorted emotions from the substance-abuse years often exaggerate the difficulties. Frequently the parents, finding it difficult to let go, attempt to manage their son's recovery program for him — or it may be the reverse: the child adversely criticizes what he sees as his parents' working Nar-Anon or Al-Anon principles "the wrong way." Quite often the conflict does not involve the young

---

1. Schneider, Max A., MD, *Medical Aspects of Co-Dependency*, FMS/ Schneider, Santa Ana, CA, 1986.

addict directly, but the parents may be in disagreement over what they perceive as their spouse's misinterpretation of what was taught at the Center.

It is in Aftercare that parents and sons begin to appreciate the depth and range of malfunctioning resulting from addiction. They look back in shock at their previously held belief that all that was needed for the family to be happy was for "the kid to get off that junk."

During the Aftercare period, patients (now former-patients) are required to attend an AA or NA meeting each day. The process of support and evaluation at RATC assures that the program is viable and synchronous with the need of the recovering persons.

RATC REQUIREMENTS FOR ACCEPTANCE

No married adolescents are accepted for treatment.

Adolescent patients must have both parents' participation in the Family Program.

If there are siblings between 5 and 13 years of age, they must participate in an eight-meeting Sibling Support Group at the Center.

To remain in treatment, patients must comply with RATC rules including the dress code. Patients using alcohol or other mind-altering substances while in the out-patient Program will be discharged.

WHEN OUT-PATIENT TREATMENT IS INDICATED

It might be asked, why do adolescents require treatment for six months and more, when many highly-respected treatment centers have 28-day programs?

Late-blooming alcoholics and drug addicts (those in their late twenties, thirties, and up) may do well in a 28-day in-patient facility. Such persons may have had a fairly normal adolescence and several years experience in handling adult responsibilities. To a great extent they are returning to former values and habits of living. In contrast, the adolescent who began drug and alcohol use at eleven or earlier has stopped maturing emotionally at the moment he became addicted to and dependent upon his chemical. For one who is from five to ten years behind in growing up, even nine months may be a crash course.

If the family can afford a long in-patient treatment, is there any reason why an out-patient facility *should* still be selected?

One factor may be that the adolescent has already been to an in-patient treatment and has relapsed. All good facilities can truthfully claim instances where their "graduates" are now attaining long-term abstinence after failing at another institution. Even if the adolescent is treated at an in-patient facility along with his parents in a good family program, there still comes a time when he and his family must leave the benign and comfortable nest of the facility and plunge back into the neighborhood, the relatives, the school, the job, and the community. With outpatient treatment as offered at RATC, this dunking experience is avoided; difficulties are discovered early and worked through.

CONCLUSION

The RATC program gives adolescents the treatment and the time needed to overcome the disturbing effect of alcohol and other drugs on their developing brains and bodies. Surrounded by their peers, and counseled by recovering alcoholics and addicts who are examples of the program's effectiveness, nearly all feel comfortable in treatment. Since the Group sessions contain no persons in the age-bracket of their parents or grandparents, the adolescents more freely express their feelings and problems.

With their parents sharing in the program and living at home with them, and while going to school and working, they more quickly and substantially build a new life. From the first they learn that AA and NA offer the best — and probably the only — chance for a happy, sober life, one day at a time.

BIBLIOGRAPHY

Alcoholics Anonymous, 3rd Ed., New York: Alcoholics Anonymous World Services, Inc., 1976.

Narcotics Anonymous, 3rd Ed. revised, Van Nuys, CA: World Service Office, Inc., 1986.

Schneider, Max A., M.D., *Medical Aspects of Co-Dependency*, FMS/Schneider, Santa Ana, CA, 1986.

Promoting Recovery
and Preventing Relapse
in Chemically Dependent Adolescents

Peter R. Cohen, MD

INTRODUCTION

The era of DSMIII-R (APA 1987), DRGs, insurance and government cutbacks, and JCAHO reviews has not been a total curse, but has been a blessing in some ways for the treatment of the chemically dependent adolescent. These new definitions and limitations have forced us to think in very specific terms about how we can help a teenager in recovery from chemical dependency. It is not enough to say that we will handle problems as they occur using our "eclectic" orientation. First, no self-respecting teenager will blindly adhere to our notions of treatment. Furthermore, our traditional psychiatric treatments have failed to help these troubled teens. Thanks to the founding work of Alcoholics Anonymous and Narcotics Anonymous and to the groundbreaking work of Stephanie Brown and Terrence Gorski, we know that there are distinctive stages of recovery from chemical dependency (Brown 1985; Gorski 1982a,b,1983). As illustrative as these works are, they do not address the unique problems of the addicted teenager—be it the purely chemically dependent or the dually diagnosed teen. This is a promising but neglected area of treatment for adolescents.

Not until recently have clinicians outlined the diagnostic and treatment tasks of the earlier stages of recovery for adolescents (Hendren 1986; Kaufman 1985; Rogers 1987; Schwartz, Cohen et al.

Peter R. Cohen is Director, Cornerstone Inpatient Program, Psychiatric Institute of Montgomery County, Rockville, MD.

1985). The later stages have been described for adults but do not account for adolescent development (Brown 1985; Gorski 1982a, b, 1983).

We know that adolescents are not adults. Although teens can demonstrate "adult" qualities of abstract thinking, intimacy, sexual behavior, humor and "sophistication," they are not financially independent, have not left home, and do not have to face the balancing act of writing checks, paying bills, putting the children to sleep, advancing a career, lighting the pilot light in the furnace, finding money to invest in one's retirement, and hopefully, making love without all of the above interferences all in the same day. At our worst we tend to treat teens like adults in treatment. Someone must have said about adolescents, "they've got the plumbing but they ain't got enough faucets to regulate the water." In other words they are missing sufficient experience and control to leave home and take on the world. This is very relevant to treating the recovering teen; historically, we have erred in assuming that once a child has embraced sobriety, he or she will naturally grow into the adult that should have been had not chemical dependency been in the way.

One must also keep in mind that there are multiple and uneven lines of adolescent development. Teens should be actively dealing with issues of independence, separation and individuation. They should be developing identity, competency, emotional control, cognitive growth, social skills, intimacy, etc. These elements of development will interact with each other and with the development of psychopathology, chemical dependency and recovery.

I am advocating what AA, NA, and Cocaine Anonymous have always promoted for the adult, but with a correction for the adolescent: recovery from chemical dependency is a dynamic and not a static process, one does not reach recovery but is recovering, and the teenager recovers in a way unique to a developing teenager.

The purposes of this paper are to introduce the concepts of recovering and relapse prevention pertaining to adolescents, and to give a practical guide of how to proceed in a specific setting with a specific teenager and family. The strengths and limitations of different settings in promoting recovering and preventing relapse, as well as the meaning and appropriateness of treatment and therapy at different phases of the recovering process, will be discussed. Case examples of recovering and relapsing teens will also provide a practical guide of how to proceed with treatment.

This model is based on a psychiatric/psychological/biological/social/cognitive/behavioral approach to the problem of recovery (Gorski 1982a). In its essence, I am describing a diagnostic and treatment plan for the recovering teenager, which can be adapted for a long-term or short-term treatment setting.

There are four points to be emphasized in this discussion. First, there are specific stages of recovery from chemical dependency that can take several years to achieve. Second, for every stage of recovery, there are specific characteristics, goals, and tasks. Third, any therapeutic technique must be adapted to the stage of recovery, because the patient can only respond to the technique based upon his or her development at that stage (Gorski 1982a). Fourth, adolescent development must be taken into account in helping the adolescent move through the stages of recovery.

RECOVERING

The recovery process is dynamic and involves stages of recovery which are partially or completely accomplished. This is a process of developmental growth which must be facilitated by peers, family, and professionals. There are eleven stages which will be described by their characteristics, goals, and their tasks. Stephanie Brown mentions only four stages of drinking, transition, early recovery, and ongoing recovery (Brown 1983). Unfortunately, these stages do not provide enough detail of the changes a teenager must make. Terrence Gorski's stages of recovery are very similar to the stages cited below (Gorski 1982a, b, 1983). Clinical experience, however, shows that there are tasks of recovery unique enough or lengthy enough in completing to warrant additional stages of recovery.

There are two important principles found in the writings of Gorski and Brown that are relevant to the recovering teenager as well as the adult. First, Gorski (1982a, 1983) emphasizes a transition from the reliance on the social environment for support in earlier recovery to the reliance on personal resources. Second, Stephanie Brown (1985) also speaks to the adolescent when she describes the significance of the concept of paradox and control in recovery. The addict must realize that he is not in control of his chemical use in order to regain control of his life. He must also become dependent on an external structure, such as AA/NA, in order to become a more independent person. As the person realizes this concept of paradox and control, he can undergo a "spiritual conversion." These are extraordinary processes to expect of an impaired adolescent who lives under the delusion that chemicals will move him toward true differentiation, independence, and competence. The stages cited below encourage the clinician to respect the enormous difficulties the teenager faces in the dynamic process of recovering.

I. Crisis Stage

When a crisis occurs usually anyone but the chemically dependent teenager will be asking for help. There is usually a repeating pattern of crisis. Social systems and rules are violated, inconsistently enforced, or relatively absent. The teen is usually in trouble with other peers unless he is very depressed. Parents are usually desperate and more overtly concerned than their child but they may deny or minimize the presence of chemical dependency. Marital strain or impending or actual divorce may also be present. Confusion abounds as one parent will say "it can't be that bad" and then blame the other parent for the child's failures. The teenager is either angry at being coerced into meeting or, strangely, shows little emotional reaction.

Why equate this pre-recovery stage as one of the stages? Because recovery begins with the first attempt to evaluate the problem, which promotes awareness of the illness and treats the denial of the family and the adolescent. Furthermore, the clinician can pay too much attention to a patient's compliance, overlook the patient's creation of family crises, and mistakenly believe that the patient is at a later stage of recovery, because he has completed a treatment program.

The tasks at this stage are designed to rally the family to problem solve and to test the mettle of the teenager. Diagnosis of chemical dependency will be incomplete and inconclusive. One will be unable to determine what problems are "psychiatric," "developmental," or "chemically dependent."

There are three qualitative rating scales which can raise the clinician's index of suspicion that an adolescent is chemically dependent. The first scale is any checklist of chemically dependent related behaviors which the parents can review with the clinician and the adolescent. The second and third scales are, respectively, the DSMIII-R Axis IV scale of severity of psychosocial stressors and the Axis V scale of global assessment of functioning (APA 1987). A multitude of these listed behaviors, greater severity of stressors, poorer functioning, and a family history of chemical dependency will lean the diagnosis in favor of chemical dependency.

Crisis intervention techniques are the hallmark of this recovery stage. The primary goal is not to foster change but to test the teenager and family's ability to adapt. The adolescent and family should be interviewed separately and together. Anticipate anywhere from one to two hours for the first meeting. Treatment is geared towards seeing if a second crisis will emerge after settling the first one: if so, suspect continuing chemical abuse.

While managing the presenting crisis, the professional is setting the tone for further treatment. The parents and the social system are motivated by encouraging the following goals:

1. more effective communication
2. a coherent hierarchy of decision making
3. better cooperation in the family
4. clear decision making by the parents
5. clear setting of consequences and contracts

These goals first introduced at this stage, will be emphasized again and again at later stages of recovery. The teenager is being tested for his or her ability to solve a crisis. You are introducing the concepts of responsibility, growth, and change as the friend of the family and of drug and alcohol abuse as the enemy.

In addition to solving the crisis at hand, always suggest an abstinence contract. For the more disturbed teen a shorter contract is necessary, because he or she is incapable of acting healthy for more than "one day at a time."

It is important to be clear about the goals of the family. Keep asking, "what do you want to know?" and "what do you expect to happen today?" Keep clear about your limits of confidentiality. If possible give the teen the chance to change or to fail. If he or she is very impulsive, or is homicidal or suicidal, move the parents toward hospitalizing their child. Be aware that parents are usually wishing for the best and fearing the worst. They want you to work hard, but may not want you to go overboard in your recommendations.

II. Assessment Stage

Parents and professionals usually want to jump the gun and carry out treatment without assessing the extent of chemical use. They can underestimate the seriousness of their child's chemical abuse and its implications for treatment. The location of assessment—be it the school clinic, hospital residential program, etc.—will dictate how quickly and thoroughly this assessment is completed. The parents, probations officers, courts, schools, and others can expect too much too soon and pressure the professional to rush to judgement and act precipitously.

The behaviors and emotional expressiveness of the parents and the teenager are usually rigid and constricted. The teen can be very resistant or too compliant. The parents can be embarrassed, hopeful, angry or pseudocompetent, mistrustful, and controlling. The assessor must guard against inflating his narcissism when the parents try to regard him as the next messiah; if not careful, he may push toward treatment without paying attention to the tasks at hand.

You must get as much data from multiple sources because the teen can be a poor historian. Specific CD interview devices, questionnaires, urine drug screens, and adherence to an abstinence contract can help one make a correct diagnosis. At this stage you are mobilizing the parents toward treatment more than the child. In order to mobilize the teen to worry about his chemical abuse, avoid judging and point out instead the discrepancies in the teen's argument that "there is nothing wrong." Empathize with this need for autonomy while pointing out how chemicals interfere with this need.

Look for leverage in the social field of the teenager because the parents may need it to coerce their child into treatment. Finally hold a meeting to present your findings to the parents and the teen.

III. Intervention Stage

The "intervention" is designed to interrupt the cycle of chemical dependency ♦ antisocial, asocial, and inappropriate behaviors ♦ family and social disruption (Gorski 1982a). You are precipitating a crisis which will motivate the teenager to realize the seriousness of his or her behavior, to agree to the first step in treatment, and to agree to a contract for treatment.

The "intervention" technique, first developed by Vernon Johnson, involves a meeting with the teen where the family and concerned others present in a loving and caring fashion the specific frightening, obnoxious, and endangering behaviors of the teen associated with chemical abuse. The teen is given the "choice" of seeking treatment (Wegscheider 1981).

This technique is especially helpful with very resistant teens and very helpless families who have "tried everything," including inpatient treatment. Be careful not to allow the session to turn into a verbal abuse forum. Professionals tend to overlook this stage assuming that the teen "knows" that he has an illness and is not in that much denial.

IV. Contract Stage

At this stage the patient realizes that his behavior has been painful and troublesome to the family. He is ready to comply with treatment. The parents begin to unite around setting limits and preparing a contract. They are trying to understand the difference between enabling and assuming guilt for their child's chemical abuse. The family is learning how to avoid the blame game and to become task oriented.

A specific contract is created to commit the family to treatment. The field of behavioral therapy has helped us understand how to create a contract. It is crucial to put the teen on the spot. Assume that he agrees that following some basic family rules and that entering treatment is a healthy step to take.

V. Detoxification/Withdrawal Stage

This stage is usually completed in an inpatient or residential setting. The impaired adolescent usually does not have the ego strengths to stay abstinent on an outpatient basis. He or she is usually sullen, volatile, depressed, and/or disorganized. It is very difficult to determine what behavior symptoms are due to therapeutic resistance or due to the physiological reaction to detoxification and withdrawal.

Drug and alcohol withdrawal signs, which are not as overt as those presented by adults, need to be monitored and managed. We can help the patient learn to tolerate discomfort of this stage through stress reduction techniques, education about detoxification and withdrawal symptoms, and immediate management of acute crises, i.e., when the patient acts as if "the world is going to end" because there is no more apple juice in the unit refrigerator. Interpret or "frame" for the family their teenager's behavior as withdrawal symptoms, treat the parental guilt of "abandoning the child to a hospital," and anticipate the teenager's desperate pleas for a "reprieve."

Those clinicians who are aware of the steps of AA may have noticed that these steps have not been mentioned yet: the patient is not ready in any way to deal with these steps seriously until the next stage, because he is too physically and emotionally uncomfortable and cognitively disorganized. This same restraint holds for the introduction of psychotherapy. Be patient and respect the progress made so far.

VI. Awareness Stage

This stage most commonly occurs at the time of inpatient hospitalization or early rehabilitation, and occasionally in a well-structured outpatient chemical dependency program. At this stage the teenager can face up to the first step of AA. He may recognize that he has a problem with illicit chemicals and has "family problems." The patient will still be furious at the parents for taking away his or her "freedom," but realizes that there are no other choices but to stay in the program. Some clinicians frequently mistake this seeming compliance for a commitment and an acceptance of treatment. They make inappropriate treatment plans, because of their over-identification with the teenager's need for autonomy and independence and because of their denial of the debilitating effects of chemicals on normal development. Be content with the face-saving adolescent who says, "O.K., I'll stay" — this statement reveals the compliance mixed with passive or active defiance, which is so typical of the awareness stage. The teen is gradually giving up his negative identity and his negative peer group affiliated with chemical abuse, but does so with a great amount of anxiety. This anxiety can present as defiance or overcompliance.

At this stage, parents experience increased relief coupled with impatience at the slowness of progress. They are cautiously dependent on the treatment team and the program. The most disturbed families will continue to enable the child to the point of displaying severe "symbiosis" and blurred ego boundaries with their child.

The tasks for the patient are as follows:

1. to begin a self-assessment of chemical dependency
2. to learn formally all about chemical dependency
3. to learn the effect of his/her behavior on others
4. to recognize the relationship of patterns of behavior and chemical abuse
5. to recognize the need for treatment
6. to learn the reality of the pathology of the "druggie" peer group
7. to regard education as positive
8. to cope with prolonged withdrawal symptoms
9. to accept the reality of concomitant psychiatric disorders
10. to begin to recognize dysphoric emotions
11. to rekindle a longing for one's family

The specific treatments for chemical dependency at this stage reflect and complement the first step of AA and other self-help groups. These treatments include drug and alcohol education, confrontation groups which focus on denial, formal AA/NA step study classes and self-help meetings, and lower level social skills groups.

Confrontation of denial and of negative image and identity should be direct but delivered in a brief and calm manner. This style of confrontation is urged in order to prevent the readily available and rigid defenses of the impaired adolescent from interfering with the message of the confrontation. Social skill groups will deal with the topics of trust, self-disclosure, making conversation, identifying feelings, and reducing stress. At the same time, the family is being formally educated about the illness of chemical dependency, is attending a self-help group, is beginning to accept the concept of powerlessness, and is learning about dysfunctional family roles and the "family trap" (Wegscheider 1981).

VII. Recovery Plan Stage

At this stage the teenager is confronted with the reality of his/her illness and its implications for seeking a new lifestyle, a positive identity, and a sober lifestyle. In any treatment facility, a written recovery plan is absolutely necessary for all concerned, because there are so many basic developmental tasks to be remembered. One must not forget that the patient is still impaired cognitively and cannot commit to what he cannot remember. You are creating a "safety net," i.e., a social network that can anticipate and treat any regressions before the patient falls too hard and begins to relapse. At the time of discharge from a facility, the adolescent's denial and grandiosity can be elicited by the confusing combination of the parent's limit setting, their new-found strength, and their enabling behaviors. This denial and grandiosity is further elicited by the anxiety-producing challenges of the real world just waiting out there for this newly abstinent man-child or woman-child.

Unfortunately the professional can be too optimistic and push the teen back into the same pathological environment from which he came. The teen is hopeful towards the future, but is still anxious and depressed about losing his negative identity, peer culture, and that ever-loving chemical high.

The family is also feeling more hope but worries for the worst and can infect the child with their feelings of helplessness. Some parents cannot tolerate their child's spending any more time in a program away from home, even if outpatient treatment is recommended and discharge is imminent. Then separation anxiety rules over the reality of the tasks of recovery.

At the recovery plan stage the second and third steps of AA are most relevant. These steps teach the teenager and the family to rely on others to stay healthy and sober. A higher power can help the teenager manage dysphoric feelings, chemical cravings, and interpersonal conflicts by binding his anxiety, promoting problem-solving, and providing hope. As the teenager begins to increase his trust in group process and to realize the seriousness of his chemical abuse, confrontation slowly shifts to a more intense and affectively laden style. Now the group can effectively confront a peer's denial, minimization of pathology, and negative identity in a direct manner.

The written recovery plan is indeed a higher power for the family. It is a contract that states specifically how the patient will schedule his or her time and what rules will be followed in the family.

The teenager will need to learn higher level social skills in order to cope with the anxiety over leaving the old lifestyle behind and to cope with the threatened loss of autonomy and "freedom" upon returning home or transferring to a residential facility. These social skills include problem-solving, giving and accepting negative and positive feedback, negotiating, and "saying no to drugs" and negative peers.

The parents learn to rely on an external structure of rules and a hierarchy of decision-making in order to cope with the challenges of recovery. They are just learning the difference between detachment from their child's chemical dependency and the need to set limits on their child as any well-functioning parents must do.

Unfortunately, we can be hard pressed to push the teen out of inpatient treatment before he has completed the above stated tasks. The professional who carries out and monitors the recovery plan after discharge from a program should not assume that in reality the teenager and the family have mastered this stage of recovery. The main tasks at this stage of recovery are to adhere to the recovery plan, to manage the teen's attempts to socialize with his "druggie" peers, and to treat his or her reluctance to associate with sober peers, continuing care programs and self-help groups.

VIII. Early Recovery Stage

The goals of early recovery are the following:

1. to manage staying sober and healthy day-by-day
2. to cope with the ups and downs of regular living
3. to prevent the creation of more problems
4. to prevent relapses while accepting without panic the possibility of relapses and crises
5. to accept sobriety as a way of life

The time for completing this recovery stage depends primarily on the number of problems which complicate recovery from chemical dependency (Gorski 1983). These problems include psychiatric disorders, learning disabilities, family problems, physical or sexual abuse, and so forth.

The adolescent can show marked emotional lability, fear of social situations, continued prolonged withdrawal symptoms, worsening psychiatric disorders, and difficulty coping with stress and peer pressure and applying appropriate social skills. Gorski (1983) warns of substitute addictions becoming prevalent at this stage. Adolescents may become addicted to work, sex, physically or legally risky situations, fighting, sports, cars, and even academics. Some of these activities may seem more appropriate than chemical abuse, but the teenager involves himself in them as a way of avoiding conflicts, dysphoric feelings, and the tasks of recovery. The clinician should warn his patient of the development of substitute addictions and of recurrent wishes of giving up and returning to the chemically dependent lifestyle. Recovering teenagers very commonly wish to test out alcohol and drugs "one more time to see if they are that bad." This is the time to help the teenager apply the learned social skills of problem-solving, of identification of feelings, and of stress reduction. This is also the time to introduce the concept and the skills of relapse prevention, which will be discussed below.

The family tends to panic when faced with the stresses of treatment, conflicts, and their child's mood lability. Every family member seems to be more needy but these needs can be disguised in the form of complaints, high expectations, and wishes to cut down on treatment, even when everything looks better.

There are a number of family tasks to be achieved. In this newly organized family, it is inevitable that more problems are created than solved. Expect the family to reduce treatment prematurely. The psychiatrist must not panic or resort to recommending psychotropic medications as first resort in order to deal with this imperfect situation. Stay calm and stick to the practical tasks at hand. Keep the family to the teenager's set daily schedule and to the recovery plan and update both of them regularly. Help the patient begin to tolerate anxiety, solve the little problems of life, and anticipate the teenager's urge to use chemicals when times are extremely rough or wonderful. The clinician must be actively looking for and confronting denial and avoidance of feelings and problems and conflicts. Be sure to meet with the patient's sponsor in order to foster cooperation and to keep the "safety net" alive. Help the family accept setting limits as the norm at this stage not to be loosened up until later on in recovery. Encourage the family to learn how to cooperate, work, and play together without conflicts erupting into rage. Put the family at ease by informing every member that mistrust of each other is normal at this recovery stage, should be tolerated, but will improve over time if everyone's behavior remains consistent. By improving the emotional bond between the teenager and the same sex parent, one is attending to the patient's need to form a primary identity. Finally, watch for and treat emerging psychiatric and chemical dependency problems in other family members.

IX. Middle Recovery Stage

Gorski has noted that in middle recovery, one will see a normal decrease in the hours of therapy and AA/NA/CA/CDA/Alanon, etc. (Gorski 1983). There is a concomitant increase in the teenager and family's committing themselves to other healthy activities. Everyone is learning to be more comfortable with dysphoric feelings and with conflict. The professional will be ready to say "welcome to becoming a real teenager!'' when he hears the teenager describe how overwhelming are the normal challenges of school, work, extra-curricular activities, romantic relationships, learning to drive, and so on. The patient is beginning to develop an identity which is positive. He needs help in facing the normal developmental challenges with optimism. Both the teen and the family are raising their self-esteem and confidence in trying to cope with problems. Everyone begins to believe that life's problems can be faced even if there are no immediate answers.

The recovering adolescent can panic, when he realizes that he is in fact acting healthy. He faces an identity crisis because he worries about keeping up this healthy state. The teenager has become more aware of his self and is ''suffering'' from the shock of being aware that he has a positive identity. This awareness is, however, so new that the teen fears that it is as evanescent as a chemical high. This crisis can lead to relapse if not predicted to the recovering adolescent.

Although the expected ''conversion'' process of spiritual recovery has taken place, the teenager will still regret that the thrills and the short-term gains of chemical use are no longer available. Boredom can be regarded as an albatross around the neck, rather than a normal occurrence in life, which can spur us to find something interesting to do in the world at large. It is difficult to determine at this stage when the teenager is regressing or progressing when he takes the first steps away from home and therapy, while still living at home.

One may also note the parents' panic and anxiety as their child begins the normal movement away from home and toward self-sufficiency. They may still try to treat the child with ''tough love'' when it no longer seems appropriate.

The tasks for the adolescent are as follows:

1. to learn how to balance the demands in one's life now that he is involved with school, work, friends, paramours, parents, etc.
2. to manage self-doubts
3. to plan ahead and therefore prevent problems from occurring

4. to keep faith with one's increasing inner controls, while maintaining a supportive network
5. to keep a recovery plan alive and to prevent premature abandonment of the plan
6. to deal with boredom, the need for thrills, and coping with being alone
7. to ward off substitute addictive behavior
8. to balance the need for challenges versus the fear of being overwhelmed
9. to focus on planning one's future including college, leaving home and letting go of the dependent role in the family.

By fulfilling these goals the patient has progressed from Step IV (making a searching and fearless moral inventory) to Step V (admitting to ourselves and a higher power the exact nature of our wrongs).

It is important to encourage the parents to refocus on their marriage, to reduce their watchful eye on the teenager, to cope with the "empty nest" syndrome and the issue of their child leaving home (Haley 1980), to treat any lingering resentments, to encourage forgiveness, and to keep active in their self-help group.

X. Later Recovery Stage

Unlike an adult, the adolescent begins to leave home during the early to middle phases of developing an identity and establishing intimate relationships. There is less emotional turmoil in the family and in the self. Noticing and managing relapse warning signs becomes second nature. He now has the psychic energy and emotional resources to focus attention towards helping others who are in need, because he is more confident of his coping skills and ability to manage his emotions and problems. The teenager is beginning to focus on treating his "defects of character," on altering these characterological problems, on making amends to others, and on spending more time helping others. In other words, he is now actively working on Steps VI through IX of AA. Patients with complicating psychiatric and family problems have worked through their denial of those problems and are focusing on underlying psychodynamics of acceptance of the reality of the problems. The need for treatment is not seen as a weakness but as a need to improve the quality of one's life. This is the time when psychodynamic psychotherapy can be effective, because a foundation of ego strengths has been built at the earlier stages of recovery. The patient is more confident in managing the dysphoria which will be elicited in psychotherapy. The parents will need help adjusting to their teenager shifting from the role of being "our child" to "our young adult."

Ironically, the adolescent may bow out of individual, group, and family therapy at the time when he or she seems most able to cope with ongoing clinical problems. The need to leave home (Haley 1980) and the need to test one's abilities in the "real world" override the need to solve one's intrapsychic problems. It may be best for the therapist to reframe and treat emerging problems as attempts to "leave home" in a successful fashion, to keep an open door for therapy in the future, to stay in touch with the patient, and to let go of the patient for the time being. The later recovering teenager needs to say "I'll come back when I really need some help—no offense!!!" and know that the elders will trust his or her autonomy.

XI. Maintenance Stage

At this stage our once impaired adolescent is emerging into young adulthood. He and his family are maintaining a dynamic recovery plan and know how to prevent relapses. As their social networks increase they are beginning to separate from treatment. They are focusing on the last Steps of AA, where one's presence inspires hope to those recovering people in the earlier stages of recovery. These families and adolescents can provide a powerful emotional influence on the "newcomers" to chemical dependency programs.

Case Examples

#1: C.M. is a 17-year-old white young man who has been living with his divorced mother. Both his mother and father are recovering alcoholics. He has abused cocaine, PCP, marijuana, and alcohol and dealt drugs. He realized that he had a problem with drug abuse and began going to AA. He also enrolled in a public school designed for chemically dependent teens and attended a three day a week outpatient chemical dependency program. In addition he saw a therapist weekly to deal with his new found recovery. He denied any symptoms of affective or cognitive disorder. He presented as a very bright charming young man who isolated his affect. The therapist noticed the urge to fall asleep during repeated sessions with his patient. One month into treatment C.M. stated a desire to stay sober and requested a prescription of disulfiram. Two months after initiating treatment, he ran away from home. He returned after several days stating that he had run away to get away from drug-using peers. Shortly thereafter he was expelled from the outpatient program for using marijuana. One month later he was expelled from the school for stealing school property. He was then admitted into a residential chemical dependency program under order of the courts. After a month of detoxification C.M. confessed to depressive moods and suicidal ideation. He was discharged from the residential facility to a hospital when he began carving on his arm. In the hospital he attempted to hang himself. He was treated with Lithium for mood swings and with a small dose of Prolixin for suspiciousness. He was then transferred to an adolescent residential facility for emotional disturbances and chemical dependency, even though he still was trying to convince parents and staff that he could manage at home.

Comment: Early in treatment this youngster attempted to present a guise of progressing quickly through the crisis to the recovery plan stage of recovery. Actually he was in a perpetual, if silent and guarded, stage of crisis. His diagnoses are polysubstance dependence, major depressive episode and conduct disorder, group type, characterized with borderline and narcissistic traits. The somnolence in a clinician can be a warning sign of denial in both the clinician and the patient, as well as an indication of severe characterologic pathology in the patient.

#2: T.K. is a now 19-year-old white single male who presented at the crisis stage at age 15 because of heavy alcohol, LSD, and marijuana use. He was living with his divorced mother, who had a middle-level administrative job. He was verbally abusive toward his mother who, he thought, was only invested in controlling him. He viewed his father, who lived in another state, as someone who was never available for him. For three months, T.K. was an inpatient in a unit designed for psychiatrically impaired/chemically dependent adolescents. He was tested in the superior range of intelligence, but had many avoidant traits. His diagnoses were avoidant disorder and polysubstance dependence. He proceeded to put little investment in the program in spite of numerous interventions. He was then transferred to a residential chemical dependency program, but he ran away after one week because "I can stay sober at home."

He was enrolled in a therapeutic day school and in an afterschool drug and alcohol program. Psychotherapy continued but remained on a superficial level, although he addressed his social shyness and low esteem. His isolated affect and emotional underresponsiveness continued. He did achieve excellent marks in school, kept a steady job and went to AA meetings. He was discharged from the continuing care program two weeks before his high school graduation.

He was not at the middle stage of recovery in spite of his progress. At this time he and an old friend dropped a few tabs of LSD. His friend proceeded to destroy cars in the neighborhood and was apprehended by the police. T.K. was caught with acid on his hands and had to confess. He had "slipped" using marijuana, LSD, and alcohol on several occasions over the past year. He kept this hidden well and had clean random drug urine tests. The only aberrant behavior was sporadic absences and tardiness over the year.

The school staff wanted immediate expulsion but consulted with the therapist who had kept in frequent contact with them over the year. The therapist suggested that expulsion would only look like punishment unless T.K. were first put to a test—after all, he had shown considerable progress over the year and teenagers do slip. His mettle would be tested by putting him through a living example of the first five steps of AA and by coercing him to overcome his tendency to withdraw, as follows:

1. he was required to confess to his peers all of his underhanded and chemical abusing behavior over the past year, to the satisfaction of his peers
2. he would have to attend AA/NA meetings by contract
3. he would face the confrontation of his peers regarding his defects
4. he would have to make amends to the school by a symbolic gesture on his own time and money.

After one week of fear, trepidation, apprehension, anxiety, etc., he fulfilled all of these goals, including his planning and coordinating the food concession at the annual school carnival. He was then allowed to graduate with his class.

Soon after graduation, he found an AA sponsor and attended meetings at least five days per week. After three months he was leading meetings and providing refreshments for the meetings. He found a girlfriend. In psychotherapy he started to identify and to learn how to manage his depression, social anxiety, and problems with his girlfriend and his mother. He was clearly in the early stage of recovery, as he had mastered the major tasks of the recovery plan stage. He became more cooperative at home and started attending a local community college, while keeping his full time job. He severed his relationship with his old drug using friend.

He is still resistant about facing the absence of his father, but has not allowed this issue to disrupt his recovery plan. He is now coping with the demands of paying bills, attending classes and passing tests, maintaining his car, spending time with his girlfriend, working daily, taking music lessons, and going to AA and NA. He knows that he can manage these demands but is still learning not to panic about his proficiency. He is clearly in the middle stage of recovery.

RELAPSE PREVENTION

The word "prevention" can mistakenly promise answers to a problem which in reality can be managed but never solved. The expert regards "relapse prevention" an integration of knowledge, skill, and clinical experience, self-actualization and creativity. The novice tends to seek out the "right technique." Ongoing supervision is necessary in order to season the novice into a professional.

Gorski (1982a, b, 1983) provides the starting point for approaching relapse prevention, because of his reliance on a comprehensive bio-psycho-social model. He contends that relapse is a process in the individual which can lead to a variety of disturbances including resumption of chemical abuse. He observes that relapse begins when the individual undergoes stress and is unable to manage the "post-acute withdrawal syndrome." This syndrome represents the presence of acute stress sensitivity and the deterioration in the functions of thinking, feeling, and memory. When the relapse syndrome emerges, the alcoholic experiences a progression of ten relapse phases. These phases are return of denial, avoidance and defensive behavior, crisis building, immobilization, confusion and overreaction, depression, behavioral loss of control, recognition of loss of control, option reduction, and the acute relapse episode. There are thirty-seven symptoms distributed under these ten phases. The acute relapse episode can be a crisis of total "degeneration," chemical abuse, psychiatric disorders, medical disorders, "physical exhaustion," suicidal behavior, "accidental proneness," and/or "disruption of social structures." This formulation is very helpful in understanding relapse but has drawbacks for the adolescent. First, there is no data available to show that these phases show the same progression in the teenager. In this author's experience with over two hundred teenagers, these phases and symptoms occur but randomly. Second, the language used in his descriptions can be extremely abstract for many teens, especially learning disabled ones. Third, few teens in early to middle recovery seem to have the attention span or interest to undergo a thorough study of these phases in a methodical manner. One can better use a methodical approach in a group format but over a long period of time in small doses.

THE TECHNIQUE OF RELAPSE TREATMENT AND PREVENTION

This author recommends a different therapeutic strategy with the relapsing adolescent in a group or individual session. This approach requires the professional to consider eight areas for assessing relapse. A gestalt is then formed out of consideration of these areas and a treatment plan is created. The clinical experience and creativity of the therapist are crucial to this approach. Throughout this process one is encouraging the teen to share his or her thoughts and feelings and to accept help in a healthy and face-saving way that does not threaten one's autonomy.

I. Identification of the problem. The patient is in trouble and knows it on some level. Details of events leading up to the problem are required. A simple sentence is needed to define the problem.

II. Stage of recovery. The stage of recovery of the teen and the tasks not yet mastered that contributed to the problem are identified.

III. Identification of post-acute withdrawal or stress symptom. An acute symptom relating to the emotions, thinking, and memory are outlined. It becomes apparent that the patient can not solve the problem until his or her mental and emotional abilities are handy.

IV. Assessment of the "social field." With the adolescent one must always evaluate the present "social field" of home, school, friends, treatment programs, extracurricular programs, work. A clinician can conduct the most creative therapy with the patient but a chaotic and enabling environment can undo any progress attained in a treatment session.

V. Assessment of diagnosis. Many patients have a psychiatric diagnosis, which can complicate the recovery process (Gorski 1983). The psychiatric symptoms must be treated or managed relevant to the stage of recovery. For example a clinically depressed young man in early recovery, whose mother died in his latency years, may need to be treated for his depressed mood, for his sleep disorder, and for his agitation on the anniversary of his mother's death, but may not be ready to deal with the loss of his mother other than to recognize that he honors her by continuing his recovery plan.

VI. Assessment of learning potential. One must determine if the patient is learning disabled, is a chronic underachiever, or is impaired secondary to chronic chemical abuse and/or "underuse" of his or her intellect. This factor can affect the ability of the patient to benefit from a therapeutic intervention, because it may be difficult to process the information discussed in treatment.

VII. Assessment of temperament. Chess and Thomas (1986) have described specific temperaments that can affect healthy functioning. A poor fit between the patient's temperament and his environment can promote emotional, behavioral, thinking, and relational disorders.

VIII. Identify the primary sign of relapse. Table I (see Appendix) describes "Signs of Relapse." These signs are written in the first person under the five categories of emotional, thinking, behavioral, relating, and commitment to treatment "warning signs." After checking off the most prevalent signs, the teen rank orders them and then picks one symptom on which to concentrate. Table II (see Appendix) is a checklist of signs of relapse for the professional. In crisis it is more important and time saving for the professional to identify the warning sign. Many early recovering teenagers have neither the attention span nor the patience to deal with an extensive checklist.

Once these eight areas are delineated, it is possible to proceed in the following two areas:

I. Exploration of the past, present, and future. Past, recent, and future situations are explored where this symptom has been present. In exploring the past, present, and future, role-playing, imagining, problem-solving and other active techniques are used to help the teen cope with the relapse sign and the present problem. As an outcome of the process the teenager will pick three options he can adopt if the warning sign appears in the future. Learning the task of a specific recovery stage may be the primary focus. Medication or a specific form of psychotherapy may be necessary to allow the process of recovery to continue.

II. Additional family, school, and program interventions. A "systems" orientation is necessary. One must pinpoint the strengths and weaknesses of the adolescent's social field and intervene to allow the social field to promote rather than sabotage his or her efforts to recover.

Example:

> E.M. is a 15-year-old white male who was recently discharged from an inpatient program that integrates chemical dependency and psychiatric treatments. He is a recovering polysubstance user, living with his mother, father and two older sisters. He is attending a private school, a continuing care outpatient chemical dependency program, and individual and family therapy. Two months after discharge he told the therapist that his parents were furious with him because he missed a school day. He had forgotten his money that day. He did not want to hassle his friends to borrow money again or to telephone his parents at their work. Therefore he went home without signing out from school, found some money and then waited forty-five minutes for a bus to arrive. He then realized

that it was too late to return to school and informed the school. He missed an important quiz at school but it was not known whether he had studied for the quiz. His father swore that he had handed his son money for lunch and the bus ride home. After a highly emotional argument, his parents informed him that he could not go out that night. He proceeded to defy them by walking out of the house. His parents then upped the ante, telling him they would not sign for his drivers learning permit until after the school winter vacation. The father wanted to send him to boarding school while the mother believed that her son had never been happier than at his school.

According to the strategy process described above the following occurred:

I. The *PROBLEM* was defined as his being understandably irresponsible, whether it was because he misplaced the money or wanted to miss the test. If the problem stemmed from his continuing to abuse chemicals, then any intervention would ultimately fail; but for one slip, he seemed to be staying sober.

II. He was in the early *STAGE OF RECOVERY*. He was no longer abusing drugs but had slipped by having two beers two weeks ago. Random drug urine tests were negative. He was still emotionally labile and continued to create ten problems as he proceeded to solve a single problem. He had little confidence that he could solve the simplest of problems.

III. He suffered from the *STRESS SYMPTOMS* of poor memory and concentration, and emotional under- and over-responsiveness.

IV. With regards to his *SOCIAL FIELD*, his school set consistent limits. His treatment program was not aware of the slip. His parents continued to set too high expectations for his stage of recovery. He regarded their remarks as too negative in tone even though he was beginning to improve in his behavior and performance at school and at home.

V. His psychiatric *DIAGNOSIS* was major depressive disorder, fulfilling the DSMIII-R criteria (APA 1987), even after a sufficient period of detoxification. Historically, he had always taken a back seat to his sisters who had demanded a great amount of attention because of their own severe developmental disorders. As a child he coped by being "the good little boy" who always pleased his parents. However, he considered his father to be too demanding and emotionally distant and his mother to be too critical and intrusive.

VI. His *LEARNING POTENTIAL* was chronically above his actual performance. He tended to prefer nonverbal forms of learning such as playing a guitar. When asked how he made certain choices in this crisis, he would begin by responding, "I don't know."

VII. His *TEMPERAMENT* was slow-to-warm-up with low activity levels. His father and mother tended to pressure him immediately without time for adjustment and would then proceed to lecture or moralize while handing out a consequence.

VIII. His *PRIMARY SIGN OF RELAPSE* was his avoidance of future thinking.

As a result of this formulation the following was done:

I. The *PAST AND PRESENT* were combined because the crisis had not been solved. He was seen alone and with his parents. Everyone was educated to understand the dynamics of his stage of recovery and to understand that he was irresponsible because he still was a novice at problem-solving. Whenever he responded with an "I don't know," the therapist countered with "come on, think!!!" and with a scheme for problem-solving. The family then proceeded to resolve this crisis. He accepted his punishment regarding the license and stayed in that night. The parents realized that their moralizing and lecturing made matters worse. Furthermore they realized that pressuring him with their high expectations and raising the emotional tone of arguments did not facilitate problem-solving. The *FUTURE* was managed by helping the patient realize that he can simply solve his problem by being more compulsive about carrying his money in the morning, signing out from school, and cooling off in his room before becoming defiant. Before the parents entered the room he practiced what he would say to his parents. The meeting proceeded with a blowup. The parents were praised by realizing that they could up the ante. They were instructed to make a list of ten consequences they could set when he was defiant. They also realized that restricting the use of the guitar should only be used for the most serious of grievances, because guitar playing was one of the only outlets he had for calming himself down.

II. The *SOCIAL FIELD* was treated in the family therapy above. In addition the chemical dependency program was notified that he had slipped. His slips were discussed in the program's peer group therapy.

SUMMARY

The above case studies illustrate the need to attend to the issues in addition to chemical dependency that can complicate successful recovery. One must constantly reassess the stage of recovery, signs of relapse, and completion of tasks. This integrative approach to assessment and treatment holds the promise of addressing effectively the chronic nature of adolescent chemical dependency. This paper is also a call for further research into the dynamics of adolescent recovery and relapse.

BIBLIOGRAPHY

American Psychiatric Association (APA). *Diagnostic and Statistical Manual of Mental Disorders*. Third Edition, Revised. Washington DC: American Psychiatric Association, 1987.

Brown, Stephanie. *Treating the Alcoholic: A Developmental Model of Recovery*. New York: John Wiley and Sons, 1985.

Chess, Stella and Thomas, Alexander. *Temperament in Clinical Practice*. New York: The Guilford Press, 1986.

Gorski, Terrence. "The Developmental Model of Recovery, Counseling for Relapse Prevention". Audio tapes. Indianapolis: Access. (317) 547-8273, 1983.

Gorski, Terrence. *Counseling for Relapse Prevention*. Independence, MO: Independence Press, 1982a.

Gorski, Terrence. *Learning to Live Again: A Guide to Recovery From Addiction and Drug Dependence*. Independence, MO: Independence Press, 1982b.

Haley, Jay. *Leaving Home: The Therapy of Disturbed Young People*. New York: McGraw-Hill, 1980.

Hendren, Robert Lee. "Adolescent Alcoholism and Substance Abuse", Chapter 21, Section 4, Adolescent Psychiatry. *The American Psychiatric Association Annual Review*. Volume 5, Edited by Frances and Hales. Washington DC: APA Press, 1986.

Kaufman, Edward. "Adolescent Substance Abusers and Family therapy", Chapter 15. *Handbook of Adolescents and Family Therapy.* Edited by Mirkin and Coman. New York: Gardner Press, 1985.

Rogers, Peter D. (ed.). "Chemical Dependency", *The Pediatric Clinics of North America.* 34:2, 275-537, Philadelphia: W.B. Saunders, April 1987.

Schwartz, Richard, Cohen, Peter, and Bair, Glenn. "Identifying and Coping with a Drug-Using Adolescent: Some Guidelines for Pediatricians and parents". *Pediatric Review,* 1985.

Wegscheider, Sharon. *Another Chance: Hope and Health for the Alcoholic Family.* Palo Alto, CA: Science and Behavior Books, 1981.

ADDITIONAL SUGGESTED RESOURCES

Brader, Thomas E. and Forrest, Gary G. *Alcoholism and Substance Abuse: Strategies for Clinical Intervention.* New York: The Free Press, 1985.

Cummings, Claudette, Gordon, Judith R., and Allen, Marlatt G. "Relapse: Prevention and Prediction", Chapter 8. *The Addictive Behaviors.* Ed. by William R. Millar. Oxford: Pergammon Press.

Dupont, Robert L. *Getting Tough on Gateway Drugs: A Guide for the Family.* Washington DC: American Psychiatric Press, 1984.

Harticollis, Pitsa-Calliope. "Personality Characteristics in Adolescent Problem Drinkers". *Journal of the American Academy of Child Psychiatry* 21, 4: 348-353, 1982.

Hellman, Jesse. "Alcohol Abuse and the Borderline Patient". *Psychiatry* 44: 307-317, 1984.

Kandel, Denise. "Epidemiological and Psychosocial Perspectives on Adolescent Drug Use". *Journal of American Academy of Child Psychiatry* 21:4, 328-347, 1982.

APPENDIX

TABLE I

SIGNS OF RELAPSE
A CHECKLIST FOR PROFESSIONALS

Relapse can be viewed in the teenager according to five major areas as follows: emotional disorders, thinking disorders, behaviorial disorders, relating disorders, and disorders in commitment to a recovery program.

I. Emotional Disorders

    A. Avoidance of expressing feelings following revelation of an emotional experience, stressful incidences, in past or present: evidenced by isolated affect, reaction formation, averted eyes, staring or inexpressive, blank eyes, speech (monotone, mournful, repeated tone pattern).
    B. Giddiness: rapid speech, smiling.
    C. Depression: mood; can be accompanied by poor sleep or too much sleep, poor appetite or overeating, poor concentration, suicidal thoughts and plans, helplessness, hopelessness, and worthlessness.
    D. Rage.
    E. Loneliness.
    F. Anxiety: low frustration tolerance, shaking, constricted affect.
    G. Fear: evidenced by rapid speech, awfulizing, giving up, bodily stiffness, widened eyes.
    H. Self-pity/low self-esteem: as evidenced by "no one appreciates what I'm doing" or "I'm here for myself".

II. Thinking Disorders

    A. Can't make obvious insights.
    B. Everything is "ok" — i.e.global denial.
    C. All or nothing thinking.
    D. Too "one day at a time" — avoids future thinking, i.e., what I can do today about the future, what do I want?
    E. Magical thinking, daydreaming, wishful thinking, asking for medication.
    F. Disorganized thinking: evidenced by "confusion", looseness of thoughts, flight of ideas, rapid shifts of topic.
    G. Reliance on oversimplistic solutions.
    H. Overgeneralizations/awfulizing.
    I. Avoidance as evidenced by the following: minimizing, denial, recognizing avoidance later on, intellectualization.
    J. Grandiosity.
    K. Homocidal thoughts.
    L. Suicidal thoughts and thoughts of violence.

III. Behavior Disorders

A. Avoidance: as evidenced by joking, goofing off, punchiness, silliness; doesn't initiate bringing up of problems; changes topics; switching ("Well, you do it too").
B. Impulsivity: tends to act before stopping, looking, listening, or thinking; gives up easily.
C. Disorganized: as evidenced by poor planning for future, where plans fail, where details are overlooked or forgotten; the more "holes in the dike" phenomenon; haphazard schedule (inconsistent in carrying out schedule and vague about commitments).
D. Hostility
   a. Overt: as evidenced by violence (against property or persons); argumentative, especially at times of stress, transition, discharge, limit setting; picks fights; sarcasm; resentments (long-lived); insults in putting down authority; argues (regarding rules, school work, chores, etc.).
   b. Covert: passive-aggressive behavior.
E. School/work (as evidenced by truancy, absenteeism, minimizing the importance of attendance and performance, underachieving, overachieving, irratic performance and inconsistent performance, changing jobs or schools frequently, suspensions or firings).
F. Homocidal behavior.
G. Suicidal behavior.
H. Accident-prone behavior.
I. Medical illnesses.
J. Beginning to drink or use drugs.

IV. Relating Disorders

A. Assumes the therapist's role: heavy involvement in a group, poor self disclosure in the group.
B. Outcast/scapegoat.
C. Socially awkward.
D. Practical joker or goof-off.
E. Emotionally withdrawn.
F. Changes friends or abandoning of them.
G. Rejects help: e.g. "Yes . . . but . . ." or "You don't understand . . ." or use of profanity as a threat.
H. Obsequiousness.
I. Fights consistently with close friends, parents, teachers, mentors, sponsors, therapists — all without resolution.
J. Avoidance most evident in assuming the therapist's role, joking, socially withdrawn behavior, rejecting help, obsequiousness, fighting consistently, unholy alliances, negative contracts with peers, switching, superiority/inferiority (overvaluing or undervaluing).

K. Avoids confronting others about obvious addictive behaviors.
L. Great difficulty in finding tasks, work projects, recreation, in common with parents and siblings.

V. Disorder in Commitment to Recovery Program

A. Denial: "I'll never drink again" or "selective user", i.e. "I only have a problem with . . .".
B. Avoidance: as evidenced by late, irregular or no attendance; forgets "homework"; stalling (e.g. getting a sponsor); makes fake commitment to contract; working the other person's program.
C. Borderline commitment
  a. Spends time with "druggie friends".
  b. Mentions chemicals at social events, job, school, "But I didn't use any".
  c. Understated stories about possible parent's/peer substance abuse are later learned to be active abuse.
  d. Performs well in one context and poorly in another.
  e. Great gains and regressions.
  f. Parents call the therapist to cut down treatment? Too costly! Or increase treatment?
D. Defiance:
  a. Active: "Make me" or "I won't".
  b. Passive: "I won't make trouble".
E. Compliance:
  a. Active: The adolescent seems too good to be true or acts like a treatment robot.
  b. Passive: "I'll go along with treatment" or "When do I go home and get out?".

TABLE II

SIGNS OF RELAPSE
A CHECKLIST FOR TEENAGERS

Once a person has made the commitment to stay sober he or she can still have problems coping with feelings, thinking, behavior, relating to people, and keeping a commitment to treatment. These are warning signs that you may be getting closer to thinking about your taking that first drink or use of a drug. If you can know the warning signs, then you can make a plan of action to keep yourself feeling healthy and make sure that matters don't get worse. Please make a check by any statements that apply to you, even if you only experience them once in awhile, sometimes, or all the time. Also put a check by any that are of interest to you or that you think might happen to you at some time.

Emotional Warning Signs

Avoiding

_____ 1. I try to avoid feeling some of the feelings described below and pretend I'm ok:

I have tried to avoid feeling (circle): sad, angry, happy, excited, disappointed, afraid, nervous, other _____.

Depression

_____ 2. I get depressed:

When I get too depressed (circle): I sleep too little or too much, I eat too little or too much, I can't concentrate, I feel helpless or hopeless, I feel like dying.

Going out of Control

_____ 3. I lose my temper easily.

a. I get too wound up and can't settle down (feeling hyper or goofy or jumpy).

Loneliness

_____ 4. I feel lonely in a crowd of people.

Frustration

_____ 5. I can't stand waiting for something I want.

Self Pity

_____ 6. Sometimes I think no one appreciates what I do.

a. I feel sorry for myself.

Self Righteousness

_____ 7. I'm here for myself now; I don't need anyone's help; you can't help me.

Low Self-Esteem

_____ 8. I worry that no one likes me; I worry I can't face the challenges in life.

Boredom

_____ 9. I can't stand being bored.

Thinking Warning Signs

Insight

_____ 1. Sometimes I don't understand why I act the way I do; sometimes everyone else understands better than me.

Denial

_____ 2. Sometimes I think "everything is ok" when nothing is going well.

All or Nothing Thinking

_____ 3. There is no in-between. I am happy or sad, up or down, bored or interested, etc. I have to fight or give up.

Wishful Thinking
_____ 4. I wish for my life to get better in one day. I daydream. I wish there was a pill to help me think, feel, behave and relate to others better.

Disorganized
_____ 5. I get confused. Sometimes I get lost in my thoughts. I change topics a lot and then lose the point of what I'm saying.

Oversimplistic
_____ 6. I can't stand an unsolved problem. I'll try a solution even if I know it won't work. I'll give advice even though it won't work.

Overgeneralizing/Awfulizing
_____ 7. "Sometimes everything seems awful". "I'll never do well". "Things won't work out well for me".

Avoiding
_____ 8. Sometimes I don't like to think about my problems. I know I can make a big problem look like it is nothing at all.

Grandiose
_____ 9. Sometimes I think I'm better than anyone and I'll be famous, even when I'm accomplishing nothing.

Homocidal
_____ 10. Sometimes I get so mad I feel like killing someone.

Suicidal
_____ 11. Sometimes I think I'd be better off dead.
_____   a. Sometimes I'd like to disappear from the world for awhile and come back later.
_____   b. Sometimes I think about killing myself.

Behavior Warning Signs

Avoiding
_____ 1. I goof, joke around, or act silly when something serious is going on.
_____ 2. I don't talk about problems with someone who could help me.
_____ 3. I change the subject when something makes me nervous.
_____ 4. If someone confronts me, I say to myself or to them "Well, you do it too."
_____ 5. I put off things I should do.

Impulsiveness
_____ 6. I act before I stop, before I look, before I listen, before I think (circle any of them).
_____ 7. I create more problems for myself than I solve.
_____ 8. I give up easily when faced with a challenge.

Disorganized
_____ 9. I have difficulty planning for the future.
_____ 10. My plans fail even when I try hard to succeed.

_____ 11. I can forget to remember important details in my plans.
_____ 12. I don't carry out my daily schedule in a consistent way.
_____ 13. I don't do what I promise I'll do for someone.

Hostility

_____ 14. When I'm angry, I hit people or threaten them.
_____ 15. When I'm angry, I destroy things around me.
_____ 16. When I am under pressure, I argue with my family, friends, teachers, etc.
_____ 17. I like to pick fights.
_____ 18. I can be really sarcastic and put other people down.
_____ 19. When I am angry with adults, I put them down or insult them or make them feel stupid.
_____ 20. Rules, homework, and chores are usually stupid and get me really angry.
_____ 21. When I am angry at people, I don't talk to them.
_____ 22. When I am told to do something, I'll say that I'll do it, but I really won't.
_____ 23. I can be too stubborn.

School/Work

_____ 24. I still skip school, miss work (circle any of them).
_____ 25. Doing well or graduating from school isn't that important.
_____ 26. I could be a really good student, but I'm not.
_____ 27. I only do well in some of the important school subjects.
_____ 28. I've been suspended or expelled from school, fired from my job.

Homocidal Thoughts

_____ 29. I've gotten close to killing someone.

Suicidal Thoughts

_____ 30. I've gotten close to killing myself.

Drug and Alcohol Ideation

_____ 31. Sometimes I think about using drugs or alcohol again and think that I won't have any problems if I do.

Drug and Alcohol Use

_____ 32. I've come close or used chemicals again.

Relating Warning Signs

"Being a Therapist"

_____ 1. I try to help others but they don't help me and they don't know my problems.

Scapegoat/Outcast

_____ 2. I don't think people like me, and my feelings get hurt by them.

Feeling Awkward

_____ 3. I don't know how to act around people my own age. I feel awkward.

Joking

_____ 4. I play a lot of practical jokes on people. I like to make people laugh even when it's not the right time to do so.

Withdrawing

_____ 5. I prefer to stay away from people and spend time alone.

Social Problems

_____ 6. I don't keep friends or I drop them quickly.

Rejecting

_____ 7. I don't want people's help. I get angry if they try to help me.

Obsequious

_____ 8. I'm a people pleaser, even when I don't want to be.

Combative

_____ 9. I fight with parents, siblings, friends, teachers, and we don't agree usually.

Negative Contracts

_____ 10. I get into trouble with my friends. Sometimes they start it, sometimes I do.

Acting Superior

_____ 11. I act like I'm better than a lot of people, even when I don't want to.

Acting Inferior

_____ 12. I act like I'm not as good as other people, even when I don't want to.

Avoiding Unpleasantness

_____ 13. If a peer, parent, or sibling does something really wrong and I think that they will be angry with me if I tell them, I won't tell him or her.

Attitude to Authority

_____ 14. There is no way you can reason with authority; they just want power and to put you down.

Making Attachments

_____ 15. Sometimes I get close to a person and then pull back quickly.

_____ 16. I can't find anything to do in common with my mother, father, or siblings. I don't know how to spend time with them.

Apologizing

_____ 17. I won't say sorry to someone even when I think I should.

Commitment to Treatment Warning Signs

Denial

_____ 1. I believe I'll never drink or use drugs again.

_____ 2. I only have a problem with alcohol or some drugs. I can use other ones.

Avoidance

_____ 3. I can be late to appointment meetings.

_____ 4. I miss appointment meetings.

_____ 5. I don't go to therapy or meetings all the time.

_____ 6. I forget to try the advice of my sponsor, therapist, or peers.

_____ 7. I don't follow the advice of my sponsor, therapist, or AA/NA peers right away.

_____ 8. I spend more time dealing or thinking about other people's sobriety than my own.

Borderline Commitment

_____ 9. I "sort of" agree to make a commitment to treatment.

_____ 10. I still spend time with friends who use alcohol or drugs.

_____ 11. I still hang around places where there are drugs or alcohol available.

_____ 12. I don't use any.

_____ 13. I fool myself into believing that some people I know don't have a problem with drugs or alcohol.

_____ 14. I can do well in AA/NA or in therapy with my peers, but I don't do well with all of them at the same time.

_____ 15. I go up and down in making progress.

_____ 16. I try to get my parents to let me cut down or stop AA/NA therapy.

_____ 17. I still don't know if I want to stay sober.

Defiance

_____ 18. People try to make me stay straight and I don't like it.

_____ 19. I won't stay straight if I don't want to.

_____ 20. I'll go along with AA/NA/treatment until I'm old enough. Then I'll do what I want to do.

_____ 21. I want to know when I can get out of going to AA/NA and when I can get out of treatment.

© Peter R. Cohen, M.D. 1988

The Chemically Dependent Adolescent: Issues with Ethnic and Cultural Minorities

Eileen Smith Sweet, PhD

In many broad aspects, adolescents everywhere resemble each other in their joys and sorrows. In many areas, however, chemically dependent teen-agers from ethnic and cultural minorities are significantly different from their majority peers. They are obviously different in cultural background. They are also different though not so obviously, in life experiences, values, educational background, vocational and life goals, use and choice of drugs and alcohol, responses to intervention and treatment, and quality of family participation in their treatment and recovery. This paper attempts to delineate these differences, both strengths and weaknesses, in an effort to help the alcohol and drug counselor and mental health provider furnish the best possible treatment for these adolescents and their families.

Adolescence is an important stage of development in which teen-agers must develop autonomy and responsibility and at the same time retain the structure and support of their family. It is normal for adolescents to be in frequent conflict with other family members as they carry out this very difficult but necessary rite of passage (Erickson, 1963). This normal level of difficulty is magnified many times, however, by the additional stresses placed on minority youngsters.

Eileen Smith Sweet is Assistant Professor at Montclair State College, Upper Montclair, NJ and is in private practice in Bogota, NJ.

STRESSES UNIQUE TO THE EXPERIENCE
OF THE MINORITY TEEN-AGER

The lives of adolescents who are part of an ethnic or cultural minority group frequently are strongly influenced by the social ramifications of being dependent on federal aid programs. The bureaucracy which has grown up around the administration of these programs has been humiliating and demeaning to many poor people, and is often perceived as cold and uncaring by the recipients of these benefits. The large urban centers which were the habitat of many minority members have been decimated by the success of the middle class and presently for the most part host only the very poor, very disadvantaged underclass (Wilson, 1987). Consequently education for these youngsters is substandard.

Poverty and disadvantage have fractured families, placing an additional strain on the adult in charge (Miller et al., 1982). Many single parents in these cultural subgroups are very loving and caring and work heroically to do a good job of parenting. One person alone coping with poverty, joblessness and substandard housing and trying to do the work of two parents creates enormous stress however, for the children as well as the adults in these families.

Many youngsters from a minority background perceive the members of the mainstream as rejecting. Consequently they feel different, isolated and unappreciated (Chun et al., 1983). Language is frequently another barrier, whether it is a foreign language spoken in the home, or rather another style of English. It can often make general communication, especially in academics, very difficult, and also make it difficult to make a bond with the helping personnel from the mainstream. All of these factors either add to the already high stress level of normal adolescence, or make it difficult to seek and accept help once problems are recognized.

On the other hand, some of the characteristics of different minority group members facilitate the growth and development of their members, or aid in the recovery process once a problem has been addressed. Many members of these cultural sub-groups are nourished and supported by a deeper and more powerful religious faith than their majority member counterparts. They frequently take great pride in their cultural heritage and supply this to the children as a bulwark in adversity (Clark, 1980).

THE IMPORTANCE OF PREVENTATIVE EDUCATION

Preventative drug and alcohol education is important for all young people, but when working with a minority community, the approach must be innovative. The typical suburban PTA seminar on prevention would be largely ignored by minorities, who because they are often overburdened and overstressed, do not attend routine school functions in large numbers. The approach for an educational program must be made through important community leaders whom the community perceives as representing their own views, and the emphasis must be on careful research to find people to whom they will listen. In a recent educational program in a large urban community, local government officials, business leaders, law enforcement personnel, hospital, clinic and local school staff, university faculty members and religious leaders were important traditional leaders in the planning. Additional less traditional leaders were nominated by people from the community and included a faith healer, a community aide and a housing program chairperson.

The manner of planning educational programs is important. It cannot be emphasized enough that mobility and motivation are continual problems. The programs must be presented as being effectively helpful in people's present lives and must be given in easy to reach locations to which most people can walk. It is a case again of being flexible and nontraditional, and willing to bring the services to where they are needed. A particularly apt setting for a series of educational presentations, for example, would be the elementary schools, since there is one within walking distance of each member of the community.

A powerful source of inspiration for young people are programs run by colleges, high schools and professional associations which introduce children to successful members of the community. They provide an alternative model for children to the neighborhood drug pusher or pimp. These people may come from the highly successful professional class, such as business executives, physicians, lawyers and accountants. An even stronger message can be given by industrious members of the working class and lower middle class such as the apartment custodian, hospital aide or local store-keeper. It is important for these people to tell youngsters their story honestly and cite those factors which helped them avoid chemical addiction, finish their education and training, and go on to lead successful lives. It is interesting to note that in the latest research on "invulnerable" children (Honig, 1986)—those unusual youngsters who grow into responsible and well-balanced adults, despite having grown up in chaotic homes—each successful adult told of an important person in his life—a school staff member, a teacher, a nurse, a relative or a neighbor, and in some instances, someone whom they had heard speak only once.

In many minority milieus, the concept of a preventative program for alcohol and other drug abuse is greeted with disapproval. Many families fear this type of program as a potential source of entrapment for their youngsters who may have recently begun to experiment with illicit drug use. It is particularly important therefore, that a chemical dependency prevention and education program be part of a total wellness approach, where the central theme is a happier and better functioning person, and where the prevention of drug and alcohol abuse is only a part of a much larger aim.

EARLY INTERVENTION TECHNIQUES WITH THE CHEMICALLY DEPENDENT ADOLESCENT

Early intervention is unfortunately a rare occurrence among minority groups. Perhaps because other serious environmental and intrapsychic problems often mask the drug dependency or because so many minority members put all their faith for solutions in their religion, or because they feel no trust for the majority member staff in the helping professions, early intervention is unusual (Dawkins et al., 1983).

Early interventions with teen-age minorities come more often through the school or the courts than through the family or the counseling centers (Brunswick, 1980). It is crucially important for drug and alcohol treatment centers to interface well with these institutions, to be willing to mail notices about seminars, to come into the schools to educate the staff as well as the students and to spend time answering questions for court and criminal justice staff members. These measures will greatly increase the incidence of early interventions.

When there is a referral, either through the courts, or through the schools, flexible procedures in the early stages such as a relaxed attitude toward appointment time and a willingness to do outreach work to the home are very important. When working with the family, each and every opportunity for an interview contact should be seized and used to the fullest. While training strictures may have suggested eight visits as the minimum to effect a successful family intervention, a single powerful family meeting which addresses important issues may be the agent of permanent positive change (Weakland et al., 1974). In the schools, a written protocol should be followed with all suspected drug and alcohol problems. It is equally important to employ staff from the same background as the minority family, as early in the intervention as possible. A nontraditional volunteer or paraprofessional, especially one who is language competent can be crucially important in helping to establish a bond at the outset. The following case history illustrates the successful use of these techniques:

> Juan was a 14-year-old boy in the seventh grade of a large urban center school. He was the oldest child of an adolescent Puerto Rican mother who had migrated to the mainland shortly after he was born and left Juan in the care of his maternal grandfather. His mother settled in the northeast, collected welfare benefits and married a man who became the father of three daughters, born within the next few years. When Juan turned five, his grandfather, who was now in poor health, sent Juan to his mother, to get a better education.
>
> By this time the mother had been abandoned by her husband and she welcomed Juan as the "little man" of the household. He was given more privileges and less responsibilities than his sisters. Juan never recovered from the loss of his grandfather. In school his poor concentration and hyperactive behavior caused problems. By fifth grade he had been placed in a class for the learning disabled.
>
> His mother had become more emotionally dependent on

him and he provided the companionship she lacked. In the seventh grade, when he was 13, his mother acquired a new boyfriend. Juan began to behave differently. His teacher complained that he had written an obscene note to her. His mother said he began to stay out late at night and no longer listened to what she said.

The drug counselor and school nurse determined that Juan had come into school drunk. A lengthy interview with the school psychologist disclosed that he had begun drinking with his older cousins every night when they played cards. When his capacity increased and they wouldn't give him more, he began to seek it other ways. He began drinking at night and soon kept a bottle hidden at home which he drank in the morning.

The child study team, nurse, drug counselor and assistant principal met and decided that Juan needed an alcohol rehabilitation program, and that since his mother had lost control over him, he needed to be in a residential program. All recognized the difficulty of persuading her to relinquish the care of her son to mainstream outsiders, but felt it could be done. The social worker made several phone calls, which were not understood because the mother spoke only Spanish. Two letters which she sent went unanswered. The psychologist sought the help of the assistant vice principal, who though black spoke fluent Spanish. They learned the mother's schedule from Juan and went together with Juan to the home. She greeted them shyly and awkwardly. The mother was told how much she was respected by them for how hard she had worked to bring up a son who was so charming. But he had gotten into bad health habits and now he was addicted to alcohol. Because of that he had behaved unlike himself in school and was suspended. The school refused to accept him back until he had received treatment for his illness, because he was a danger to himself and others. The school staff recommended a rehabilitation center which was about a half hour away in the suburbs. The mother said she could not let her son go away and stay with strangers. Besides, she said, Juan would not agree to it. The staff told the mother that Juan really wanted her to be a strong parent for him, and that it would help him to stop worrying so much about himself. He might be unhappy about her decision right now, but he would be grateful after he felt better. The vice principal offered to drive her to visit the alcohol center. They asked to return in a week. The next week the staff was greeted with coffee and cake. The vice principal drove the mother to the center with Juan. The mother at this point trusted the administrator. She was persuaded to allow Juan to be admitted.

EVALUATION

Interview instruments and questionnaires which are typically used with adolescents to help make decisions regarding treatment modalities may not be useful with minority young people. All evaluation instruments contain cultural bias, and some, like the MacAndrew alcoholism scale, may be useless with some minority populations (Walters et al., 1983). Others, like the widely used intake interviews, may be helpful when used with special populations, if interpreted with caution.

OUT-PATIENT TREATMENT

Every out-patient treatment center which is located near a recognizable percentage of minority groups must make the hiring of appropriate minority staff members a visible goal in employment practices. The available trained minority staff is scarce, but employment practices must include efforts to make their employment conditions and benefits and salary attractive to minority staff. It is also important to give support to some of the programs which are training minority members as drug and alcohol counselors. Also, if there are no available staff members at senior positions it is useful to hire entry level minority members, such as aides, and encourage them to further their training through tuition reimbursement and help with locating appropriate federal educational financial aid.

When majority staff members are working with minority youngsters, an important and continuing aspect of supervision must be the attention which is given to forming a bond with the counselor, what measures are being used to make the youngster comfortable in his or her "differentness" and what the staff members own feelings are about bridging this gap. it is also important when hiring minority group staff members whom it is expected will work often with minority youngsters, that not just an open and accepting attitude toward minorities but an actual eagerness to learn about other cultures is demonstrated. It is important that they learn to treat the child and his or her family with respect rather than condescending friendship.

When assigning caseloads at an out-patient treatment center, less clients should be assigned to those who are working with minorities. The staff will find it difficult to cope with learning the system with these families. It is sometimes a problem to train staff to accept that a large part of their duties will include phone calls, paper work and making agency connections to help solve reality problems regarding housing, clothing, jobs, medicaid insurance and welfare benefits. It is hard for many not to feel that they are cheated of what they perceive as the "meat" of job counseling. The staff must be educated to accept these duties as important, worthy and necessary.

Transportation difficulties for young clients can often be solved by the outpatient treatment center providing a mini-bus for the minority youngsters who have no transport. This can also be done through the Board of Education of the local school district.

Perhaps because of severe physiological, environmental and social stress, more minority member adolescents have an additional psychiatric problem or "dual diagnosis" (O'Brien et al., 1984) and the treatment center must be prepared with additional allotment of time from mental health personnel. It should be a thrust of weekly staff meetings that the supervisor make it plain that only with the full cooperation and interfacing of chemical dependency counselors and mental health therapists can each client be given everything he or she needs and that a dual diagnosis is difficult to treat and needs the best from everyone.

Any rehabilitation program for minority youngsters must include a strong academic component. These youngsters are often struggling academically and it is important that the treatment plan takes into account the importance of furthering academic aims. Again, flexibility of both concepts and practice is advocated. Often, a minority teen-ager may be surrounded by friends who exhibit flagrant school drug abuse. It should be considered whether it is wise to return the student to this environment. Sometimes a connection with a high-school-equivalency tutoring service and a part-time job may work out better. A further consideration is vocational training. Many of the minority youngsters who show up in treatment programs have poor academic histories. Even when they have tried the vocational program offered in some school systems, there is no link between the school program and the real working world. Specialized governmental off-site vocational programs may prove more effective. Many of these follow a regular academic half day program at the local school with a half day off-site at the agency, employing the newest in sophisticated equipment. The case of Robert suggests techniques which are useful in out-patient situations.

Robert was the youngest child of a middle class couple, whose mother was a homemaker and whose father worked for the city in an administrative capacity. Because of the father's job they were required to live within the city. Instead, they bought a home in a nearby suburb and used the grandmother's city home as their legal address. Robert attended school in the city. He had two older sisters who had disappointed their father by marrying soon after high school and refusing to go to college. Robert was the fair haired child in the family and his father talked to him about college plans when he was in the early elementary grades.

Robert's father used political influence with school administration to place his son in the elementary school with the best academic reputation. His plan was to transfer him to the suburban college preparatory school as soon as his son achieved the required grades. Robert's father came to school often, checking on his son's progress. According to a child study team evaluation, Robert suffered from a learning disability. It was recommended that Robert be placed in a special program, which included repeating one year of school, and attending a remedial learning laboratory for two class periods a day. His father rejected these plans out-of-hand and his mother agreed with his father. After several lengthy conferences with the child study team and teaching staff, he was convinced to try his son in the new program when he understood that it was not permanent, but would end when Robert made sufficient progress.

The frequent visits continued. The father's favorite saying was "He could do it if he wanted to." At home, his father bought books of high difficulty level and corrected Robert's mistakes as he read aloud. At this point Robert's teachers said he began "showing off," would frequently talk out in class, speak disrespectfully to the teachers and sarcastically to the other students who consequently rejected him. He had become quieter as home. His mother protected him from his father's anger by shielding him when he neglected his home chores, or got complaining notes from school about incomplete homework, or unacceptable behavior.

After Robert's father chauffeured him to school 15 minutes early in the morning, Robert got into the habit of wandering across the street to watch the drug sales. He always had money with him, because his father did not want him to be embarrassed by lack of funds. He began to try crack and was happy that it helped him feel better and forget his problems. In the beginning it was once a week but over a period of several months it became a daily occurrence. His spending money was no longer enough to pay for his habit. He became inventive in obtaining more funds from his mother. He "lost" the money on the way to the bank, the storekeeper "cheated" him. The "gang" at school got money through threats of beating him up. His mother was quick to accept his stories, and concealed this from his father at Robert's request. The mother at first was happy to comply because initially Robert seemed to be happier, and more productive with his school work, and school complaints about his behavior decreased. After several months more, things became worse than before. His behavior regressed and he was doing no homework at all because "I just can't concentrate" and quarrelling constantly with his mother about money. He took the entrance exam for the private high school and performed miserably. His father was convinced he was reading "trash" and searched his room. He found his supply of crack.

Robert confessed immediately, almost in relief. As always,

his father wanted the best. He took Robert to a highly regarded area psychiatrist. Luckily for Robert, the doctor had experience with teen-age dependency and recommended an out-patient program for him.

Robert's father acted on the suggestion quickly and Robert was enrolled in the program. But Robert's father was unhappy because many of the other clients were not middle class and many of the staff did not have advanced degrees. He complained about this and asked for an individual interview with the Director who did have a graduate degree. Robert's father was told that many different staff members would be important to Robert's recovery, but it would not take place unless they had the full cooperation of the family. Both Robert's own racial group and advanced level staff from the majority group had much to offer.

The staff selected a buddy for Robert and instructed him to help Robert feel part of the group. The staff were all part of the group. At a staff meeting it was stressed that Robert's father's ambitions for his son were not totally unrealizable but perhaps misdirected.

The family was helped so that Robert and his father grew closer, the mother became less involved with her son, and the mother's views were given as much importance as the father's. Robert's father changed his mind about a private high school for his son. The entire family was advised that college for Robert, with a program geared toward his disability was not out of the question. It was, however, Robert's decision and his effort which would be the determinant. The family took the pressure off and began to accept Robert for himself for the first time.

PROBLEMS UNIQUE TO RESIDENTIAL PROGRAMS

For minority teenagers, residential programs present both positive and negative facets. The transportation problem is solved. On the other hand, with some minority groups, especially the Hispanic, letting go of a child to reside with unknown people produces insurmountable anxiety (National Institute on Alcohol Abuse and Alcoholism, 1980). In many instances, there is no approach which can successfully alleviate this anxiety. Since teen treatment centers are so few and hence so often so far away, it is often impossible for the family to come either for the family program component, or to visit their relative.

When families of minority youngsters do not have savings, it is impossible for them to raise the money for what may be an expensive and extensive treatment program. Many do not have private insurance benefits and Medicaid disallows nonhospital chemical dependency treatment claims, thereby effectively closing doors to minorities. It is important for every treatment center to have a fixed number of beds available for indigents. The money for this might be raised through private solicitations, or as contributions from industry, especially those near the area served by the facility.

One way to cope with nonattendance of family members is through the use of modern technology. With either three-way phone conversations or conference phones, families can participate in a telephone visit with their youngster, or take part in a family session with the counselor and the client. The following case history illustrates the use of some of these methods.

Tyrone was a 15-year-old ninth grade boy who was being raised by his alcoholic grandmother. He had learning problems in school as well as behavioral problems, and was classified and put into a class for the emotionally disturbed. His grandmother really loved him and to protect him when she drank, locked him indoors with her. When he was younger he accepted this and watched TV when he was locked in. As a result, however, he had little experience in making and keeping friends. When Tyrone entered his teens he began to rebel against his grandmother's strictures and escaped from the apartment or never came home. His grandmother contacted his mother, who had given over his care to the grandmother when he was a very young child. Regularly employed, she sent a small check monthly. She had moved to another city and had gradually lost touch with her son except annually at holiday time. She had married and had other children and currently lived within a car ride of Tyrone. She came instantly when she was called, visited a few times and exacted from him a promise of better behavior. Tyrone brightened up considerably. As soon as reports from the grandmother improved the visits ceased. Tyrone was inconsolable and became depressed. He reverted to rebellious behavior and began to spend time with the youngsters in the part which was a drug haven. At first he started with marijuana, progressed to crack, and began using heroin.

His habit became expensive and through his contacts with friends in the part he was put in touch with a "chop shop" operation. He stole parts from cars and sold them to an intermediary who had connections with an illegal auto parts business. Most of his work was done at night so he began coming in very late, sleeping late in the morning, and missing a lot of school. One night he was caught by a policeman. Since it was his first offense he was released. The second time he was fined. The third time he was caught with possession of the drugs and ordered to a drug rehabilitation program. His mother offered to pay the cost of an eight week program, but the only program with available space which would accept an adolescent was several hours drive away. His grandmother was too ill to visit but his mother did make the trip to deliver him and pick him up and once in between. The mother and grandmother participated in a family meeting with Tyrone and his counselor once a week by conference phone and Tyrone was allowed to speak to them each week by means of a supervised telephone call.

His mother was encouraged to become an ongoing part of his life. His grandmother was encouraged to give up drinking. By now Tyrone had turned 16 and the family and staff thought it better that he did not return to his school since he had no positive base of friends, but only the negative base of the drug culture. Tyrone was encouraged to study at night with a local college program to attain his high school diploma. Since he found it easier to concentrate on an individual basis, he got his high school equivalency within a year, went into a job training program and by the time he turned 18 had a full time job as a car mechanic. Tyrone was not able to get to many 12-step meetings but he had several AA pen pals from the drug center. He also kept in touch by phone with others who lived near. He subscribed to the "meeting by mail" and was able to stay sober. He refused to leave his grandmother who cut down considerably on her drinking. With all he had learned about chemical dependency he could accept his grandmother, illness and all, and appreciate everything she had done for him. Tyrone did not go for counseling but his mother did and Tyrone became part of her life once again.

AFTERCARE AND RELAPSE PREVENTION

The post rehabilitative stage is probably the most neglected phase of minority adolescent chemical dependency treatment. In many minority homes, young people are often needed to assist with child-care and domestic chores or to earn money to help support the family. Transportation is again a problem. For these reasons it is difficult to return to the treatment center for follow-up counseling and meetings. The milieu from which the youngster came may not be conducive to maintaining sobriety, e.g., a high school where buying, selling and using drugs is common and where the "straight" student is almost an exception. An informal survey of three major cities disclosed few AA meetings attended in any significant numbers by minorities (Maxwell, 1984), and of these, even fewer had young people in attendance.

Some solutions to these problems might be to establish AA groups right in the school, perhaps during study hall, so the teenager would not have to lose valuable work time or battle transportation in the evening to attend a meeting. They might be scheduled by the Guidance department to provide maximum confidentiality. These groups could at first be led by retired long-time members and then eventually be taken over by the students themselves. The treatment center might offer any or all of four alternative services: round trip transportation for the weekly follow-up counseling session, weekly in-home counseling for the first post-treatment month, regular scheduled telephone counseling sessions and the privilege of making "hot-line" calls to the counselor during specified times daily for any emergency post-treatment problems which might arise.

It would be helpful if Alcoholics Anonymous World Service Organization made the attendance problems of minorities a forthcoming platform plank. Groups all over the country could be sensitized to the discomfort of minorities walking into a meeting for the first time with majority peers, and an extra measure of friendship and understanding might be directed their way.

It is important to take care before the rehabilitation to let the school or vocational program know that there will be a hiatus because of the treatment program, and alert them as to what to expect when the adolescent returns. It seems to facilitate the post-rehabilitative stage if agencies and institutions are previously told what kinds of program modifications may be expected when the adolescent comes back. For example, the weekly number of days in the vocational program could be reduced during the first four weeks, following their return and it might be necessary to leave school an hour early for the counseling follow-up at the treatment facility. It is also important that the rehabilitation center make itself available for questions from the family, school, vocational agency or employer and that this availability is clearly understood by them.

As with all other groups, relapses should be dealt with before they occur (Marlatt et al., 1985). This is best done by teaching youngsters what the warning signs are and what to do to combat them when they occur. It is also important to stress the acquirement of a natural "high." These youngsters may have had little experience with them as the following case of "Rosa" illustrates.

Rosa was the middle daughter of a Cuban American mother who had immigrated to this country when Rosa was a toddler, and had become widowed shortly thereafter. The family had been part of the professional class in Cuba but reduced circumstances due to the husband's death necessitated a move to the inner city. The mother was high strung and nervous after the loss of her husband and unable to hold onto a permanent job. She sporadically did clerical work to supplement her government benefits.

From the time she was very young, Rosa felt she "never got

254 Practical Approaches in Treating Adolescent Chemical Dependency

it right,'' that she was unable to please her mother. Her mother had very high expectations for all her children, in school and in the community. Rosa's sisters were good students, but Rosa barely passed from one grade to the next. Her mother's criticism grew more carping, and Rosa became more despondent. In high school she failed virtually every course in the first year. The Guidance department recommended a half-day vocational program and Rosa with the help of the vocational staff chose beauty culture as her field. She did very well and enjoyed it very much. However, her mother's negative attitude continued. Since the other daughters spent more time with homework and visiting friends, Rosa was expected to wait on her mother on days when the mother felt more nervous than usual.

Rosa began to use marijuana to get high with the other girls in school. She noticed it made her not worry as much about her problems. Soon it was every day and eventually Rosa had a "joint" outside of school before going in. Her school grades and attendance grew worse and her interest in her vocational program waned. When she stopped helping her mother with the younger children and a neighbor reported seeing her engaged in an activity which looked suspiciously like street walking, her mother was persuaded to take her to a local mental health clinic. They soon discovered her drug dependency and involved her in a treatment program.

Rosa and her family made a strong effort to have her complete the month's program but afterwards after-care became a problem. The school, vocational agency and drug center worked together in a flexible and cooperative way to solve the main problems which were lack of transportation and the necessity of Rosa being home to attend to her mother's illnesses and the care of the younger children. The treatment center and the Guidance program set up a 12-step program in school. Rosa was given round trip transportation weekly, telephone counseling from the center's drug counselor and hot-line privileges for emergencies. She continued in school and vocational training, stayed sober and got a job as a hair-dresser after she graduated. Her mother's health deteriorated and she was eventually able to gain the services of a community nurse. Rosa continued the major care of the younger children. Her mother was taught to show appreciation for her daughter and to respect her job in beauty culture.

APPROACHES FOR SPECIFIC MINORITY GROUPS

Cultural differences have important implications for treatment (McGoldrick, 1982). Although not everything discussed in this section is true for all minority members, clinical experience has suggested that both the assets and problem areas mentioned for each different group are often observed. The intention is not to categorize or stereotype different cultural minorities, but rather to share information which has been helpful in treating these clients.

Blacks

Many black families are in the grip of despair after enduring several generations of "welfare" existence. They often feel a sense of hopelessness about breaking out of the bind (Watts et al., 1983). Education, the key to the exit door, is often denied to these young people, who drop out of school at an alarmingly high rate during the middle teen years, because of school failure, the pressure to work and bring in more money to support the family or gratify short term longings, early pregnancy, or drug involvement. One of the greatest strengths of this group, their abiding religious faith, can also be a difficulty in treatment (Hines & Boyd-Franklin, 1982). Blacks are accustomed to finding the solutions for all their problems in the church, and often are reluctant to accept help from other sources regarding drug and alcohol dependence.

Black adolescents are very often highly physical, like to be active, and can be refreshing to work with. For example, accepting responsibility for chores is not usually a problem in a residential program. A highly structured, disciplined approach to treatment with clear rules and sanctions for misbehavior is readily accepted. Black youngsters are often referred for drug treatment through the court system (Dawkins et al., 1983). Since they often come from a father absent home, accepting authority may be difficult for them and initial resistance to group leaders is common. This is dealt with best by clearly stating that "the group leader is the boss" is just another one of the rules to follow. It is also important to show respect, e.g., many black teen-agers forego nicknames and prefer to be addressed by their full first names.

Individual drug counseling might be an approach which emphasizes an action solution for the here and now, such as a gestalt or reality type (Perls, 1969). It is important to show respect for the family of the patient by appropriate staff apparel. Many blacks seem to feel more comfortable using the staff member's honorarium, and being addressed by their own honorariums in turn, rather than to be subjected to the affected friendly or condescending use of first names. Appreciation should be shown for the heroic behavior of the single parent who has persevered in trying to do the best for his or her youngster, in the face of impossible odds. Family treatment is often successful when it empowers the parent to deal successfully with family problems as in structured therapy (Minuchin, 1974).

Mexican-Americans

This is a large heterogeneous group largely from the Southwestern and Western parts of the United States, made up both of those who have been here for several generations and are a part of the successful middle class, and those who have recently migrated in order to escape dire socio-economic privation in Mexico. These groups differ markedly from each other, but there are some characteristics which they share (Gilbert, 1985).

The family network and relationships are stressed among Mexican-Americans (Falicov, 1982). Outsiders are mistrusted at first, but once they show their sincerity and desire to help the family, they are accepted and in most ways treated no differently from other members of the family network.

The approach of the treatment staff should be formal at the outset and formality should be expected from the client and his or her family. If a bond is forged between the worker and the clients, this initial reticence quickly gives way to physical demonstration of affection.

The idea of "machismo" has important ramifications in the treatment of this group as well as other Hispanic groups (Carillo, 1982). Except in the successful middle class, the Mexican-American male is frequently disenfranchised through discrimination and lack of education and training from holding a job which will support his family. Since he has been effectively stripped thereby of power and authority, he often plays out the other parts of the machismo stereotype. Hispanic men who drink hard do so in order to be "real men" and are also frequently absent from the home. This paradigm facilitates the perception that out-of-control drinking is normal and encourages wives and mothers to make it easy for this behavior to flourish.

Another behavior which is frequently seen with the disenfranchised father, in his frustration with feelings of powerlessness, is scapegoating his son. Frequently, the relationship between father and son is very poor because of this.

Although Mexican-Americans often go to church only on holidays, their reverence and respect for church clergy makes this an area of possible affiliation during decision making time. It is important for staff members to show respect for their "honest and hardworking" ethic. An approach which encourages respect for the family group and the participation of the patient and siblings, such as Haley's family therapy (1976), is a good starting point for the family program.

A cultural anomaly of dissimulating negative feelings, especially anger, may make these youngsters appear unreachable in the beginning of treatment. Techniques of modeling and role reversal (Bandura, 1977) will help these teen-agers accept that it is healthy to experience and express so-called negative emotions. Qualities of affiliation, cooperation and affection make group therapy a good experience for these young people.

Puerto Ricans

It is not unusual for Puerto Rican families to have moved several times between Puerto Rico and the mainland, before the children in the family have reached their teen years (Carrillo, 1982). The frequent moving is often due to shifting economic conditions for the family and the availability of extended family members for help with child care as well as to serve as a source of support. Nevertheless the phenomenon acts to create a sense of rootlessness in the children. When they reach their teens it frequently causes these youngsters to have difficulty making commitments, whether in making friends, attending school, forming career goals or cooperating in their own recovery from chemical addiction (Robles et al., 1980).

These adolescents have been culturally impressed with the habit of trusting and complying with the wishes of adult authority figures. This, together with the ease with which they form an affectional bond can be used as treatment tools. This compliance in different situations can at times verge into passivity (Robles et al., 1980). In a treatment facility, with other youngsters from differing backgrounds whom they are meeting for the first time, they are in danger of being bullied. Staff must take care that this is averted, by being alert and watchful for the possibility, discussing this potentiality with the "buddy" and making assertiveness training a part of the group content.

Schedules and contracts, the favored tools of the behaviorally oriented, may be difficult for Puerto Rican youngsters to comprehend, since this has not been an important aspect in their upbringing. Social rewards, in the form of the counselor expressing verbal pleasure at growth or improvement, would probably be more powerful a reinforcement than a tangible reward. They have been taught to believe that the highest good is to please the person who loves you. An emotionally expressive style of counseling will work best with this group.

In the family program, it is difficult for the family to accept that it is sometimes for one's child's best interest to take action which may make them unhappy. The precepts of "tough love" are totally alien to this culture. Often in a father absent home, when the male child reaches mid-adolescence, he follows the "macho" path, role reversal occurs, and the mother turns over decision-making to her ill-equipped son. An approach which will allow the parents to know that reassuming their authority roles will reduce their youngster's tensions, such as Minuchin's structural method (1974), would prove most effective (Garcia-Preto, 1982). They can be taught effective techniques in encouraging their child to succeed with a strategic approach (Rohrbaugh & Eron, 1981).

Cuban-Americans

Many of the problems associated with chemical dependency with Cuban-Americans date to the last immigration wave of the 1980s. Large numbers of this group were disenfranchised in their native land and were drawn from the residents of jails and psychiatric hospitals. As with the black inner city population, numerous members of this group are troubled with a multitude of problems in addition to the chemical dependency (Carrillo, 1982).

The middle class group, on the other hand, have either been here longer, or are first or second generation descendants of earlier immigrants. Their problems are quite different. Middle class and professional Cuban-Americans have, as a group, been remarkably successful and quickly assimilated into the majority culture. High expectations are communicated by the group to other adults, and by adults to children. Failure in school or in business is seen as a sign of weakness, and greeted by much negative pressure.

Partly perhaps because of years of political upheaval in their native land, and severe loss of relatives and other loved ones, as well as property and income, many Cuban-Americans employ a philosophy with an existential dimension. Success is not expected to come easily, but to be instead the fruit of hard work. Suffering is an accepted part of life, and each person has the responsibility of working out his own destiny with the cooperation of his extended family and friends. The use of humor and self-deprecation are charming defenses, to which the counselor is expected to respond positively (Bernal, 1982).

What may seem to the mainstream staff to be the enmeshment of the youngster with the family may be instead the result of deliberate training for responsibility on the part of the parents (Page, 1980). For example, it is not uncommon for a Cuban-American teen-age girl to take pride in caring for younger siblings.

These young people are not usually characterized by humility. On the contrary, Cubans often have a sense of being "special" (Bernal, 1982). For example, they may incorporate their drug dependency into a perception of themselves as being creative. A therapy which accents the recognition of feelings as modified by attitude such as cognitive therapy might be useful in drug counseling (Beck et al., 1979).

The family counseling portion of the family program would work best with emphasis on duty, how one wins a special place for oneself by doing good for others, and the importance of loving family relationships. Bernal (1982) suggests that this is found in contextual therapists (Boszormenyi-Nagy, 1980) and is a good fit for this particular culture.

Native Americans

Many native Americans live on a reservation and this artificial existence presents some unique problems. The severe employment difficulties, the education of children away from their families and the lower level of general health are some of the chief difficulties affecting native American adolescents in this group (Levy & Kunitz, 1974).

In this cultural group, trust is not easily obtained by outsiders. "Testing" may last for a long period of time (Attneave, 1982). These parents will do anything for their children. There is immediate surface cooperation with helping personnel, but deeper levels needed for important and lasting change must wait until the "outsider" is completely accepted. The way for staff to achieve this is through total honesty. Since genuineness is highly prized (McBride & Page, 1980), it is unwise for majority member staff to make an affected effort to affiliate with the American Indian culture. Manipulation is instantly recognized, so that the use of covert strategies as in strategic therapy, is ineffective. A method which recognizes the role of suffering and destiny, such as an existential approach (Ofnan, 1980) works best.

Family treatment must be flexible enough to include all important adults in the adolescent's life. Surrogate parenthood, whether for insufficient parental health or strength, or educational or vocational advantage, is alive and well in the native American community. There may be adults in the youngster's life who are as important as the parents and they must be allowed to make their contribution to his or her recovery. The participation of these other important adults is important for another reason. The native American culture can be an enabling society. People may make excuses for each other and adults may make excuses for children. To break this cycle, it is necessary to work with all the relevant members.

The chemically dependent adolescent is very comfortable interacting with a group, as long as an effort to bridge the culture gap is made. Group work in which all have an equal voice is similar to the tribal culture mechanism. Motivation is difficult to establish. Young people do not have many successful role models (Bard et al., 1987). It is important to put them in touch with those who have succeeded. In most cases, in the native American community, it is those who have achieved sobriety who have achieved success in education, government, business, the professions and their own personal and family life.

During the chemical dependency treatment it is wise to fit the idea of sobriety into the ideal of total health. This is a concept which is an integral part of the native American belief system.

Flexibility has often been missing in treatment of native Americans who are on reservations. Treatment centers are often located far from the reservation. It is unusual for these places to provide outreach services to the isolated communities, despite their severe problems with time, distance and transportation. Aftercare is troubled in much the same way. Although there are AA and Alanon meetings every night of the week, they are often 40 to 80 miles away, and it is difficult for even a committed individual to take advantage of them. Holding meetings on the reservation could be an important part of a post-rehabilitative outreach program.

CONCLUSION AND IMPLICATIONS

The foregoing discussed suggestions for dealing with issues in the treatment of minority chemically dependent adolescents. Leadership regarding policy change in high government and educational levels is crucial to success in this area. Emphasis on the training and hiring of minority staff as well as supervision which accents the acquisition of knowledge and understanding of minority clients by majority staff is important.

Flexibility and spontaneity in treatment methods and techniques which stress cultural strengths seem indispensable. Program adjustment to suit minority adolescent needs at treatment centers is important. Willingness to interface with staff from other fields, as well as nontraditional and noncredentialed family and community leaders facilitates lasting change with these adolescents. Above all, in working with these special populations respect and caring form the core of successful treatment for these minority adolescents and their families.

REFERENCES

Attneave, C. (1982). American Indians and Alaska native families: Emigrants in their own homeland. In M. McGoldrick, J.F. Pearce & J. Giordano (Eds.) *Ethnicity and family therapy*, (pp. 55-83). New York: Guilford Press.

Bandura, A. (1977). Self-efficacy: Toward a unifying theory of behavioral change. *Psychological review*, (pp. 191-215).

Beck, A., Rush, A.J., Shaw, B.F., & Emery, G. (1979). *Cognitive therapy of depression*. New York: Guilford.

Bernal, G. (1982). Cuban families. In M. McGoldrick, J.F. Pearce & J. Giordano (eds.), *Ethnicity and family therapy*; pp. 187-207. New York: Guilford Press.

Bobo, J.K., Snow, W.H., Gilchrist, L., & Schinke, S.P. (1985). Assessment of refusal skill in minority youth.

Boszormenyi-Nagy, I., & Krasner, B.R. (1980). Trust based therapy: A contextual approach. *American Journal of Psychiatry, 137* (7), 767-775.

Brunswick, A.F. (1980). Perspectives on black youth's drug abuses. *Youth & Society, 11*(4), 449-473.

Burd, L., Shea, T.E., & Knull, H. (1987). "Montana Gin": Ingestion of commercial products containing denatured alcohol among native Americans. *Journal of Studies on Alcohol, 48*(4), 388-389.

Carrillo, Carmen (1982). Changing norms of Hispanic families: Implication for treatment. In E. Jones & S.J. Korchim (Eds.) *Minority Mental Health*. New York: Praeger.

Chun II, J.C., Dunston, P.J., & Ross-Sheriff, F. (Eds.), (1983). *Mental health and people of color*. Washington, D.C.: Howard University Press.

Clark, K.B. (1980). The role of race. *New York Times Magazine*. October 5, p. 24.

Dawkins, R.L., & Dawkins, M.P. (1983). Alcohol use and delinquency among black, white and Hispanic adolescent offenders. *Adolescence, 18*(72), 799-809.

Dworkin, A.G., & Stephens, R.C. (1980). Mexican-American adolescent inhalant abuse: A proposed model. *Youth & Society, 11*(4), 493-506.

Erikson, E.H. (1963). *Childhood and Society*. New York: Norton.

Falicov, J. (1982). Mexican families. In M. McGoldrick, J.F. Pearce, & J. Giordano (Eds.), *Ethnicity and family therapy*, (pp. 245-272). New York: Guilford Press.

Garcia-Preto, N. (1982). Puerto Rican families. In M. McGoldrick, J.F. Pearce & J. Giordano (Eds.), *Ethnicity and family therapy*, (pp. 164-186). New York: Guilford Press.

Gilbert, J. (1985). Mexican-Americans in California: Intracultural variation in attitudes and behavior related to alcohol. In L. Bennett & G. Ames (Eds.). *The American experience with alcohol*, (pp. 255-277). New York: Plenum Press.

Gorski, T.T. (1987, June). *The developmental model of recovery. The recovery relapse grid*. Paper presented at 1987 Rutgers Summer School of Alcohol Studies, New Brunswick, N.J.

Haley, J. (1976). *Problem-solving therapy*. San Francisco: Jossey-Bass.

Higgins, P.C., Albrecht, G.L., & Albrecht, M.H. (1977). Black-white adolescent drinking: The myth and the reality. *Social Problems, 25*(2), 215-224.

Hines, P.M., & Boyd-Franklin, N. (1982). Black families. In M. McGoldrick, J.F. Pearce, & J. Giordano (Eds.), *Ethnicity and family therapy*, (pp. 84-107). New York: Guilford Press.

Honig, A.S. (1986). Stress and coping in children. *Young Children, 41*(4), 50-63.

Kaufman, E. (1985). *Substance abuse and family therapy*. Orlando, Fl.: Grune & Stratton.

Lawson, G., Peterson, J.S., & Lawson, A. (1983). *Alcoholism and the family: A guide to treatment and prevention*. Rockville, Md.: Aspen Systems Corp.

Levy, J.E., & Kunitz, S.J. (1974). *Indian drinking; Navaho practices and the Anglo-American*. New York: Wiley.

Liepman, M.R., & Nirenberg, T.D. (1987). Beginning treatment for alcohol problems. In *Treatment and prevention of alcohol problems: A resource manual*. New York: Academic Press.

Marlatt, G.A., & Gordon, J.R. (Eds.). (1985). *Relapse prevention: maintenance strategies in the treatment of addictive behaviors*. New York: Guilford Press.

Maxwell, M.A. (1984). *The A.A. experience; a close-up view for professionals*. New York: McGraw-Hill.

McBride, D.C., & Page, J.B. (1980). Adolescent Indian substance abuse: Ecological and sociocultural factors. *Youth & Society, 11*(4), 475-492.

McGoldrick, M. (1982). Ethnicity and family therapy: an overview. In M. McGoldrick, J.F. Pearce, & J. Giordano (Eds.). *Ethnicity and family therapy*, (pp. 3-30). New York: Guilford Press.

Miller, S.O., O'Neal, G.S., & Scott, C.A. (Eds.). (1982). *Primary prevention approaches to the development of mental health services for ethnic minorities*. New York: Council on Social Work Education.

Minuchin, S., (1974). *Families and family therapy*. Cambridge: Harvard University Press.

National Institute on Alcohol Abuse and Alcoholism. (1985). *Alcohol and Hispanic Americans*.

O'Brien, C.P., Woody, G.E., & McLellan, A.R. (1984). Psychiatric disorders in opioid-dependent patients. *The Journal of Clinical Psychiatry III, 45*(12), 9-13.

Ofnan, W. (1980). Existential psychotherapy. In H.I. Kaplan, A.M. Freedman, & B.J. Sadock (Eds.). *Comprehensive textbook of psychiatry III.* New York: Williams & Wilkins.

Page, J.B. (1980). The children of exile: Relationships between the acculturation process and drug use among Cuban youth. *Youth & Society, 11*(4), 431-447.

Pandina, R.J., & White, H.R. (1981). Patterns of alcohol and drug abuse of adolescent students and adolescents in treatment. *Journal of Studies on Alcohol, 42*, 441-456.

Perls, F.S. (1969). *Gestalt therapy verbatim.* New York: Real People Press.

Reilly, D.K., Hegg, J., & Wwyman (1984). A systems approach to the management of drug-related problems. *Australian Alcohol/Drug Review, 3*(2), 53-57.

Robles, R.R., Martinez, E., & Moscoso, M.R. (1980). Predictors of adolescent drug behavior: The case of Puerto Rico. *Youth & Society, 11*(4), 415-430.

Rohrbaugh, M., & Eton, J.B. (1981). The strategic systems therapies. In L.E. Abt & I.R. Stuart (Eds.). *The newer therapies: A workbook.* New York: Van Nostrand Reinhold.

Smart, R.G. (1980). *The new drinkers; teenage use and abuse of alcohol.* Toronto: Addiction Research Foundation.

Stephenson, J.N., Mobert, D.P., Daniels, B.J., & Robertson, J.F. (1984). Treating the intoxicated adolescent. *Journal of the American Medical Association, 252*(14).

Walters, G.D., Jeffry, T.B., Kruzich, D.J., Greene, R.L., & Haskins, J. (1983). Racial variations on the MacAndrew alcoholism scale of the MMPI. *Journal of Consulting Psychology, 51*(6), 947-948.

Watts, T.D., & Wright, R., Jr., (Eds.). (1983). *Black alcoholism: toward a comprehensive understanding.* Springfield, Il: Charles C. Thomas.

Weakland, J., Fisch, R., Watzlawick, P., & Bodin, A.M. (1974). Brief therapy focused problem resolution. *Family Process, 13*(2), 151-168.

Welte, J.W., & Barnes, G.M. (1987). Alcohol use among adolescent minority groups. *Journal of Studies on Alcohol, 48*(4), 329-336.

Whitaker, C.A. (1982). Power politics of family psychotherapy. In J.R. Neill, & D.P. Kniskern (Eds.). *From psyche to system: The evolving therapy of Carl Whitaker.* New York: Guilford.

Wilson, S.J. (1987). The truly disadvantaged. *The inner-city, the underclass, and public policy.* Illinois: University of Chicago Press.

A.A. and N.A. for Adolescents

Philip D. Gifford, MA, CSACR

HISTORICAL BACKGROUND

No discourse on adolescent chemical dependency can be complete without a substantive examination of Twelve Step recovery programs. The effectiveness of these programs is without parallel. Both Alcoholics Anonymous and Narcotics Anonymous have had quite high success rates if the recovering person wants help, and, *if* the recovering person is referred to the *more appropriate* fellowship. Although there are other Twelve Step programs such as Cocaine Anonymous, Addicts Anonymous, and Drugs Anonymous, only N.A. and A.A. have proven their worth over a sustained period of time.

Alcoholics Anonymous is the originator of the Twelve Step concept. Other organizations using this philosophical base owe a major part of whatever success they have managed to achieve to them. However, as A.A. progressed in its theoretical development by borrowing from predecessor organizations and then improving and modifying their program according to the specific needs of its targeted population, so, also, has Narcotics Anonymous. Both A.A. and N.A. spent their formative years fitting their programs to the personality characteristics of those people who arrived at their doors and whose needs became vitally obvious to them. These two major recovery organizations now differ considerably in practice, attitude, content, and behavioral mechanics.

Much of the development of both organizations was experiential. Both were intensely aware that what had preceded them was not at

Philip D. Gifford is Substance Abuse Specialist, St. Clares-Riverside Medical Center, Boonton, NJ 07005.

all adequate. Many died as A.A. and N.A. were seeking to understand what was necessary and important and what was not.

Our concern here, is to examine the parameters of both fellowships, and, by so doing, establish a referral protocol which will best serve the recovery needs of the adolescents we seek to serve. There can be no question that because of their differences, A.A. and N.A. have different strengths and weaknesses. All chemically dependent people seem to be served better by one or the other. The question then becomes, "who should go to which fellowship?" And, a following question, "why?"

Discussions of the appropriate recovery program for addicted adolescents tend to arouse passion. It was not always so. As long as Alcoholics Anonymous was the only generally available support group, there was no controversy. The powerful emergence of Narcotics Anonymous has changed all that. The debate continues, only slightly abated at best, more acrimonious often, and vicious at worst. It is reminiscent of lines from William Butler Yeats poem, *The Second Coming:* "The best lack all conviction, while the worst are full of passionate intensity" (Yeats, 1920). If professionals are truly and honestly committed to assist recovery, then hidden agendas (which at best will tend to sabotage such efforts) can have no legitimate place in the recommendations for post-treatment referrals.

An analysis of the psycho-social traditions and historical development of both A.A. and N.A. is essential to the understanding of what each of these Twelve Step fellowships can do best. To begin with, neither can be mistaken for the other. The psychodynamics diverge quickly and dramatically. The often heard put-down that "N.A. is a poor carbon copy of the original" is totally without merit. Both organizations are brilliant. But, they are not at all the same: they treat problems and symptoms differently, and, for the appropriate person, both organizations afford marvelous results. This last concept, "for the appropriate person," should be well established in the minds of treatment professionals. Jellinek's seminal work, *The Disease Concept of Alcoholism* (Jellinek, 1960), once and for all set the stage for us to understand concepts of differentiation, that there is more than one "alcoholism" and, then, of course through analogy, more than one "addiction." Depending on where an individual fits in Jellinek's typology, there are quite dissimilar physical and behavioral manifestations in "addiction" which turn out to be important distinctions.

In A.A.s early history, A.A.ers determined that adolescents who sought recovery from "alcoholism" would have a separate forum and early in the 1940s Young People's A.A. was born. It was to be among the first of many special interest groups in Alcoholics Anonymous. Unfortunately, Young People's A.A. has had a varied consistency. In many such groups, relapse rates have been huge and repetitive.

And, as the drug devastation started its incredible inroads into the adolescent population, Young People's A.A. faced an enormous array of different mood-altering substances, deficit behaviors, and anti-social despair, none of which they had adequate guidelines for. Bill W., a co-founder of A.A., stated very concretely in an A.A. pamphlet, *Problems Other Than Alcohol*, that "Sobriety — freedom from *alcohol* (emphasis ours) — through the teaching and practice of the Twelve Steps, is the sole purpose of an A.A. group" (W. Bill, 1958). Further on in the same article, Bill W. states that *pill and drug troubles are in no way the business of an A.A. group* (emphasis ours).

No wonder there has been confusion! That article was copywrited in 1958, perhaps a direct reflection of the increasing drug-related problems that were then being foisted inappropriately onto A.A. It was, perhaps, a problem aided and abetted by those of us who sought to help. Unfortunately, for those with "drug" problems it often offered only temporary respite, for the uneasiness that these drug issues engendered turned to resentment by many in the A.A. membership and often led to effective disenfranchisement of the "druggie" who sought to stay clean in A.A.

In fact, N.A. was encouraged to start an entirely new organization after its plea to develop another special interest group was rejected (A.A. for addicts), and A.A.ers helped get it started in 1953.

Bill W.'s input on this matter was another stroke of intuitive genius; it certainly anticipated the important theory of Marshall McLuhan's *The Medium is the Message* (McLuhan et al., 1967.) And, the medium of Alcoholics Anonymous is the so-called Big Book, an *alcoholism-specific* manual of recovery. For those who were sent inadvisedly to A.A. and then relapsed, there was often only blame, — "If it can work for them it can work for you!" But, why should we even consider that A.A. can be all things for all people?

This was (and is) a classic case of blaming the victim. Unfortunately it continues today. Inappropriate referral reinforces a sense of abandonment, betrayal, and failure in the victim and to a sense of chaos in A.A. Alcoholics Anonymous certainly deserves better than an insistence that it accept and be successful with everyone sent to its doors! And A.A. doesn't deserve any implied criticism that it change its mission and its genius by altering its language and practices. There would be no end to the revisions, no end to the wrangling, and no end to a legitimate heartfelt loss that would inevitably occur.

No, A.A.'s great strength is in being what it is. The drug addictions, other than alcoholism, present other insuperable issues which prevent allegiance or affiliation. Importantly, there are also other "alcohol dependencies" and "alcoholism" (which A.A. has been uncomfortable in accommodating) which are handled well in N.A. and this is essential for us to realize. This can be as true for those with an alcohol-only history as well as for those with a mixed substance abuse pattern which included alcohol.

PSYCHOSOCIAL PARAMETERS

For a variety of reasons which we will present following, I believe that A.A. is almost never the more appropriate Twelve Step recovery program for adolescents now that N.A. is more generally available; because of the powerfully different psychodynamics in the two organizations, that no one should ever be referred to both! In my experience, those who do go to both organizations seem not to establish their footing in either camp; they often wind up confused and angry, a position which can and has led to relapse. Jargon, style, substance, and social tradition are considerably diverse. Today I think it absurd to advice a recovering person to try both and then stay where they are the most comfortable. *Any* chemically dependent person worth his or her salt will tend to avoid the levels and preciseness of confrontation which they need the most, and, obviously, A.A.ers are not as aware of the machinations of the drug culture as are N.A.ers.

In order to understand some of the differences between these two fellowships, we will have to try to understand the psycho-social milieu of the age during which each of them formalized their canons — *The Big Book* for A.A. and *The Basic Text* for N.A. The separate and disparate influences of radically different times directly determined the components that dissimilarly exist in A.A. and N.A. today. Professional understanding and utilization of these differences for the client's benefit can and does save lives.

Alcoholics Anonymous was formed in 1935 and *The Big Book* was copywrited in 1939. This was in an America that was emerging from the Great Depression. It was a conservative age. Drugs other than alcohol were not thought of in the same vein. The two co-founders of A.A. both viewed their personal unmanageability as having been caused by alcohol and it was to abstinence from that one drug that their survival allegiance was born. There was no end to the availability of prospective members. But, it could have been disastrous for their fledgling organization to include programming for those with "other" drug problems.

It was not an affluent age; the Great Depression was just winding down. Economic survival was paramount. The disciplines of living tended to be well instilled. Families tended to be intact, communities stable. All forms of communication, although somewhat florid at times, seemed firmly based in morality. The electronic age was but a glimmer in a very few eyes. Trains, not planes, were still the center of long distance travel. In short, the world was a lot slower place.

The impact that Freud and his dominions would make later was yet only a "pseudo"-science which prompted great suspicion, many put-downs, and much antagonism. Because alcoholism was often looked at by psychiatry as a symptom rather than as a primary disease, much ineffective treatment resulted and an unofficial A.A.er skepticism toward this field was the result. Because of such widespread prejudices, early attempts at rehabilitation treatment which included psychological assessment and management were often hindered.

Social attitudes towards government and the establishment were generally conservative. Intellectualism flourished. Compared to the 1980s, it was a time of cliches, simple answers, and a stubborn work ethic.

It was into this world that A.A. was born. The time of its beginning influenced its social customs and traditions, its approaches and its content. It could be no other way.

And for N.A.? It can be ventured that Narcotics Anonymous, since it was founded in 1953, might have similar influences in the development of its formal and informal structures. However, that wasn't the case. The very success and popularity of A.A. hindered the practical development of N.A. for a long time. Most professionals in the field knew many other-than-alcohol addicts who did gain their recovery in A.A. Unfortunately many others didn't stay clean and died as a result. Many addicts couldn't or wouldn't identify; many addicts were made to feel rejected; many addicts became angry that A.A. didn't have them in mind. And because N.A. was new and not generally available, just sending all recovering people to A.A. accommodated professional familiarity (but it did not make good sense).

I think it can be logically argued that the most important development for the continued best success of A.A. has been N.A. It has clarified philosophies, engendered more appropriate referrals (or can), and, finally after many years of discontent, allow A.A. to go back to what it does best — treat the recovering alcoholic who belongs there and not get involved in the alien issues of poly-drug or other-drug abuse.

N.A. has had a slow growth. In many places, just as A.A. had, it started and stopped. Its social acceptance was poor. It did not have the brilliance of a *Big Book*. It smacked of illegality and other unsavory auras. But, it survived because it had to survive; the N.A.ers who stuck it out knew that they had many other issues that they needed to address for their recovery and that a successful forum for these problems was generally unavailable in any other organization.

In some N.A. groups, A.A. literature was used; in some, religious materials were the only written guidelines; others used no written material at all. During this time, the constituency of N.A. was changing as well. A fellowship that primarily started out as recovery for the narcotic addict found itself being besieged by those who used other classes of mood-bending drugs as well. They, too, had no place to go and wound up casting their lot with the only Twelve Step program which would accept them. And a wild lot they were! — all the way from the needle-junkie "shooting" heroin, to the glue sniffer, to the elderly matron on pills: the pot-head, the acid-freak, and the "duster" all found refuge. And it became more and more evident that a drug-specific language and approach such as A.A. employed could not possibly encompass all of the myriad drug-using patterns of their membership. It was this fact that led N.A. to the beginning of a very different approach to addiction recovery, equally as brilliant as A.A.'s, but substantially dissimilar in content and practice.

This varied population made it impossible to focus on the effect of any one class of drugs, or on the physiological after-effects of any one class of drugs, or of symptoms, or of the various psychological changes their membership had sought to obtain. They were forced into dealing with the unmanageability of addiction in general as well as the sick behavioral constituents, which if left unchanged, would eventually lead them back to the revitalization of the active drug use. Narcotics Anonymous saw a pitfall looming in approaching addiction physiologically. Many N.A.ers were never physically hooked on any one drug, but were addicted to *the changing of their mood by any means whatsoever.* And, this, adolescents can really identify with! Many were "garbage-heads" using anything at all to escape the uncomfortability of the reality they hated, often with good reason.

They finally embarked on writing their *Basic Text.* N.A. asked for written contributions from the entire membership and thousands replied. Literature Committees were set up on a regional basis which then began the job of collating and separating ideas and concepts. Gradually the work of these committees was brought to fruition at the N.A. World Level and final draft work began. That amazing behemoth of work resulted in sending the printer's proofs back to the membership for their approval. *The Basic Text* finally took form and in 1982 the "finished" product was published. (There have been many small, but important, revisions in language and substance since.)

But (and this is an important "but"), the first published *Basic*

Text wound up reflecting the milieu of the late Seventies and early Eighties, not of the years when N.A. began. An information and treatment explosion had occurred in the fields of addiction, psychology, pharmacology, behavioral research, recovery, and rehabilitation in the interim. Narcotics Anonymous internalized many of these new developments and directions as well as incorporating the sociology of their own experiential past. Chief among these developments had been the progress of psychotherapy with its emphasis on emotional insight and sharing rather than on intellectual approaches. N.A. members encouraged this gut-level sharing (and the trust it engendered) into the commonplace out of the rare; its membership learned to put things into one's own voice and has tended to avoid using cliches and slogans. N.A. has also somewhat integrated the rehabilitation center teaching of equating other compulsive activities and other self-destructive mechanisms with the basic addictive behaviors and attitudes that prompted them to use drugs in the first place. Narcotics Anonymous, then, is a much broader spectrum program.

> Our inability to control our usage of drugs is a symptom of the disease of addiction. We are powerless not only over drugs, but our addiction as well. We need to admit this in order to recover. Addiction is a physical, mental, and spiritual disease, affecting every area of our lives. (*The Narcotics Anonymous Basic Text*, 1986, p. 18)

> The Twelve Steps of Narcotics Anonymous, as adapted from A.A., are the basis of our recovery program. We have only broadened their perspective. We follow the same path with a single exception; our identification as addicts is all-inclusive in respect to any mood-changing, mind-altering substance. "Alcoholism" is too limited a term for us; our problem is not a specific substance, it is a disease called "addiction." We believe that as a fellowship, we have been guided by a Greater Consciousness, and are grateful for the Direction that has enabled us to build upon an already-proven program of recovery. (*The Narcotics Anonymous Basic Text*, 1986, p. xiv)

Since the 1940s, radically new sets of social influences have assisted in altering the behavioral rigidification of these young addicts. It has to be considered that the economic affluence that developed in the Fifties brought with it an emotional spending and wasting spree. Another major impact has resulted from the significant changes in child-rearing styles that were promulgated in that era: those changes have severe implications for clients who are the results of such permissive practices. The high-energy, high-tech world that has given us rock music, and SSTs, computers and stimulation without end; social tech which has led us away from the teaching of ethics and morals and into the inherent risks imposed upon latch-key kids and associated with one parent families; and science-tech which has given the world a set of highly available illegal and pharmaceutical chemicals (and their combinations); all to invent new complexities of addiction. All of these powerful societal developments have altered the "personalities" of treatment needs.

Cultural engineering and a proliferation of genetically-at-risk offspring have infected huge new populations. As affluence has made more money available to parents, adolescent pressure and peer styles have resulted in the fact that a significant amount of those monies wind up in the hands of those kids, a group not exactly noted for responsible behaviors concerning cash. And this access to money has given kids the access to the drugs (alcohol and others) which wind up rotting the fundamental fabric of society.

For a variety of social, political, and economic reasons, American skepticism has replaced American hope. It has been said that this adolescent generation is the first in this country which cannot look forward to a standard of living as high as that of their parents; this lack of opportunity has led many kids to adopt a characterological depression—a negative affective state used as a defense, fertile geography for drug experimentation.

Exposure to tacitly approved systems such as television, ads focusing on the sexuality of teeny-boppers, sexually explicit communication in magazines, soap operas, and lowered sexual standards throughout all, have led to a jaded boredom. Fatalism has replaced promise. And laziness, both physical and intellectual, has replaced creativity, responsibility, and normal necessary development with nothing but plastic illusions. Age-appropriate differentials have been obliterated and rites of passage minimized to the extent that "right" has replaced "privilege." Innocence is mocked at the same time inappropriate experience has become too heavy a psychic load for teens to handle.

While much rock music is superb, there are other groups which focus on the desirability of drugs, bestiality, self-defeating sexuality, and other perversions: most adults don't bother to listen to rock's lyrics and so their silence is mistaken for approval.

And for adolescents whose limit boundaries have been abrogated by many of the social systems which used to see to their enforcement, their lack of borders has led to aimless wandering. An often promiseless past seems rooted in what many of these adolescent addicts view as a future whose opportunity has already been spent.

The age at which children have access to and are encouraged to use drugs (including the drug alcohol) has been getting lower and younger. It is not at all unusual anymore to come across an addicted person who has been using chemicals since age seven or eight. And, of course, all of the developmental processes which kids have to grow through in order to become minimally functioning adults are blocked as long as that child is using. A most important tool in adolescent growth should be the development of the ability to think abstractly. Without that ability, frustration, anger, and intolerance are the result. Many members of Narcotics Anonymous do not yet have this ability, but, N.A. can and does accommodate it. On the other hand, Alcoholics Anonymous utilizes many abstract concepts (most notably in slogans and other *bon mots*) which are most suitable for the population that they were originally attempting to serve. It does create a dilemma for the adolescent. The relative lack of slogan use or other one-liners is merely one more reason why kids can do better in Narcotics Anonymous.

Love, itself, seems to be more and more divorced from the family system. In this regard, the N.A. custom of hugging each other in greeting has often reduced newcomer adolescents to grateful tears: for some it is the first time in their lives that they were given a hug without an ulterior motive attached; and some kids have never had one, not of any kind.

N.A. calls itself a family. Here again, for many kids this is the only feasible family they have ever had. Coast to coast, world without end, this emotional bonding among N.A. family members of all ages and status, among gays and straights, among blacks, whites, and whatever, has forged a fellowship based on unconditional acceptance.

Unconditional acceptance is paramount for adolescent recovery. Few adolescents have the ego-strength to withstand rejection. The fact that N.A. is a broad spectrum addicted fellowship insures that any kid can be totally honest and aboveboard about their drug-using or behavioral history without fear of rejection or implied abandonment by its membership. Kids who use have come from abandoning environments! (For a professional to place a recovering adolescent "alcoholic" or other-drug-addict in risk of segregated or systemic rejection in a Twelve Step Program is tantamount to saying, "But I don't care if you can't handle the rejection and you relapse as a result!")

This N.A. egalitarianism has created many other dynamics. If humility is a necessary ingredient in recovery (and I believe it is), it becomes a truly potent force for adolescent assimilation when a newcomer fifteen-year old correctly confronts a quiet senior N.A.er with years of recovery.

There are major reasons why N.A. has developed as it has. Its members, by definition, share a history of anti-social behavior, incredible loneliness, social ostracism, anti-authority tendencies, insecurity, and immaturity. The average age of N.A.ers is younger than that of A.A. The A.A. literature was written from a very responsibility-taught adult perspective while the N.A. literature was written by those who were earnestly seeking that role. And with all this preamble, it is only fair to say that the N.A. *Basic Text* is a brilliant piece of work. It has its own eloquent and spiritual elegance.

But these two major canons were written in different ages and from different experiential models. The style of the N.A. *Basic Text* seems to appeal to adolescents. They have no problem with the language. They can identify. N.A., then, has accommodated and integrated these later social problems and psychological parameters. N.A., then, has updated the Twelve Step concept into a modern framework of therapeutic solidity.

In an important article in *Health and Social Work*, "Use of Paradox in the Treatment of Alcoholism" (Shore, 1981), is a piece which points to the power of the therapeutic paradox. Alcoholics

Anonymous was remarkably brilliant in its instinctive use of this often sound technique. A.A. itself was formed on the basis of a paradox—that one "drunk" couldn't stay sober alone but could do so in fellowship with another "alcoholic." In 1935 that must have been a startling concept! Yet, as time has gone on, the skeptic's stance which gave so much of the power and effectiveness to early A.A. (through paradox) has changed to a position of acceptance (because it works!) and in matter of fact, A.A. has become a quite established authority. The pariah mantle has fallen to Narcotics Anonymous as it has become the new "outcast" on the therapeutic "block," another low-man-on-the-totem-pole paradoxical position which has had great appeal for many adolescents (and, again, if it works don't fix it). Many of these kids really want to get better but would prefer to do so in a not-too-socially-accepted fellowship!

To many adolescents A.A. represents parental admonishment. For these adolescents anything that smacks of parental anything tends to lead to oppositional postures. It is even more true, that for a child of an alcoholic, (a most common situation) Narcotics Anonymous is the less distasteful alternative (just because it is not *Alcoholics* Anonymous).

It is rare to find an addicted adolescent who has not used more than one drug of abuse. And it is a truism that addicts (especially young ones) have difficulty translating through analogy. Asking kids who are deficient in abstract thinking to understand the word "alcohol" as meaning "all drugs" is demanding a quantum accomplishment. Since the A.A. literature is drug-specific (alcohol only) and since members are required to identify themselves as "alcoholics," the life-saving necessity of appreciating that any drug will lead one back to acute addictive unmanageability is a point often masked by the one-dimensional A.A. literature.

It is also unfortunate that many addicts seek to hide themselves in A.A. so that they won't be confronted as easily if they don't stop using drugs other than alcohol. N.A. is very clear that it is a program which demands abstinence from all drugs. It is also unfortunate, despite many A.A.ers advice to the contrary, that some A.A.ers continue to use other mood-altering chemicals sometimes even after many years of "sobriety." (Of course it must be questioned whether any "alcoholic" is truly qualified to share at a meeting if they are continuing to abuse any mood-changing, mind-altering chemical be it street drugs or prescriptions. It has to be asked if anyone is truly "sober" if they are "high.")

Kids are very astute at ascertaining whether or not someone is using mood-bending chemicals. If they see one person "getting away" with it while attending A.A., then they have a very welcome role model to imitate. And, yes, to be fair, that could happen in N.A. too, but peer pressure of other N.A.ers in such a situation is usually quickly forthcoming and is most powerful in putting an end to it (either that or the person tends to stop attending N.A. if they're not ready to stop *all* drugging yet).

There can be no substitute (for the professional and other caregivers who might refer someone to A.A. or N.A.) than to frequent both of these organizations on an intensive basis for perhaps six months or so. Those professionals who are recovering in A.A. cannot assume without potentially fatal danger that they know all there is to know about recovery and that only A.A. offers it. Patients who might die cannot afford the luxury of an unknowing (or unyielding) professional. How can any of us advise any therapeutic modality (and A.A. and N.A. are that!) unless we truly know from broad-spectrum personal education what both of these fellowships accomplish differently? And vested interest prejudice, which occasionally rears its ugly head, can do nothing but injure some patients terminally.

I find it more than disconcerting to observe recovering addicts who identify themselves as "an addict and an alcoholic." How dangerously redundant! An alcoholic *is* an addict and to state that one is "both" is to imply that one has two diseases. The concept of addiction is difficult enough to grasp without encouraging an obfuscating inaccuracy in identifying one's self when a major part of the problem for these adolescents (and a major part of the recovery solution) is clarification of identity. Truth in labelling is (or should be) a stalwart base of the "honesty" part of the program. Such oxymoronic slickness can only disarm the clarity of logic we so desperately seek to establish in recovering people.

If our intent in allowing such designations is to avoid clinical diagnosis, to avoid our own uncomfortability with the word "addict," or to "get-over" in some fashion, I believe we ought to

reexamine our own qualifications to treat; if we are seeking to strad-
dle the A.A. requirement that its members identify themselves as
"addicts," (both of which are fair propositions), what solid good
can we accomplish by doing so?

N.A. meetings are high-energy, emotionally up-front (as compared to intellectual), and not slogan oriented. Because of the gut-
level sharing and emotional catharsis which is encouraged, N.A.
might be considered to be based on a "psychotherapeutic" model.

In the past few years, N.A. has grown enormously. For example,
in the period between June 1982 and January 1988, N.A. in New
Jersey has grown from thirty meetings a week to approximately
three hundred meetings a week. All areas of any population density
in that state are quite well covered. The number of people attending
all of these meetings is increasing at perhaps the same rate.

It is a superb, though very different, brand of recovery. Many
hospitals and rehabs have actively encouraged the development of
N.A. by allowing meetings on their premises. An examination of
the brochures that rehabilitation centers send out reveals that the
N.A. Program has been seen to be of extreme value and that most of
these facilities now try to make sure that their patients have access
to it.

Because N.A. has become an effective modality in recovery from
all mood-altering addictions, to deny its value and its existence will
often result in denying life to a suffering addict who could have
made it in N.A. It can no longer be considered responsible chemical
dependency treatment if N.A. is not included in case management,
particularly with adolescents. An institutional philosophy which ig-
nores such a major therapeutic regimen must certainly be called into
question as to the degree of true care and ethics they afford their
patients. There are professionals who will not refer any chemically
dependent person to an institution which accepts drug-users for
treatment and which does not include N.A. in its programming.

Whether we like it or not, we must put kids' interests and procliv-
ities above that which can be afforded by traditional adult models.
Instead of stifling their emotional energy, we must encourage them
to enter a Twelve Step forum where that energy can be functionally
advanced, developed, and channeled into a self-constructive rebirth. Kids own their feelings more than they own intellectual con-

cepts. As they amortize their pain, they will learn how to handle it. They will heal. By practising healthy emotional action, they will learn to think as well. Demanding that they learn to "think" before they learn what to do with their feelings is an order these kids cannot follow.

It is absurd to think that the Twelve Step concept cannot develop, progress and be improved upon. For adolescents, N.A. seems to have accomplished a conceptual revision which is much more favorable to their needs and growth. Because of their notorious risk-taking behaviors, it is vital that they internalize the concept of addiction. "Addiction" is a word that is already part of their conceptual vocabulary. But the words *"alcoholic"* and *"alcoholism"* *do not instill the same awareness of the need for total behavioral change that the words "addiction" and "addict" can and do instill.*

Identifying as an "addict" means you have identified your basic personality flaw. Identifying as an "alcoholic" or "cocaine-ic" or "marijuana-ic" etc. merely means you have identified yourself as your drug of choice. I don't believe that is therapeutically sound. To identify one's self with a (frequently despised) chemical is a put-down. It does nothing to help raise self-esteem and, in fact, probably lowers it. Adolescents *desperately* need clarification of their identity and to impose an abstract and (what they see as) pejorative label doesn't help matters. It makes them worse.

Another advantage of the word "addict" is that it leads to an understanding of the process of any instant gratification tendencies and impulse control deficiencies; the drug-specific "-isms" or "-ics" do not.

What is recovery and how do we judge the quality of the process? I believe we can do this by accumulating collective frames of reference, never by incorporating or by giving rampant reign or blessing to our own. Thomas Merton, in his book *The Ascent to Truth*, states, "We must know the truth, and we must love the truth we know, and we must act according to the measure of our love" (Merton, 1981, p8). This is a demanding proposition, but a minimal one if we are to help others and avoid pretense. *We* must learn what is "truth" for others, not impose our own preconceived "truth" upon them, especially when our "truth" has afforded these kids a dismal rate of success.

Richard Bach wrote in *Illusions*; "Within each of us lies the power of our consent to health and to sickness, to riches and to poverty, to freedom and to slavery. It is we who control these and not another" (Bach, 1977, unpaginated). In healing ourselves we develop the right to help heal others: it is only in the power of our own consent to health, to power, and to freedom, that we teach such consent to others.

Recovery and the quality of it is first our own: we don't have to have been addicted ourselves to have to do that.

Then, I believe we must recognize certain things:

1. That recovery cannot take place if an adolescent cannot stop using any and all drugs, and stop exhibiting other addictive behaviors; that's our first task;
2. That only those who respect and love kids are qualified to treat, that only those who put kid's interests above their own are qualified to treat;
3. That only those who once again are willing to identify as adolescents can be effective with this population;
4. That only those who refrain from imposing their own values can help instill values in children;
5. That we must encourage these adolescents to engage in a recovery program where they will be accepted unconditionally, where they will not be rejected, where their views will be respected, where their presence is welcomed and not just tolerated, where they will have equal rights and privileges and the opportunity for responsibility as have all other members, and where they can tell the complete story of their addiction without violating the precepts and conventions of the Twelve Step Program to which they are referred (most often, only Narcotics Anonymous can afford that).
6. That, if what we often perceive as regression to more childish ways during recovery is nothing more than an integration of a childhood they never had to begin with, we not criticize it. Hopefully, this might allow these adolescents to have a full range of healthy nondestructive developmental experience.

7. That we understand that these kids are different than we and with different needs, and we will see that they often have childish ways of being children but can also have very adult ways of staying clean one day at a time;
8. That we offer all of them the best opportunity for a loving surrogate family and a highly developed spirituality in the Twelve Step Program to which we send them (N.A., again, excels in this area).

CONCLUSION

In contradiction to announced anarchic games, chemically dependent adolescents do seem to want stability and they seem to be able to find it in N.A. Often, however, they have to be told by other adolescents what it is that they are looking for—a love that passes all understanding. One of the reasons that chemically dependent kids so often say, "I don't care!" is because they care so very much and they are afraid to let anyone know. Rarely have they risked healthy intimacy because of the rejection they know all too well. Real love seemed to have missed them. Expressions of caring, hugs, emotional closeness based on emotional openness, and a shared and similar behavioral history with those they find in N.A. meeting rooms, are an N.A. way of life. Words and openness emphasize to new-comers, "We know your pain, we know your words, we know your patterns and you can't fool us. Besides, there is no longer any need to hide. You are loved here, you are home. We are your family."

There is much confrontation and "ass-kicking" in N.A. They aren't civilly gentle and they aren't afraid of wounding someone's "delicate sensibilities." But how much easier it is to take this from someone who has shared your old "values" and experience than it is from someone who hasn't, and who, perhaps, doesn't care enough to learn.

Young and older addicts mesh in a sometimes awkward generational alliance in N.A. but there is encouragement to do so. There is something that becomes apparent, though, to those young people who stick, and that is that most of the somewhat older N.A.ers seemed to have retained elements of a Dionysian approach to life—

a playful, laughing, yet controlled appreciation of absurdity. Like Peter Pan, most of them just don't seem to want to become card-carrying members of an analytical and intellectual world. At the same time many N.A.ers have returned to their schooling successfully. Many of them operate their own business.

But having these values does not preclude them from having a strangely disciplined sense of responsibility. Their commitments to the N.A. Program, to each other, and to themselves, tend to be deep. Often they are thrust into significant positions of N.A. responsibility early in recovery and they handle these trusted servant positions well. Their new way of doing things and hanging out with each other allows them to be constructive rather than destructive. Most of all it allows them to grow and to hold onto life. Their recovery drums do play differently; it's a nice sound!

Intellectualism and snobbery is out in N.A. ("We don't want to hear your head, we want to hear your gut!") Dress codes are not observed (something else not to rebel against), but N.A.ers can rise to the occasion as exemplified by their dressing up at N.A. convention banquets. But, if some people don't dress up for those recovery galas, they are loved and accepted just the same. Even here, the need for some not to conform yet is understood. They are *becoming* responsible, productive members of society; they haven't all necessarily arrived there yet.

N.A. grows because it is effective, because it fills needs, and because society desperately needs it to work. Professionals need to help the process.

N.A. draws its population from a wide array of backgrounds and employment classifications. The meetings tend to be very heterogenous. Street people share with medical professionals, lawyers share hugs with men and women whose primary addresses have been the jails of America. There is class and there is "clash" all united in the identification of shared feelings and in the secure knowledge that their program works. Drugs are truly an equal opportunity employer. There is immensely more than tolerance at work here. There is a dedication and devotion to each other that only hugs can forge.

It may be that the pioneers of any positive social movement can sometimes resemble a mother cat protecting her kittens. The protection of the N.A. Program by its members is noteworthy. There is deep faith in its message of recovery.

N.A. meetings emphasize not only an emotional sharing, but a deep spiritual commitment. N.A.ers seem to talk very frequently and emotionally about the God in their lives. Few N.A.ers seem to be angry with God or to be agnostics: for an N.A.er to reject God completely is rare. Spiritual fare is a staple at N.A. conventions, camp-outs, meetings, and in one-on-one discussions. (Without this spirituality, many N.A.ers would seem to feel bereft.) To hear the tough elegance of God on an N.A. camp-out, in the middle of a wilderness, under the stars, can be an incredibly moving experience. It is the form and not the formality of God which seems to count with them. Most often it's a very down-to-earth God and very immanent. God-with-them seems to afford a very pragmatic partnership. In such a significant spiritual atmosphere it might be feared that spiritually might merge with cultism, but such has not been the case.

Meetings, though centered in form, are nonetheless spontaneous affairs. There is a vibrancy and vitality which is much colored by street smarts and some very practical coping mechanisms. Druggies seem to be very verbal in recovery.

N.A. has also come of age! After years of observation of both fellowships, I now believe that N.A. should be the preferred Twelve Step program of referral for adolescents with but the rarest exceptions. N.A.ers understand, expect, and allow adolescent behaviors as long as they don't threaten anyone's recovery or the reputation of the program. It affords an environment of acceptance that is truly beautiful to see.

In N.A.'s formative stage, many seemed bent on its destruction. Those years and steeling experiences were invaluable. The tests of outrageous indifference, of ostrich-like lack of vision, and, yes, even those attacks of professional anger, have only served to anneal the N.A. way of life. The survival instincts of both N.A. and of its formerly "no-deposit, no-return, throw-away" membership have granted its beautiful soul a special place. For those who care about the world's addicted children—N.A. can effectively offer them rebirth.

If we started with a quote from *The Second Coming*, perhaps we can end with two more:
If this can represent the drug world's problem;

> Things fall apart; the centre cannot hold;
> Mere anarchy is loosed upon the world, The
> blood-dimmed tide is loosed, and everywhere
> The ceremony of innocence is drowned; (Yeats, 1920)

Then this can imply the solution;

> And what rough beast, its hour come round
> at last,
> Slouches toward Bethlehem to be born? (Yeats, 1920)

BIBLIOGRAPHY

Anonymous, *Narcotics Anonymous*. Van Nuys, Ca.; World Service Office, Inc. (Third Edition) 1986.

Bach, Richard, *Illusions, The Adventures of a Reluctant Messiah*. U.S.A.; Delacorte Press/Eleanor Friede 1977.

Jellinek, E.M. *The Disease Concept of Alcoholism*. New Haven; Hillhouse Press, 1960.

McLuhan, Marshall and Fiore, Quentin, *The Medium is the Message*. New York; Bantam Books, 1967.

Merton, Thomas (Father M. Louis Merton, O.C.S.O.), *The Ascent to Truth*. New York; Harcourt Brace Jovanovich Inc. 1981.

Shore, Jeffrey, J. "Use of Paradox in the Treatment of Alcoholism," *Health and Social Work* (Journal), 11-20, 1981.

W., Bill "Problems Other Than Alcohol" (pamphlet). New York; reprinted by permission of the A.A. Grapevine, Inc. by A.A. World Service, Inc. 1958.

Yeats, William Butler "The Second Coming" (poem) (reprinted in numerous anthologies) (1920).